Humanistic Critique of Education

Humanistic Critique of Education

Teaching and Learning as Symbolic Action

Edited by
Peter M. Smudde

Parlor Press
Anderson, South Carolina
www.parlorpress.com

Parlor Press LLC, West Lafayette, Indiana 47906

© 2010 by Parlor Press
All rights reserved.
Printed in the United States of America

SAN: 254-8879

Library of Congress Cataloging-in-Publication Data

Humanistic critique of education : teaching and learning as symbolic action / edited by Peter M. Smudde.
    p. cm.
  Includes bibliographical references and index.
  ISBN 978-1-60235-157-8 (pbk. : alk. paper) -- ISBN 978-1-60235-158-5 (hardcover : alk. paper) -- ISBN 978-1-60235-159-2 (adobe ebook)
  1. Education--Philosophy. 2. Education--Aims and objectives. 3. Learning, Psychology of. I. Smudde, Peter M.
  LB14.7.H8645 2010
  370.1--dc22
                        2009053934

Cover image: "Golden Library" © 2008 by Alex Nikada. From istockphoto.com
Cover design by David Blakesley
Printed on acid-free paper.

1 2

Parlor Press, LLC is an independent publisher of scholarly and trade titles in print and multimedia formats. This book is available in paper, hardcover, and Adobe eBook formats from Parlor Press on the World Wide Web at http://www.parlorpress.com or through online and brick-and-mortar bookstores. For submission information or to find out about Parlor Press publications, write to Parlor Press, 3015 Brackenberry Drive, Anderson, SC 29621, or e-mail editor@parlorpress.com.

Dedicated to Bernard L. Brock (1932–2006)—
teacher, scholar, mentor, colleague, friend.

Contents

Acknowledgments   *ix*

Introduction: A Prelude to Critique   *xi*
    Peter M. Smudde and Bernard L. Brock

1 Linguistic Approach to Problems of Education   *3*
    Kenneth Burke

2 Kenneth Burke as Teacher: Pedagogy, Materialism, and Power   *42*
    Andrew King

3 The Both-And of Undergraduate Education: Burke's "Linguistic" Approach   *61*
    Elvera Berry

4 The Education of Citizen Critics: The Consubstantiality of Burke's Philosophy and Constructivist Pedagogy   *92*
    Peter M. Smudde

5 Extending Kenneth Burke and Multicultural Education: Being Actively Revised by the Other   *115*
    Mark E. Huglen and Rachel McCoppin

6 Preaching What We Practice: Course Design Based on the Psychology of Form   *127*
    Richard H. Thames

7 Motives and Metaphors of Education   *143*
    James F. Klumpp and Erica J. Lamm

8 A Burkeian Approach to Education in a Time of Ecological Crisis   *166*
    Robert Wess

9 "By and Through Language, Beyond Language":
Envisioning a Burkeian Curriculum   *187*
   Bryan Crable

10 Educational Trajectories for Open and Democratic Societies:
Kenneth Burke's "Linguistic Approach"   *208*
   David Cratis Williams

Contributors   *233*

Index   *239*

Acknowledgments

This book has been a wonderful exploration of education and Kenneth Burke's applicability to it. Along the way certain people were especially helpful, and I want to briefly express my appreciation and acknowledge them here.

First is the late Bernie Brock, for whom this book is dedicated. He embraced my idea for this book with his usual enthusiasm and sound counsel to help me get it going. The fact that he also wanted to work with me on writing the brief introduction to frame the book was a special joy. I am sorry he did not get to see the final product, but I believe his spirit is somehow gratified.

Second is a small but mighty group of believers in this project. Foremost among them are the contributors to this volume, for without them this book would not exist. I am grateful to the National Society for the Study of Education in Chicago for granting permission to reprint Kenneth Burke's complete, original article, "Linguistic Approach to the Problems of Education," which appeared in the NSSE's 1955 volume, *Modern philosophies and education: The fifty-fourth yearbook of the National Society for the Study of Education, Part 1 of 2*. I also thank Jim Chesebro, whose wisdom, energy, and sage advice meant a lot to me and will long influence my thinking and management of future projects. Also there is Jeff Courtright, whose friendship, coaching, soundboarding, and humor have been great blessings upon me and my work. Plus David Blakesley, Parlor Press's curator-in-chief, gave me marvelous support throughout the process, especially in refining the book's focus. Parlor Press's anonymous reviewer gave me excellent comments that helped me and the contributors make this book into a sound contribution to the literature. And Joan Leininger always has been interested in and supportive of this project, especially through her special relationship with Bernie Brock.

Last but certainly not least is my family. My wife, Patty, and my boys, Matt and Jeffrey, put up with a lot of my musings about this and my other projects. Their love and support of me every step of the way means more than they know.

Introduction: A Prelude to Critique

Peter M. Smudde and Bernard L. Brock

Fifty years hence we may well conclude that there was no "crisis of American education" in the closing years of the twentieth century—there was only a growing incongruence between the way twentieth-century schools taught and the way late-twentieth century children learned.

—Peter Drucker

America's approach to education is terribly outmoded and should be updated to the realities of the 21st century.[1] The contributors in this volume would like to breathe some new life into the education system and set a new direction. This book's central focus, then, concerns Burke's philosophy of education and how his larger system informs us about education as a specific arena of human symbolic action. Isolating a Burkeian pedagogy is simple enough, if and only if one were to depend on his only formal treatise on education from 1955, "Linguistic Approach to Problems of Education," published here in the first chapter. But Burke scholars would strongly caution against such an approach, citing at least the explanatory power of Burke's canon to truly illuminate his thinking and apply to humanistic education. This orientation is particularly true when it comes to the symbolic action of education and all that transpires in this specialized realm of human relations.

Kenneth Burke's philosophy and critical method have been extended into many areas of human relations, but perhaps the least-often addressed area for extension is that of education. A search of published scholarship on the application of Burke to specific and general areas of education (see Chapter 4) reveals only a handful of work, and most of it was published sporadically within the last quarter century and focused on applying only selected Burke "tools" (especially the pentad). Other scholarly work done around the turn of the 21st century was presented at National Communication Association conferences in 1999, 2000, 2003 and 2004, all of which largely targeted ways to teach Burke's ideas and only began to examine his system as it applies to broad matters of pedagogy.

This book does not develop or advance any singular view on education, except to have Burke as the nexus for thinking about and acting on education. Accordingly, in true Burkeian fashion, this book allows for multiple perspectives. As Burke once said of himself and the critical enterprise: "I think that there has to be a lot of leeway in this business. I see no reason for being authoritarian. . . . The fundamental notion of choice in my scheme is difference" (as cited in Chesebro, 1992, p. 365). The fact that Burke created an open system—one that welcomes others' views that are similar and different, converging and diverging—allows it to grow beyond what he originally set forth. This book seeks to do just that for education.

Humanistic Critique of Education's collection of critiques about education addresses the subject on both general and specific levels. On a general level this book concerns the rhetoric of contemporary teaching and learning. *Humanistic Critique of Education* focuses on education as "symbolic action" that is "equipment for living" and the foundation for discovery. In this way the book sparks dialog about improving education in democratic societies through a humanistic frame. On a specific level, this book takes the lead from Burke's only focused piece on education to address matters about the design, practice, and outcomes of educational programs in the new millennium. Concepts like cognitive motivational outcomes, student development, literacy, active learning, constructivism, problem-based learning, cooperative educational movement, learning communities, student retention, community responsibility/service, technology, curriculum development, and others are featured. Such specificity grounds *Humanistic Critique of Education* in the current context of pedagogy and public policy. This book takes the position that Kenneth Burke's approach to humans as "bodies that learn language" and rhetoric as symbolic action has a great deal to contribute to a rebirth of education. The chapters that follow will describe aspects of that rebirth.

Readers may wonder why a 50 year old educational treatise can help improve today's and tomorrow's education situation. Burke is a pivotal figure in twentieth century rhetoric and social criticism, and we can use his ideas to help us learn from the past and, especially, better prepare for the future of education in America. The guiding principle for *Humanistic Critique of Education* is that education is the foundation for citizenship and community. This principle is humanistic in its origin and serves as the perspective from which the book analyzes the subject of education. Kenneth Burke's work is the inspiration for the book's humanistic perspective on education. The central question raised and answered in the book is, "How does Burke's philosophy of education and, especially, his larger system, inform our understanding of the nature and activity of a humanistic education, and how would that understanding be applied to education?" The book also answers a natural follow-up question: "Why is a Burkeian perspective important as we critique education in this new millennium?"

Timeliness for Critique

An accumulation of problems is throwing American education into crisis, derailing it from its goal to prepare students to become positive, contributing members of society. The traditional signs of crisis are overcrowded classrooms, school buildings in dire need of repair, and under-prepared teachers. Silent dropouts and HIV rates continue to increase. Charter schools have seen mixed results, especially for those where students did not score better than those from traditional public or private schools or scored worse (cf. Planty, Hussar, Snyder et al, 2008; Snyder, Dillow, & Hoffman, 2008). Some students are receiving excellent educational experiences, but this simply is not happening for many children throughout the country, many of whom score below their grade in reading, writing, or mathematics (cf. Bracey, 2007; Ginsberg & Lyche, 2008; Loveless, 2007; Mead & Rotherham, 2008; McCoog, 2008: Murnane & Steele, 2007; Ogden, 2007). *No Child Left Behind* has been either a praised or vilified public policy (cf. Bracey, 2007; Lips, 2008; Nelson, McGhee, Meno & Slater, 2007; Ogden, 2007). Its antecedent report, *A Nation At Risk*, in 1983 has also been cited as a watershed to the increasing federal influence—for better and for worse—on the nation's educational policy and curricula, including the benefits of standardized testing (cf. Casey, Bicard, Bicard, & Nichols, 2008; Ginsberg & Lyche, 2008; Hewitt, 2008; Lips, 2008).

These are just a few of the problems that have brought about the crisis and suggest the timeliness of this critique. However, we cannot solve the crisis by simply adding more money and doing more of what the schools have traditionally done. The following concepts, the detail of which are laid out in Figure 1, frame the tone for that new direction and are central to this book. First, the Western world is experiencing a paradigm shift in thought from a scientific to a humanistic orientation. This does not mean that the technology created by science will be dismantled. It only means that it will be placed in a new context. Instead of people being at the mercy of science and technology, humans will control them for the betterment of society. Education must reflect this shift in values.

Table 1. Comparison between status quo and humanistic views of education.

Education in the Status Quo	Education as Symbolic Action
past orientation	future orientation
content/knowledge focus	behavior/action focus
curricular	participative (increase intellectual involvement)
intellectual	functional
scientific	poetic humanism
life phase (milestone)	life-long learning
individual	sociological
students	learners (holistic)
technology as end	technology as agency
authoritarian	egalitarian
hierarchy	pluralism
metaphor	community
grades	outcomes (learning quality; performance measurement)

Next, education traditionally has been constructed and marketed around the idea that individuals should advance themselves as fast and as much as they possibly can. This approach, by focusing exclusively on the individual, has created a self-centered society that has had significant negative consequences. People looking out only for themselves can exploit others, especially the weaker members of society—the young, the elderly and the handicapped. Instead, education should be based on people balancing rights and responsibilities. This would hopefully teach a greater sense of responsibility to the others and to the community.

Finally, the metaphor operating in education today is the "workplace." It fosters thinking such as "school is a student's job," "that behavior is unacceptable on the job," "school is measured by how well it trains a person for a specific job," and schools are evaluated based on "job placement" to name a few ideas.[2] This approach might have been appropriate when we had a manufacturing economy. However, manufacturing jobs have been disappearing, and we're moving from an information economy to a creative economy, requiring a dramatically different approach to education and therefore a new metaphor. Either a creative or a community metaphor would be far superior to the current approach, or they could be combined into a "creative and humanistic community" metaphor that would be far superior for the needs of the 21st century.

Additionally, instead of problem solving, people must understand creative thinking that shapes the future. This pattern of thought could breathe new life into education because it requires a dramatically different structure and curriculum. As McCoog (2008) argues, "To acquire 21st century skills, students must be encouraged to create new ideas, evaluate and analyze the material presented, and apply that knowledge to their previous academic experiences. This is achieved by changing the methods of instruction" (p. 4). These changes are necessary to be consistent with the emerging humanistic context for thought. The inspiration for a "creative community" approach to education is Kenneth Burke's writing on rhetoric and education.

Fit Within the Literature

Numerous books have been published about individual pedagogical thinkers, ranging from Socrates to Dewey to Bloom. These works have been formative on the discipline of education, and many played a role in Burke's thinking. What is so important about this new book about a humanistic, Burkeian frame for pedagogy? There are three vital reasons for this book:

- Only one other book, Blakesley's (2002) *The Elements of Dramatism*, has ever been published that is dedicated to specifically extending Kenneth Burke's ideas into the realm of teaching and learning. To this end *Humanistic Critique of Education* further fills that gap and serves as a solid steppingstone to additional study and refinement of Burke's work for scholarly and professional application in education.

- Textbooks that address the communication of teaching focus on behaviors and strategies. But these same books do little to address the *rhetorical* dimensions of teaching and learning, with the notable exception of Mottet, Richmond, and McCroskey (2006). Such texts, including trade books, treat education as a communication phenomenon and present a montage of perspectives.

- No volume has been published that focuses solely on a single rhetorical perspective's illumination of education theory and praxis. Such a focus—framing education as symbolic action among humans—hits on specific purposes of teaching and learning that span the range from elementary and secondary education, to higher education curricula, to training seminars, to special education. It also includes specific matters, ranging from the impact of technology to changing the public-policy environment for education.

The rhetoric of teaching is sorely missing in the literature, with the exception of Petraglia's (1998) work that focuses on how constructivist pedagogy is most informed by an understanding of education's rhetorical challenges. *Humanistic Critique of Education*, offers a broad range of appeal to target readers that break into three categories, admittedly with some overlap among them but enough uniqueness to secure individual appeal:

- Academics—professors and practitioners who teach, research and serve in rhetoric, English, communication, and education fields

- Students—graduate students plus motivated, advanced undergraduate students in rhetoric, communication, and education

- Professionals—educators attending graduate school looking for a humanistic perspective to education that would be helpful to them as they enhance their credentials with a master's degree and move up in careers in the field but not to go on for a doctorate; also teachers wanting to build their knowledge about education through independent reading on the subject

The book's subtitle, "Teaching and Learning as Symbolic Action," positions the entire critique in the realm of Burke's philosophy and method. It would appeal to Burke scholars while also emphasizing the centrality of communication that other target audiences can reasonably understand without specific familiarity with Burke's ideas.

In this volume, the chapters are arranged to progress from Burke's "Linguistic Approach to Problems of Education" (Chapter 1) and address issues about effective education in our nation. Chapters 2 through 5 present analyses about Burke's ideas that reveal much about the potential of his work in education in terms of pedagogy and curricula. In Chapter 2, Andrew King places Burke's teachings on power within the frame of his educational ideas and practice. The key is that Burke gives us practical tools for life in the world of the publicly engaged intellectual and teaches how to assess, critique, and resolve power conflicts that undermine the effectiveness of social hierarchies, including those of education itself. Elvera Berry, in Chapter 3, next argues that Burke's extensive analysis of human beings, as defined by their linguistic capacity and activity, and his observations concerning education in a democracy are incorporated in a trans-disciplinary perspective as "equipment" for learning. Berry, then, proposes a framework within which to examine education and a heuristic by which to generate educational agendas and shape curricula. In Chapter 4, Peter Smudde reveals that a very small collection of research has applied Burke to education, and its application is restricted overwhelmingly to teaching Burke's ideas and never to contemporary pedagogical perspectives. Smudde demonstrates how Burke gives us a philosophy of education and that, together with his larger system, it is directly applicable to the field of education through constructivist pedagogy and problem-based learning, ultimately building up to an educational design for the development of "citizen critics." In Chapter 5, Mark Huglen and Rachel McCoppin develop pedagogical strategies specifically from Burke's four "rungs of learning." Huglen and McCoppin argue that the educational curriculum ought to place primary emphasis upon the two latter rungs, applying several anecdotal examples to demonstrate the importance and challenges of this kind of positioning.

Chapters 6 and 7 address matters largely focused on humanistic teaching and learning *in situ*. Chapter 6, by Richard Thames, approaches education from a student's perspective—that the material cannot bear the burden of repetition. Teachers may constantly update their courses with new information, which tends to work for "hard" sciences and fields whose content frequently produces new information. More humanistically/philosophically oriented courses must be built on a "psychology of form," which may include some repetition but is far more interesting initially because there is a dramatic arch to such courses. In Chapter 7, James Klumpp and Erica Lamm reveal metaphors' potency in education because they direct people's attention to the ends that they name, such as student as container, as consumer, as apprentice, as unmolded clay, as computer have marked perspectives on education. Klumpp and Lamm then trace such metaphors' implications on the attitudes about and practices of education among students, teachers, and the public at large.

Chapters 8, 9 and 10 round out this volume's humanistic critique by examining education in the bigger, social-democratic picture. In Chapter 8, Robert Wess explains that Burke's studies of symbolic action and rhetoric offer a new conceptualization of what it means to be human, based on the idea that we are "symbol-using animals" or "bodies that learn language"—all of which stresses language and biology brought together to show humankind as intimately ecological beings. Wess argues, then, that ecological literacy—what it means to be human both biologically, as part of the ecosystem of the earth (ecological science), and linguistically, as distinctive in the way we inhabit the earth (verbal or symbolic action)—may prove to be the paradigm best suited to flesh out Burke's vision about humanity fully, particularly as it bears on education. In Chapter 9, Bryan Crable summarizes the foundational assumptions and concepts of Burke's dramatistic perspective of education, and offers suggestions about how this perspective might be used to provide an overall framework for reconceptualizing the aims and goals of American education. For Crable, a truly dramatistic curriculum would start with language in early childhood to form the basis of all educational efforts, rather than traditional emphases on math, writing, and science. Primary and secondary education, thereafter, features a complete developmental program for linguistic appreciation. Finally, in Chapter 10, David Williams observes abundant current concern with the condition of U.S. civic engagement and democratic culture. Accordingly, Williams frames Burke's "linguistic approach" to education to contextualize that approach in the problems of and prospects for democratic culture and to discuss the implications of the Burkeian approach to education and democracy for the renewal of American democratic culture.

Humanistic Critique of Education: Teaching and Learning as Symbolic Action fills an important scholarly niche by bringing together excellent scholarship while extending Kenneth Burke's ideas into a rarely touched area of inquiry, thus providing an opportunity to foster new research and application of his system in new and fruitful ways. Research findings based on ideas applied *in situ* from *Humanistic Critique of Education* would be the next important step to contributing knowledge through the scholarship on teaching and learning.

Notes

1. Bernie Brock and I wrote this introduction several months before his death, and I carried on our work for publication. This chapter is likely the last (or at least one of his last) projects, which he embraced with his usual enthusiasm and critical perspective. Through this brief chapter we wanted to apply some of his selected critical observations about America's education system and bolster them with evidence from other sources—to help me frame this volume's role in bridging scholarship about Kenneth Burke and education.

2. A related metaphor to these is "student as customer," which many institutions use to define both their relationships with students and their institutional missions. The problem with this metaphor is that it, essentially, equates education with the mere purchasing of a product or service (cf. McMillan & Cheney, 1996; chapter 7 in this volume). Although education, strictly speaking, may be viewed as a service, it certainly is not like buying a product, such as a toaster. And if education is viewed as a service, it is unlike having a carpet cleaned, for example, where people who want it done may be those who cannot do it well, do not want to do it at all themselves, or find it easiest to pay someone to do it for them. Education, if viewed as a service, is unique from all others, at least because of the particular symbolic action inherent in educational settings among instructors, students, alumni, and administration.

References

Blakesley, D. (2002). *The elements of dramatism*. New York: Longman.

Bracey, G. W. (2007, October). The 17th Bracey Report on the condition of public education: The first time "everything changed." *Phi Delta Kappan*, 119–136.

Casey, L. B., Bicard, D. F., Bicard, S. C., & Nichols, S. M. C. (2008, April). A much delayed response to *A Nation at Risk:* Recent innovations in general and special education. *Phi Delta Kappan*, 593–596.

Chesebro, J. W. (1992). Extensions of the Burkean system. *Quarterly Journal of Speech*, *78*, 356–368.

Ginsberg, R., & Lyche, L. F. (2008). The culture of fear and the politics of education. *Educational Policy*, *22*(1), 10–27.

Hewitt, T. W. (2008, April). Speculations on *A Nation at Risk:* Illusions and realities. *Phi Delta Kappan*, 575–579.

Lips, D. (2008, April 18). A nation still at risk: The case for federalism and schools. *Backgrounder*, *2125*, 1–10. Retrieved October 21, 2008, from http://www.heritage.org/Research/Education/bg2125.cfm

Loveless, T. (2007). *The 2007 Brown Center Report on American education: How well are American students learning?* Washington, DC: Brookings Institution. Retrieved October 21, 2008, from http://www.brookings.edu/~/media/Files/rc/reports/2007/1211_education_loveless/1211_education_loveless.pdf

McCoog, I. J. (2008). 21st century teaching and learning. *ERIC Digest*. Retrieved October 21, 2008, from http://www.eric.ed.gov/ERICDocs/data/ericdocs2sql/content_storage_01/0000019b/80/3f/65/1e.pdf

McMillan, J. J., & Cheney, G. (1996). The student as consumer: The implications and limitations of a metaphor. *Communication Education*, 45(1), 1-15.

Mead, S., & Rotherham, A. J. (2008). *Changing the game: The federal role in supporting 21st century educational innovation*. Washington DC: Brookings Institution. Retrieved October 21, 2008, from http://www.brookings.edu/~/media/Files/rc/reports/2008/1016_education_mead_rotherham/1016_education_mead_rotherham.pdf

Mottet, T. P., Richmond, V. P., McCroskey, J. C. (2006). *Handbook of instructional communication: Rhetorical and relational perspectives*. Columbus, Ohio: Allyn & Bacon.

Nelson, S. W., McGhee, M. W., Meno, L. R., & Slater, C. L. (2007, May). Fulfilling the promise of educational accountability. *Phi Delta Kappan*, 702–709.

Ogden, W. R. (2007). Mountain climbing, bridge building, and the future of American education. *Education*, *127*(3), 361–368.

Petraglia, J. (1998). *Reality by design: The rhetoric and technology of authenticity in education*. Mahwah, NJ: Erlbaum.

Planty, M., Hussar, W., Snyder, T., Provasnik, S., Kena, G., Dinkes, R., KewalRamani, A., Kemp, J. (2008). *The condition of education 2008*. Washington, DC: National Center for Education Statistics, U. S. Department of Education. Retrieved, October 21, 2008, from http://nces.ed.gov/pubs2008/2008031.pdf

Snyder, T. D., Dillow, S. A., & Hoffman, C. M. (2008). *Digest of education statistics 2007*. Washington, DC: National Center for Education Statistics, U. S. Department of Education. Retrieved, October 21, 2008, from http://nces.ed.gov/programs/digest/d07/

Humanistic Critique of Education

1 Linguistic Approach to Problems of Education*

Kenneth Burke

Basic Orientation

Beginning absolutely, we might define man as the typically language-using, or symbol-using, animal. And on the basis of such a definition, we could argue for a "linguistic approach to the problems of education." Or we could settle for much less, merely pointing to the obviously great importance of the linguistic factor as regards both education in particular and human relations in general.

Language in Educational Theory

For symmetry's sake, we would build upon the more thoroughgoing of these positions. Yet, for prudence' sake, we would remind the reader: Even if he will not go so far with us, there are still many points in favor of restoring (however differently) the great stress once placed upon language in educational theory. (Recall that the medieval *trivium* comprised grammar, rhetoric, and logic or dialectic.)

In either case, whether the more thoroughgoing or the less thoroughgoing of these positions is adopted, we shall be considering our subject in terms of symbolic action. We shall look upon language-using as a mode of conduct and shall frame our terms accordingly. We could call this position "dramatistic" because it thus begins with a stress upon "action." And it might be contrasted with idealistic terminologies, that begin with considerations of perception, knowledge, learning. In contrast with such *epistemological* approaches, this approach would be *ontological*, centering upon the *substantial-*

---

* Educational Consultant: Professor Kenneth Benne, Boston University, Boston, Massachusetts.

ity of the *act*. Also, a "dramatistic" approach, as so conceived, is *literal*, not *figurative*. Man *literally* is a symbol-using animal. He *really does* approach the world symbol-wise (and symbol-foolish).[1]

But a "dramatistic" approach, with its definition of man as the typically language-using or symbol-using animal, points two ways. First, the principles of symbol-using must be considered in their own right, as a separate "realm" or "dimension" (not reducible to "nature" in the nonverbal or extraverbal sense of the term). Second, the formula should warn us not to overlook the term "animal" in our definition. Man *as an animal* is subject to the realm of the extraverbal, or nonsymbolic, a realm of material necessity that is best charted in terms of *motion*. That is. in his sheer animality, man is to be described in terms of *physical* or *physiological motion*, as contrasted with the kind of terms we need for analyzing the realm of verbal action.

Professor Brubacher has touched upon an analogous problem, when referring to the classical definition of man as "rational animal." As regards those who "subscribed to a humanistic theory of education," he says: "They held with Aristotle that the distinctive nature of man which set him off from other animals was his rationality. The principal function of education, therefore, was to develop this rationality."

In general, this partial *nonsequitur*, in leading some thinkers' to overstress the differentia (man's "rationality"), led others to an antithetical overstress upon the genus (man's "animality"). And if we are to abide by our somewhat similar definition, we must watch lest, in our zeal to bring out the *formal* considerations of the differential (language-using, or symbol-using), we slight the *material* considerations of the genus (animal). Or, otherwise put: We must guard lest, in our zeal for a terminology of *action*, we overlook the areas properly chartable in terms of *motion*.

Accordingly, a "dramatistic" terminology built about this definition for man will not exalt terms for "action" to the exclusion of terms for "motion." If, by the physical realm, we mean the nonverbal ("subverbal" or "extraverbal") realm, then the *physical realm* is properly treated in terms of motion. And "action" (ethics, "personality," and the like) will be confined to the realm of symbol-using, with its appropriate principles. Thus, a "dramatistic" perspective, as so conceived, would *decidedly not* oblige us to treat of "things" in the terminology proper to "persons" or vice versa.

The problem is complicated by the fact that, while there can be motion without action (as with a falling material object, or the operations of some purely mechanical device), there can be no action without motion (as one cannot think or speak or carry out a decision without a corresponding set of sheerly neural and muscular goings-on). Thus, there is a sense in which every human act is merged with its sheerly physical or physiological ground.

For instance, whereas the *actions* of a game are motivated by the logic of the rules, such acts also involve the sheer physical *motions* of the players and their instruments, in varying quantitative distribution about the field. *(Nulla actio sine motione.* A team can't win a game unless it knows how to "throw its weight around.")

Or consider cases where moral attitudes affect physiological functioning (as when emotional disturbances produce disorders of the bodily organs). Here the realm of action (and its "passions"!) is seen to infuse the realm of motion in ways grotesquely analogous to the powers of a "grace" that, according to the theologians, "perfects" nature.

Thus, though the realms of "action" and "motion" are *discontinuous* in so far as the "laws" of action are not in strict principle reducible to the "laws" of motion (quite as the rules of grammar could not properly be reduced to terms suitable for electronics), the two realms must be *interwoven* in so far as man's *generic animality* is experienced by him in terms of his *specific "symbolicity."*

Suppose, for instance, that we tried to conceive of "property" in as purely "physical" a sense as possible. We might note respects in which an organism "accumulates private property" by adapting to its particular needs certain portions of its environment. *Its* food, *its* air, *its* water, *its* sunlight, *its* space, *its* shelter, *its* mate—some or all of these things may be "appropriated," in accordance with the specific nature of the organism. In this sense, assimilation could be said to involve a purely *physiological* kind of "private property," however mutual may be the relationships prevailing among various organisms, or "substances," in their "ecological balance."

Here is the realm of "animality," of sheer physical "necessity." If the organism is denied the proper "motions" of assimilation or digestion needed for its survival, it dies. It *must* take into itself alien substances, in accordance with the nature of *its* substance. Some degree of such purely *material* appropriation, with the many material "motions" involved in these processes, is necessary to sheer animal survival. And man, as an animal, confronts the same necessities.

Think next of the many ways whereby such rudimentary needs are transcended, once we move into the realm of "symbolic action." Here we come upon the vast structure of "rights" and "obligations" that takes form when "property" is conceived *legalistically* (as with the "legal fictions" of a modem financial corporation, which the courts treat as a "person"). Surely no one would hold that the "needs" of such a "body" are reducible purely to terms of a few biological necessities. Ownership, as so conceived, involves a fantastically intricate network of purely *symbolic* operations, as evidenced by the army of *clerics* who in one way or another are occupied with promulgating, recording, interpreting, and enforcing the sheerly *man-made* laws of property.

To consider this realm intelligibly, we must discuss symbolic manipulations as such. For obviously, they have a "perfection" of their own, a formal resourcefulness that transcends the nonsymbolic or extrasymbolic realm of purely biological functioning. And such a realm of "personality" goes so far beyond the needs of sheer "animality," that whereas a physical organism can "biologically own" only so much as it can take into its body, or as it can by purely physical powers deny to another, a member of the symbol-using species may "symbolically own" resources that, in his capacity as a sheer physical organism, he could not exhaust in a million lifetimes.

Indeed, once ownership becomes modified by the conditions of purely symbolic action, a realm of fantasy and paradox arises. Does a great leader, for instance, "own" his office as head of a state? Or is he not rather "owned" by his subjects who consider themselves "consubstantial" with him, so far as their sense of participation in a common cause is concerned? Whatever your answer to this quandary may be, you will grant that such thoughts confront us with a great *drama* of *human* relations. For quite as a state is held together physically by a network of purely *material* communicative resources (things that exist and operate in accordance with the laws of *motion*), so this network itself is guided in its construction and control by a network of purely *symbolic* acts and symbol-guided purposes, ranging from the lowly processes of bookkeeping and accountancy to the over-all terminology of "right," "justice," "beauty," "propriety," "truth," the "good life," etc., in which the logic of a given social order comes to an ideal, theoretic head.

Above sheer human animality, then (above man's genus as rooted in the laws of material motion), there has been erected a social complexity that could not have existed without the aid of man's differentia (his capacity for symbolic action). And in this sense, though we would warn against the temptation to forget the genus in our concern with the differentia, we would hold that the proper approach to the genus is *through* the study of symbolic action, as such action takes form in the drama of human relations. Otherwise, for reasons that we shall consider as we proceed, the failure to detect the full scope of the "linguistic dimension" in human affairs and human attitudes obscures our undemanding of both the linguistic and the extralinguistic. According to the position here advocated, there is a "pageantry" in objects, a "socioanagogic" element imposed upon them, so far as man is concerned, because man necessarily approaches them in accordance with the genius of his nature as a symbol-human species. Since language is social in the political, administrative sense, the purely physical sociality of nonlinguistic things thus subtly partakes of this purely symbolic spirit, so far as human dealings with "nature" are concerned.

Here is the problem at the bottom of our search, as at the bottom of a well. Our motto might be: By and through language, beyond language. *Per linguam, praeter linguam.*

The "dramatistic" is to be distinguished from the "dramatic," in that drama proper is the symbolizing or imitating of action, whereas the "dramatistic" is a critical or essayistic analysis of language, and thence of human relations generally, by the use of terms derived from the contemplation of drama.

But the dramatistic can take great dramas as its point of departure. They provide the set forms in conformity with which we would construct our terminology. Since the real world of action is so confused and complicated as to seem almost formless, and too extended and unstable for orderly observation, we need a more limited material that might be representative of human ways while yet having fixity enough to allow for systematic examination.

In this respect, great dramas would be our equivalents of the laboratory experimenter's "test cases." But this kind of "controlled conditions" would differ from the arbitrary controls of a typical laboratory experiment. The losses are obvious, the gains less so, unless one stops to realize how hard it is to set up laboratory conditions for establishing instances of symbolic action that, while having a form sufficiently stable to be methodically observable, are also sufficiently complex and mature to be representative of human motives.[2]

But we may be on less cogent ground when laying primary emphasis upon the examining of written texts. Professor Benne has tellingly raised this objection in correspondence, pointing to the many elements besides the literary text that figure in a dramatic performance, and suggesting that the present writer's occupational psychosis as a specialist in literature may be partly responsible for this textual emphasis. To be sure, though we can at least point to the example of Aristotle, who rated the text of a drama higher than its performance, we must never forget that many fresh exegetical insights come of witnessing actual performances (as when we compare different actors' readings of the same lines); and a sympathetic auditor may be mysteriously moved by a performance given in a language he doesn't even know). Yet, although histrionic and choreographic elements (tonal, plastic, and scenic) contribute critically to the enjoyment and understanding of drama, don't all such modes of expression regularly build their logic *about the interpretation of the text itself?*

Professor Benne has further objected that we tend to neglect the fertile field of drama-like situations in real life (situations that may arise spontaneously, or may be set up partly by the deliberate cunning of an impresario; as with some "candid" radio and television programs). This is a particularly important objection, since education is so largely in the realm of public relations generally. Our point here is simply that one should not *begin* a "dramatistic" analysis with such cases. But co-ordinates *developed from the analysis of formal drama* should certainly be applied to fluctuant material of this sort. Further, such applications, made by a different class of specialists, should reveal notable respects in which the drama-like situations of real life *differ* from drama proper (a difference probably centering in the fact that situations in real life lack *finality*, except in so far as life happens to "imitate art"). Professor Benne's desire to place more weight upon drama-like situations in life ("a playground fight, for example") led us to realize that, given the new recording devices for motion and sound, such new-style documents do resemble the text of a formal drama, in allowing for repeated analysis of a single unchanging development (an "action" that, in its totality, remains always the same). Here, in effect, the new means of recording, or "writing," have extended the realm of the "text" into areas that once lay beyond it. Such material comes close to the "textual" ideal we have in mind; since an observer can repeatedly observe the identical object, thus having the best opportunity to mature his observations.

Still (in an "occupationally psychotic" way) we feel that the written word comes nearest (so far as "records" go) to a merging of "linguistic anatomy" with "linguistic physiology." For single words (many of which are recurrent in the given text) are in their singularity quite "dead"; yet they are very much "alive," as regards their ways of taking part contextually with one another. And in the beginning of our culture was the assurance that in the beginning was the word.

On the other hand, we do not by any means equate "symbol-using" with "word-using." All the arts, such as music, painting, sculpture, the dance, even architecture, are in various ways and to varying degrees symbolic activities. Verbal symbol-using (like its variant, mathematics) enjoys a special place among the lot because the individual word has a kind of conceptual clarity not found in individual notes, colors, lines, motions, and the like (except in so far as these are in effect *words*, as with the conventionalized doctrinal representations in some traditional ritual dance).

In this connection, Professor Benne has suggested that the justification for featuring language among symbolic media may "lie in the fitness of word-symbols for the *criticism* and *analysis* of the others, including word-symbols themselves." This observation suggested to us another step in the same direction, thus: Inasmuch as education merges into the philosophy of education, we may note that verbal symbols are the best medium for "philosophizing" about anything.

Professor Benne adds:

> Mr. Burke seems not quite to have met my point about the selection of cases to be used educationally for dramatistic analysis. True enough, "great dramas would be our equivalents of the laboratory experimenter's, 'test cases.'" And teachers, under the influence of dramatistic philosophizing, would in their education have analyzed these "test cases" and would have acquired an appreciation of the folly and grandeur of man's differentia, symbol using, as well as skills in analyzing the complexities of language within the far-flung drama of human relations. But would children under the tutelage of such teachers delay their educational experience with dramatistic analysis of human action until they had gained the maturity to deal with these "test cases"? I would hope not. I do not pretend to know at what age students might profitably analyze the great dramas dramatistically. Let's guess arbitrarily they might begin at fifteen or sixteen. Long before that time, of course, they are acquiring orientations and habits toward using and being used by language, toward enacting the follies and grandeurs of human (symbolic) action. Shouldn't their education incorporate elements of dramatistic analysis before they are ready for the "complete texts"? I think it should. And some of the materials for such analysis might well come from the dramas of human relations in everyday life in which they take part, using whatever devices of mechanical recording, spontaneous dramatization, participant observation, etc., which might advance the learning. Perhaps students so brought up would be more ready to profit from analysis of the "test-cases" par excellence when they were mature enough to deal with them directly than students who had had no previous orientation to dramatism and its methods.

Language and Problems of Human Relations

But for our over-all principles, we necessarily select terms so highly generalized that they apply to work greatly varying in quality (just as both an "excellent" play and a merely "representative" one might be said to have beginning, middle, and end, or to be written in blank verse, or to be a tragedy).

All told, the project approaches the problem of human relations through a study of language in its four major aspects: (a) the logical or indicative; (b) the rhetorical or persuasive; (c) the poetic; (d) the ethical or personal. But only some of the theories and rules of thumb on which this essay is based are directly relevant to the philosophy of education. And in trying to decide which parts of this material should be stressed here, we shall follow the very helpful lead of an article by Professor Benne, "Toward a Grammar of Educational Motives," published in the January, 1947, issue of *Educational Forum*. The article is built around a review of the present writer's book, *A Grammar of Motives*, which outlines the "dramatistic" view of language and of motivational problems generally. The article makes the following main points:

The *Grammar* "may be read as a reaction against 'scientistic' attempts to 'reduce' the explanation of human conduct to the influence of various conditions and causes—physical, chemical, biological or generally environmental." Burke "finds an irreducible minimum of terms necessary to the adequate discussion of human motivation," and he derives these "from his analysis of dramatic action." There are five such terms, which "'point' in any human action to an actor, a scene, some agency (means), a purpose, as well as the over-all action in which the other terms are united."

Again, "Whatever the various motivations of the semanticists, one may see Burke as a semanticist, seeking to give an interpretation of meaning and its transformations in a 'dramatistic' as opposed to the 'scientistic' perspective which has prevailed in most semantic studies."

"Still another approach" might stress the fact that "in focusing on the language of *any* discussion of motives," the book "is a 'grammatical' approach to discourse about motives." Hence, "on this view, various philosophies become 'casuistries' seeking only to apply these grammatical principles in and to 'the case' of some actual and given cultural situation." Accordingly, Burke attempts a "'casuistry' of his own, taking major philosophic systems as 'cases' and developing their distinctive characters in terms of their varying stress upon one or another of the terms of his pentad," as materialism features the "scenic" element in motivation, idealism stresses "agent," pragmatism "agency" (instrument), mysticism "purpose," and realism "act." (We might here add that the book also stresses the ways whereby the terms become functions of one another: Thus, by the "scene-act ratio" is meant a statement where the substance of an act is said to have been potentially or analogously present in the scene, and to be derived from the scene; similarly, an "agent-act" ratio derives the quality of the act from the corresponding nature of the agent; the "purpose-agency ratio" concerns the relation of consistency or consubstantiality between end and means; etc.)

The project as a whole (including portions still to be published) aims at an "extended comic treatment of human relations, of the 'foibles and antics" of "the Human Barnyard.'" Reaffirming "the parliamentary process," it is motivated by a "humanitarian concern to see how far conflict (war) may be translated practically into linguistic struggle and how such verbal struggle may be made to eventuate in a common enactment short of physical combat."

Other details noted: "encouraging tolerance by speculation"; a "Neo-Liberal Ideal" that proposes to accept with ironic resignation "the development of technology, a development that will require such a vast bureaucracy (in both political and commercial administration) as the world has never before encountered"; would "confront the global situation with an attitude neither local nor imperialistic"; and is designed to embody its attitude in a method of linguistic analysis.

In his "howevers" (and howevers are of the essence in this perspective) Professor Benne finds that Burke's book is not sufficiently "normative, preferential." But there is a partial however to this however: "Nevertheless, one can find implicit norms in his description of his method," as with Burke's stress upon the *dialectical*, which is equated with "dramatism" at one end and with "scientific method" at the other, and with an over-all complexity of view that is ironic. (For irony "arises when one tries, by the interaction of terms upon one another, to produce a development which uses all the terms," in the methodic search for "a 'perspective of perspectives' in which the values of each partial perspective are in some measure preserved.")

Calling the book "a methodology of practical judgment," Professor Benne next refers to another work, *The Discipline of Practical Judgment in a Democratic Society* (by Raup, Benne, Smith, and Axtelle), which "attempts to do justice to the meaning of Burke's pentad of dramatistic terms in the act of judgment, though without the employment of his terminology." These two books "seem fruitfully to supplement each other"; and they "make at least a beginning in this task of the interpretation of rationality and of contemporary symbolic adequacy." Or, in sum: "'Symbolic adequacy' can only be developed," and "mastery of our linguistic resources (which are ultimately our rational resources) can be achieved if acquired in the dramatic perspective of the significant conflicts of our time."

Among other considerations stressed in this perspective, we night list briefly: Their systematic concern with the principle of "identification" that prevails, for instance, when ruler and subjects, however disparate their ways of living, feel themselves united in some common cause; the gleams of "mystery" and corresponding feelings of guilt that arise when beings of different status are in communication; the modes of *symbolic purification* ingrained in the nature of symbolic action, and culminating in acts of *victimage;* the principle of *completion* to which language vows us, as when we round out a judgment upon others until it returns upon the self (cf. the Kantian "categorical imperative"); the verbal resources of *transcendence,* implicit in the initial momentous fact that the word transcends the thing it names; and, above all, the workings of that marvel of marvels, not present in nature, and found only in the resources of symbolism, the *negative* (with its "completion" or "perfection" in the "thou shalt not").

The approach to human relations through the study of language in terms of drama makes such concerns primary and seeks to build a systematic terminology to treat of human quandaries in such a spirit. It contends that the basic motives of human effort are concealed behind the clutter of the machinery, both technological and administrative, which civilization has amassed in the attempts to live well. It contends that by a methodic study of symbolic action men have their best chance of seeing beyond this clutter, into the ironic nature of the human species. Yet it seeks to be as instrumentalist as the instrumentation it would distrust. But while it would completely grant that terminologies of motion are properly cultivated in those fields of applied science dealing specifically with aspects of motion (as the physical sciences), it would categorically resist any quasi-positivistic tendencies to treat of the human realm in such terms.

We must here leave many relevant questions unanswered. But we might close this section by a reference to the kind of "short-cut" which we consider primary, where the analysis of particular linguistic structures is concerned:

We refer to the notion that the study of symbolic action in particular literary works should begin with the charting of "equations." That is: When you consult a text, from which you hope to derive insights as regards our human quandaries in general, you begin by asking yourself "what equals what in this text?" And then, next, "what follows what in this text?"

The study of such "equations" is a way of *yielding without demoralization.* One cannot know in advance what the "equations" are to be (what "hero" is to equal, what "villain" is to equal, what "wisdom" is to equal, etc).[3] Yet in one search for such "equations," which the author himself *spontaneously exemplified* rather than upheld as conscious doctrine, one is guided by method. Accordingly, such analysis is no mere surrender, though it does set up a preparatory stage in which one wholly "yields" to the text.

Having thus, without heckling, systematically let the text say its full say, even beyond what its author may have thought he was saying, we have the basic admonition as regards man, with relation to his specialty, "symbolic action." We see "exhortations" of terrifying importance being prepared for, even when a writer has no such intentions in mind. For, if certain elements equal "good" and certain elements equal "bad" (or, what is often more important, if certain elements equal "socially superior" and certain elements equal "socially inferior"), then in contemplating the "dynamics" of such "equations" (their implied hortatory value), do we not contemplate the very essence of human foibles?

And, at least within the ideality of our educational pursuits, are we not thereby admonished to watch and wait—and not just preceptorially, but technically?

"Dramatism," the approach to the human situation "linguistically," in terms of symbolic action, fulfils its purposes only in so far as it makes methodical the attitude of patience. The "dramatic" may thunder. It should. The "dramatistic," in a commingling of techniques and hypochondriasis, will "appreciate" man's ways of thundering.

Educational Aims and Values

Education, as so conceived, would be primarily admonitory. It would seek to become a sophisticated and methodized set of parables, or fables. Noting how man's distinctive trait, his way with symbols, is the source of both his typical accomplishments and his typical disabilities, education as so conceived would be first and foremost "of a divided mind," and would seek to make itself at home in such divisiveness.

Far too often, education is wholly under the sign of the promissory. The serious student enters school hoping to increase his powers, to equip himself in the competition for "success," to make the "contacts" that get him a better-paying job. Vocational courses almost inevitably confirm such an attitude, since their main purpose is to perfect technical ability, to teach special skills.

The "humanistic" aspect of the curriculum is usually approached in the same spirit, even by those who think of themselves as opponents of the vocational emphasis. The courses are expected in some way or other to help students "get ahead" as individuals. Humanistic education thus becomes the attempt to teach and to acquire the kind of "insignia" that are thought to be proof of cultural election.

This pragmatic emphasis may not always be individualistically motivated. With the project of *The Republic* for the training of the guardians, for instance, the emphasis was rather in the direction of Plato's yearning that education might serve for the triumph of all Greek states, united in a common cause against the "barbarians." And nationalistic emphases in general would belong here; for although there is conceivable an ideal world of nationalisms that would be related to one another as peacefully as the varied portraits in an art gallery, we need no very difficult fables to admonish us about the ever-ready dialectical resource whereby national "differences" may become national "conflicts."

Only a truly "universal" attitude toward educational purposes can modify this intrinsically *competitive* emphasis. Such an attitude would be grounded in the thought that all mankind has a major stake in the attempt to discipline any tendencies making for the kind of war now always threatening. In this spirit, we would aim at the discovery of methods that would be a *technical* equivalent of such uneasiness as, in religious terms, has been called the "fear of God." And we would seek for a *technical* equivalent of "mortification," thereby hoping to make active and mundane a kind of scruples now too often confined to the separate realm of the cloister.

But such "technicalizing" would produce notable changes of emphasis, since we are here discussing purely *secular* modes of education. In this realm, the pious "fear of God" would be replaced by a partially impious "fear of symbol-using" (that is, an ironic fear of the very resourcefulness that is man's greatest boast). And "mortification" in the religious sense would have, as its secular "dramatistic" analogue, a methodic distrust of competitive ambitions which goad us either as individuals or as groups. Or, more accurately: We would try, *at least within the limited orbit of theory, or contemplation*, to perfect techniques for doubting much that is now accepted as lying beyond the shadow of a doubt.

A mere inculcating of "tolerance," "good will," "respect for the rights of others," and such, cannot be enough. Such attitudes are all too airily "positive." And the educational training here advocated would be in its very essence *negative*, as negative as the Ten Commandments.

Yet its negativity would be of a paradoxical sort; we might label it "Faustological," since it would center in the study of ambition as a *disease*. At the same time it would concede that we had all better be very, very ambitious and sufficiently exacting in our ambitiousness to cancel off the many prompter ambitions that, given the new weapons, threaten to destroy us.

The *pragmatic*, the *admonitory*, and the *appreciative* thus merge. For we would study the means by which men have been able to increase their assertiveness; thereby we should be "appreciating" human genius, yet doing so with fearsomeness (albeit a fearsomeness which our technical approach enables us to temper in the kindly spirit of comedy, while we tentatively seek to develop ways of looking upon us all as fools rather than as knaves). But in such tripleness of emphasis, the admonitory (the "negative") is to be treated as "foremost among the equals."

The aim, then, is to droop, at least *ad interim* (within the special conditions of the educational enterprise, considered as but one stage of a person life)—but to droop so methodically, with such an emphasis upon method, that each day can bristle with assertions, as we attempt to perfect our lore of the human scramble (what Goethe calls the *Zeitenstrudel*, and Diderot the *grand branle*).

Education, as so conceived, would brood, as with the Flaubert who wrote *L'Education Sentimentale*. But in its attempts to perfect a technique of brooding, it would learn to cherish the documents as never before. No expunging of records here. All must be kept, and faithfully examined; and not just that it may be approved or disapproved, but also that it be considered as a challenge to our prowess in placing it within the unending human dialogue as a whole.

If we temporarily risk being *stopped* by such a discipline, let us realize that the discipline is ideally designed precisely to that end. Education must not be thought of merely as a means of preparing students for market, though that's what much of it now is. Education must be thought of as a *technique of preparatory withdrawal*, the institutionalizing of an attitude that one should be able to *recover at crucial moments*, all along the subsequent way.

Admittedly, this view of education as a kind of smiling hypochondriasis presents some difficulties. The promissory, by its very nature, likes to look forward. And there is apparently danger lest youth would either too greatly resist such doctrines as a mere "counsel of despair," or would accept them only too thoroughly, if a whole educational program were undertaken in such a spirit. Perhaps, the world being what it is, this enterprise could be but one course in a curriculum, rather than the guiding principle behind educational policy in general. But if so, at least it would be conceived of as a kind of "central" or "over-all" course, a "synoptic" project for "unifying the curriculum" by asking the students themselves to think of their various courses in terms of a single distinctive human trait (the linguistic) that imposes its genius upon all particular studies.

Also, there can be much very active enjoyment in approaching the precious documents from this point of view. When the mortifying "fear of man as symbol-user" has been "comically" *technicalized*, such an attitude does not by any means close our horizons but opens many new vistas, making all aspects of symbolic activity somehow "contemporary" with us.

"Drooping," as so qualified, can be quite muscular.

Educational Process

Methodology

Primarily, we are ever to be on the lookout for grammatical and dialectical resources in general, while inspecting particular works for the discovery of special cases that forever keep threatening our frame of generalizations. In this respect, the procedure is not different from the traditional modes of inquiry and placement. But it has a somewhat "existentialist" aspect, in that we constantly re-begin from unique experiences (since each book that we take as our point of departure leads into our generalizations from one unique set of conditions, and accordingly compels us to see them in a perspective never quite duplicated, if we take any other book as our "informing experience"). Later, when discussing the negative, we shall consider another point at which this position closely parallels the existentialist one, if we have interpreted it correctly.

The study is thus built pedagogically about the "indexing" of some specific "symbolic structure," in the attempt to study the nature of a work's internal consistency and of its unfolding. But in contrast with courses in "literary appreciation," the generalizations at which we aim are not confined to a concern with the work's "beauty." Our quest concerns its linguistic nature in general; and then, beyond that, the insight it may afford into man's ways as symbol-user.

We proceed on the assumption that the "perfect case" for analytic purposes is a definitive literary text. This view, in turn, is doubtless but a variant of the traditional analogy whereby "nature" was likened to a "scripture" which would be legible if one but knew the language it was written in. In this case, the "signs" manifested by a human personality or by a social incident (or social order, or social movement, or cultural trend in general) would be treated as relatively obscure aspects of motivational structures that are least obscure in literary texts. There would thus be no difference "in principle" between textual analysis and social analysis. But though textual analysis would be the "ideal norm" here, there is no reason why specialists in other sciences could not apply the same procedures, *mutatis mutandis*, to their subjects (as with Freud's systematic attention to the "free associations" of his patients, or the use of questionnaires in polls of public opinion). Our major difference (if there is any essential difference!) is in the over-all direction we would give to such procedures.

When the great executive has finished his murder thriller, and relaxed into a well-earned sleep after having gone, by a certain disciplinary route, from the killing of the victim to the killing of the mystery, our vigil has but begun. We must ask: "What does the victim equal? . . . What does the killer equal? . . . What does the virtuously or disingenuously instigatory heroine equal? . . . What are the stages of this journey?" etc.

And we do this, not just to learn something about the given work, but ultimately in the hope of learning something about the ways in which the "personality" of the work relates to the "personality" of a social order; and then, in accordance with our project for methodic drooping, we look for ways whereby the work embodies, however assertively, even militantly, the *malaise* of a given property structure (with the goads, and "mortifications," and demands upon our "patience," and invitations to victimage, that are intrinsic to any such order).

Tragedies are quite convenient for our purposes, since we accept Aristotle's statement that tragic poetry aims at a kind of "catharsis"—and the explicitly civic, stately, or courtly nature of the tragedies traditionally accepted as great, makes easier our search for routes that clearly link mere "personal equations" with the "great persecutional words," such as fate, law, right, justice, Themis, Moira, Nemesis, necessity. But other species of expression are also inspected for kinds of catharsis or transcendence proper to their nature.

There are principles and rules of thumb to guide the task of "indexing." And one has available a set of at least partially coordinated statements about the nature of symbolic action in general. With this to start from, teacher and class are on a voyage of discovery together. Ideally, we keep open the channels that take us back and forth between general principles and casuistry, and, whereas certain methods for tracking things down have already been developed, teacher and class are engaged in a joint enterprise for perfecting these. But, whereas the original reading might have sought to track down a "villain," we rather would seek to track down the nature of the author's idea of "villainousness" conceived, not just historically, with regard to the "climate of opinion" that prevailed in a given social order but, universally or formally, with regard to the modes and motives of such symbolizing in general.

We proceed by systematically "suffering" a given text, in the hope of discovering more about the symbolic activity in its particular kinds of sufferance. "Formal discipline" is identical with the carrying out of such an investigation. "Truth" is absolute, in the sense that one can categorically make assertions about certain basic resources and embarrassments of symbols. It is nearly absolute, as regards certain "factual" statements that can be made about the terms of a given work. It is highly problematical, as regards the question that ultimately concerns us most: What is the nature of a symbol-using animal? Here, at least ideally, however emphatic we may become on the spur of the moment, we adopt as our primary slogan: "All the returns aren't in yet." And we would continue to keep alive this attitude (the "Dew-eyite" emphasis) by embodying it in methods that practically *compel* one to be tentative, at least during the preparatory stage when one is trying to locate all the significant correlations in a book, without deciding whether they are "good" or "bad," but trying rather simply to find out exactly what they *are.*

Since every course in the curriculum is a symbolically guided mode of action, a placement of all courses from the standpoint of symbolic action violates none of them, though with regard to many scientific disciplines the linguistic approach can be irksome to instructors who would persuade themselves and their classes that they are talking about "objective reality" even at those times when they happen to be but going through sheerly linguistic operations. Since every specialty has its terminology, it can be studied like any poem or philosophic treatise, for its "equations." And, indeed, if you inspect any given scientific writer's terminology closely enough, you can hope to find the bridges that join his purely technical nomenclature with the personal realm.

But though such statements are required for a full account of human action in the realm of physical motion, a "dramatistic" approach by no means requires that laws of motion as such be equated with action. Indeed, we have tried to show how the very self-consciousness of our stress upon action forces us to distinguish action from sheer motion (a distinction that is obscured, for instance, in Aristotle's term *kinesis*, though that very ambiguity is helpful in warning us how the two usages can cross, as when Aristotle himself "dramatistically" discusses the realm of physics in terms of "action" and "passion").

Though the student would not be abiding by the spirit of the enterprise if he merely set about such a fragmentary search as often characterizes doctoral theses, in all methods there is a large percentage of "neutrality," in the sense that a theory of ballistics could be called "neutral," since it could be employed by either side to slay the other. Accordingly, analysis can be carried into lines that take us far from our primary search (any method being ambiguous enough in its potentialities to become detached from the attitude for which it was designed).

Indeed, one can even imagine situations where, even if mankind did amass an authoritative lore on the odd kinds of "somnambulism" to which our nature as symbolists makes us susceptible, there might arise some calamitously endowed "throw-back" who used it all to make things worse rather than better, somewhat as when rules for the cure of souls are transformed into the techniques of "psychological warfare." For, since every point of view has its corresponding "pragmatics," this dilemma of the ambiguities in power or method is not confined to pragmatism. And, at least, the admonitory aspects of our position can prevent us from thinking of any human resource, such as "mind," "spirit," "eloquence," "imagination," "intellect," "understanding," "rationality," as intrinsically good, rather than as prone to the trickeries (and the grandeurs!) of the symbolic order upon which such resources so strongly rely.

The principle of "negativity" which is basic to the "dramatistic" approach, being essentially of a "repressive" nature (in contrast with liberal practices that often seemed to do all in their power to avoid the spirit of the thou-shalt-not), this approach must cope with the great threat to student interest that goes with such a concern. However, as contrasted with earlier modes of scholastic regimentation, it says no with a difference. It says no *by studying "no,"* by trying systematically to discover just how vast a domain the principle of negativity does actually govern, despite our assumptions to the contrary. Nor is such an investigation undertaken purely in the hope that, by such insight, one may be better qualified to emancipate one's self from the "reign of no." One must take it for granted that negativity of some sort is inevitable to social order, as conceived and constructed by an inveterately symbol-using species. And one must remember that the "negatives" of property and propriety are very "positive" in the sense that they affirm the given society's co-operative norms. Negatives shared in common can be like wealth shared in common.

It is not for us a question whether man is naturally good or naturally depraved; it is simply a question of realizing that, as animality in general comprises a set of positive needs, appetites, and gratifications (ultimately reducible to terms of material motion), so the distinctive trait of man, his way with symbols, or languages, centers in his ability to use the negative of "conscience," a symbolically guided ability that is also interwoven with the thou-shalt-not's, or no-trespassing, of property.

Curriculum Organization

To guide our search, we keep in mind a curricular distribution of this sort:

First, there are the sciences of motion, such as physics, mechanics, chemistry, astronomy, geology, mineralogy, oceanography. Though the building of such disciplines is in the realm of symbolic *action*, their subject matter is exclusively the realm of nonsymbolic motion, *except in so far as they must criticize their own terminology.*

The biological sciences would also fall under the heading of motion, though less absolutely. One may argue that there are the rudiments of symbolism in all living organisms, as attested by experiments with "conditioning" and "unconditioning," alterations of behavior which might be classed as the lowest kind of "learning," or "interpretation." But though one might possibly contend that there are respects in which nonhuman animals could be said to "read the signs," no one, within our present range of knowledge at least, considers any of these species "typically language-using, or symbol-using."

Recent studies of the motions of bees and ants would seem to indicate that these species have a highly organized code of signals whereby individuals can communicate precise information to one another. So it is remotely conceivable that eventually investigators may "crack" the expressiveness of animal gestures sufficiently to find even the rudiments of a grammar in the ways whereby dumb animals behavioristically influence one another by the use of posture and sound to convey the sheerly "motive" equivalents of "meaning."

In any case, we could still propose a way of distinguishing "symbolic action proper" from what we might call "sign-affected motion." Symbolic action proper is attested by a kind of "second-level" possibility. There is a sense, for instance, in which monkeys could be said to use tools as with situations wherein, if two sticks are so constructed that the end of one can be inserted into the end of the other to make a longer stick, the monkeys can learn this operation and apply it to procure something that was beyond the reach of either stick singly. We might call such behavior the rudimentary "inventing of a tool." Yet we should not expect the monkeys to go a step farther and construct the device that made the two sticks joinable. That is, they do not manifest the rudiments of such "second-level" behavior as the making of tools for the making of tools. And human intelligence is marked by this second-level kind of activity, which we dramatistically attribute to the kind of intelligence implied in the ability to use language. For language readily uses not only signs but also signs about signs, as general words can be used to sum up a set of particular words, or as the written word "table" can be a sign for the spoken word, which in turn is a sign for the thing itself, or as we can talk about talk, a glory that attains its somewhat unwieldy flowering in a critic's critical critique of the criticism of criticism.

Empirically and experimentally, at least, that would be our basis of distinction, until or unless further insight discloses the need for different dividing lines. And in view of the respects in which colonies of ants and bees are like burlesques of human social orders, presenting a set of motions that are crudely analogous to the actions and passions of a political community, we think it significant that these species seem to be the ones closest to being capable of human language. Presumably, such complex technology-like regimentation is possible only to a species capable of signalling fairly precise information or instruction.

Though all action involves motion, we may next make a distinction between practical and symbolic action (each of which requires a mediatory ground of motion). Practical action would be ethical (the doing of good), political (the wielding and obeying of authority), economic (the construction and operation of utilities, or powers). To say as much, however, is to realize that the practical realm is strongly infused by the symbolic element (since ideas of goodness, right, and expediency so obviously play a part in these practical acts). Yet in extreme cases at least, there is conceivable a clear distinction between practical and symbolic activity. It is a practical act to get in out of the rain, and a symbolic act to write a poem about getting in out of the rain; it is a practical act to eat, and a symbolic act to speak of eating.

On the *symbolic* side of our alignment, we would make a further distinction, between the "artificial" and the "neurotic." A poem would be an "artificial" symbolic act; and so likewise with a philosophy or scientific theory. While pure theory would be on the symbolic side of our chart, the various *applied* sciences would fall on the practical side, though *books* about them would be but symbolic artifice. Historiography would thus be an aspect of artificial symbolic action, for however real the *man* Napoleon may have been, his place in a history or a biography is that of one symbol among others. He is a *word*.

Rhetoric would likewise be artificial symbolic action. Aristotle calls it a "counterpart of dialectic," thus putting it in the realm of sheer words. But its use for ethical, political, and economic purposes also brings it close to the practical side. For example, Longinus's *On the Sublime* deals largely with examples from oratory that was originally designed for a practical end but, long after the practical occasion had passed, was "appreciated" by him purely a: poetry, because of its beauty or "imagination" as a robust symbolic exercising to be enjoyed and admired by readers in and for itself.

The other aspect of the purely symbolic, the "neurotic," might be subdivided into a distinction between those pathological conditions wherein the sufferer is still within bounds of communication and pathological conditions beyond communication. The latter kind (as with complete schizophrenia) might seem almost like a return to sheer motion, as though the sufferer had become but a vegetable; yet indications are that purely symbolic activity may here have attained a "simplicity" and "perfection" of inner consistency not possible to a symbol-system under normal conditions. Within communication would be the various partial "mental" disorders, high among which would also be the realm of "psychogenic illnesses," wherein the *motions* of the body have been radically disturbed by the *passions* that go with disorders of linguistic action. The artificial symbolic action of a poem becomes symbolic action of the neurotic sort in so far as the poem reflects the poet's attempts by purely symbolic means (by "beauties of the imagination") to solve problems that require practical solutions (ethical, political, economic).

But as soon as one stops to think how readily the *artifice* of a poem's symbolic action takes on *neurotic* ingredients, one may congratulate one's self that one's own favorite poets do not thus succumb; or one may congratulate one's self that one is not a poet but a "practical man of action." A linguistic approach to the study of human relations, on the other hand, would suggest rather the possibility that we are "poets all." Maybe, then, with a typically symbol-using creature, no solution of his difficulties but a *perfectly symbolic one* could content him, no matter how practical or normal he may think of himself as being.

The educational process as here conceived is guided by this ironic likelihood: That man can be content with nothing less than perfection, and that a typically symbol-using species will conceive of perfection in a way that is essentially symbolic, somewhat as "angels" are sheer "message." Our study of poetic ritual, for instance, would be guided by this notion. And some of Santayana's ingenious conceits, concerning the aspirations of the spirit to so transcend material conditions that the mind dissolves into the realm of pure being, would be interpreted by us linguistically as the ultimate human hankering for a condition so thoroughly in keeping with man's differentia that his generic animality would be transformed into a perfect symbol-system. A visible burlesque of such transcendence is seen in the Cyberneticists' dream of reducing all mental operations to their counterparts in the order of *pure* motion. And we all know of journalistic critics who read books so fast and write on them so quickly, their minds are hardly more than a telephone exchange where messages automatically converge and are automatically rerouted.

But here again, we come to the point at which, having stated our absolute position, we can settle for much less, as regards the processes of our study. We need but look for the respects wherein the sociolinguistic dimension is observable in all our actions, whereat these actions become *symbolic* of the principles infusing both a given social order and social order generally. This sociolinguistic nexus is headed in the principle of *negativity*, the astounding linguistic genius of *no*, which merges so perfectly with the conscientious thou-shalt-not's of property.

Thus, in accordance with this view, whereas we would divide the curriculum in ways that allow for the traditional autonomy of the various disciplines, we would so conduct our investigations that we might glimpse, brooding over the lot, a lore of the *universal pageantry* in which all men necessarily and somewhat somnambulistically take part, by reason of their symbol-using natures.[4]

School and Society: Social Philosophy

Imagine an educational ladder of this sort:

On the lowest rung would be the training of students in accordance with immediate local purposes, a mode of "indoctrination" designed to assert a narrowly partisan point of view in subjects of a "controversial" nature, and to deflect attention from any social philosophy at all in subjects of a "free" nature, such as "pure" literature.

The kind of education on the next higher rung would be just as narrowly partisan in its aims but more prudent in its ways of working toward such aims. It would be wider in its range so that the student would also know something of other views, because such knowledge would better equip him to combat them. Looking upon all enemies, or even opponents, as instruments of the devil, it would nonetheless seek to give the devil his dues, not because we owe the devil anything, but because we owe it to ourselves to know his powers.

Next above the second rung would be a more "humanitarian" view of alien ways. Holding that people generally have great moral virtues, it would, like the ethnologist, anthropologist, or sociologist, seek to describe and "appreciate" other groups, in all their varied habits, strengths, and shortcomings, not for partisan purposes, but purely in accordance with ideals of "truth" or "scientific accuracy." Although its findings would have been made in an impartial spirit, they could also be applied to narrower ends. In this respect, the third rung would be but the highest region of the second rung. Otherwise. it would be on a new level, having passed a "critical point."

A fourth rung would be involved in a much more complicated set of maneuvers. Here, the kind of material assembled in investigations on the third rung would be treated as voices in a dialogue. One would try to decide how many positions one thinks are important enough to be represented by "voices," and then one would do all in one's pourer to let each voice state its position as ably as possible. No voice deemed relevant to the particular issue or controversy would be subjected to the quietus, and none would be inadequately represented (as were one to portray it by stating only its more vulnerable arguments). But although one would be as fair as possible in thus helping all positions to say their say, a mere cult of "fair play" would not be the reason. Rather, one hopes for ways whereby the various voices, in mutually correcting one another, will lead toward a position better than any one singly. That is, one does not merely want to outwit the opponent, or to study him, one wants to be affected by him, in some degree to incorporate him, to so act that his ways can help perfect one's own—in brief, to learn from him.

This fourth principle of education is the most mature of the lot, and the one that would surely be aimed at, in an ideal world of civilized and sophisticated people. But for that very reason, it is very difficult to maintain, except in glimpses and at happy moments. What actually happens in education is that, to varying degrees, all four of these emphases fluctuantly prevail. And if each were signalized by a different light that came on when it happened to be the dominant educational motive in the classroom and went off, to be replaced by the glow of whatever light signalized the motive that next took over, doubtless during a typical session the four would be flashing on and off continually. And though the one signaling the fourth rung would certainly wear out last, it would have its moments, too.

Though a linguistic approach to education could somewhat fit the needs of all four emphases (naturally being most cramped when used for rung one, which might be called the "*Us über Alles*" rung), it is not quite identical with any of them. Nor could we arrogate to it a rung still higher than the fourth. Rather, there is a sense in which, as we said regarding "free" subjects taught in the lowest rung, it would in principle deflect attention from *any* social philosophy. For social philosophies are partisan philosophies, and the study of man as symbol-using animal would deal with *universal* traits of the symbol-using species. (We shall later discuss reasons why such a principle cannot in all purity prevail.)

Thus, whether confronting a "conservative" philosophy or a progressive" one, we should set out dramatistically to analyze the structure of its statements, considered as symbolic acts. We'd ask what terministic devices are used here, how they combine, etc.

In this sense, a linguistic point of view would be not so much a step "up" or "down" as a step to one side. It offers a technique for stopping to analyze an exhortation precisely at the moment when the exhortation would otherwise set us to swinging violently. It confronts a *practical* use of language for rhetorical effect by a *theoretical* study of such usage.

A linguistic approach to human relations would probably be happiest with democracy, of all political systems, since democracy comes nearest to being the institutionalized equivalent of dialectical processes (with such hopes of maturing an opinion as we discussed in connection with the ideal dialogue of education at rung four). But Plato, greatest master of the dialogue form, has warned us that democracy is liable to degenerate into tyranny, owing to an unmanageable excess of liberty. And in practice, democratic states move toward a condition of partial tyranny to the extent that the channels of expression are not equally available to all factions in important public issues. Thus we see democracy being threatened by the rise of the enormous "policy-making" mass media that exert great rhetorical pressure upon their readers without at the same time teaching how to discount such devices; and nothing less than very thorough training in the discounting of rhetorical persuasiveness can make a citizenry truly free, so far as linguistic tests are concerned. But we can say that *ideal* democracy does allow all voices to participate in the dialogue of the state, and such *ideal* democracy is the nearest possible institutional equivalent to the linguistic ideal.

As for the question whether schools should be leaders or followers of social change, the linguistic approach confronts us with some paradoxes, which are due in part to the fact that the labels on social philosophies can rarely be accurate. For one can never be quite sure how a doctrine will perform, once it enters into combination with many other factors in life that are beyond its control, and even beyond its ken. We can always expect "unintended by-products." Think how many determined Marxists have been produced by anti-Marxism, while Marxism has produced quite an army of determined ex-Marxists. And sometimes an unreasonable teacher in a grade school can serve as an object-lesson more effective than precepts for teaching students how not to be unreasonable. Nothing is more unforeseeable than the fate of a doctrine at the hands of its disciples.

There is a sense in which the study of man as symbol-using animal can be tied to as many different local faiths as can the view that there is or is not a personal God. The analysis of language quickly teaches us the importance of *combinations*. A thinker can start with an unpromising term but can surround it with good ones, while another person can start with an excellent term and surround it very dismally indeed.

But secondarily, a linguistic approach involves us in a social philosophy because of its accidental relation to certain social forces that may happen to favor or hinder it. It must be secular, for instance; for though it is not antagonistic to religious doctrine, it must approach such doctrine *formally* ("morphologically") rather than as doctrinally true or false. Accordingly, churchmen themselves can admit of such a formal approach, and often have done so; but where they would not do so, the linguistic approach would find itself accidentally allied with a *secular* "social philosophy." Or, if pressure groups who are so minded and can exert sufficient influence objected to the stress upon linguistic sophistication, then "dramatism" would find itself allied with a liberal social philosophy, even in a militant sense. And, of course, the position is uncompromisingly liberal in the sense that its first principle must be the systematic distrust of any social certainties as now set (our position here necessarily reaffirms the Deweyite prizing of the experimental attitude, backed by experimental method).

Naturally, we identify such a program with both patriotism and international co-operation. It should be an aid to patriotism by helping to make demagoguery more difficult and by fostering an attitude that would make international co-operation easier. It would sharpen our sense of the fact that all men, as symbol-users, are of the same substance, in contrast with naïve views that in effect think of aliens as of a different substance. Dramatism thus, by its very nature, implies respect for the individual. Again, we should recognize that our stress upon the major importance of the negative may seem "reactionary" to some Liberals, particularly those who have striven valiantly to find ways of "not saying no" to children.

Perhaps we might best indicate the nature of our social philosophy by referring to the kind of "linguistic exercising" that we think wholly in keeping with the spirit of this project:

If one should read in a newspaper some "factual" story that obviously produced a pronounced attitude for or against something, while reading it one would try to imagine how the same material might have been presented so as to produce other attitudes, It is not, thus, a matter of deciding about the "factual accuracy" of the story, a matter about which in most cases you will not be equipped to make a decision. You will permit yourself speculatively a wider range of freedom as regards its *stylization*. That is, you counteract "slanting," not by trying to decide whether the reporter is honest or a liar, or even whether he is fair or unfair, but by leaving unquestioned the facts as given and merely trying to imagine different ways of presenting them, or by trying to imagine possible strategic omissions.

Or, were the earlier pedagogic practice of debating brought back into favor, each participant would be required, not to uphold just one position but to write two debates, upholding first one position and then the other. Then, beyond this, would be a third piece, designed to be a formal transcending of the whole issue, by analyzing the sheerly verbal maneuvers involved in the placing and discussing of the issue. Such a third step would not in any sense "solve" the issue, not even in the reasonable, sociological sense of discovering that, "to an extent, both sides are right." Nor would we advise such procedures merely as training in the art of verbal combat. For though such experience could be applied thus pragmatically, the ultimate value in such verbal exercising would be its contribution toward the "suffering" of an attitude that pointed toward a distrustful admiration of all symbolism, and toward the attempt systematically to question the many symbolically-stimulated goads that are now accepted too often without question.

Or a student might write an essay analyzing the modes of utterance in two previous essays he had written, one of which traced man's progress "upward" from "savagery" to the "high standard of living" provided by modem technology, while the other treated this same development as deplorable "degeneration," with profound tribal conscientiousness overgrown by a wilderness of superficial abstract law.

We can never sufficiently emphasize, however, that we are thinking of education as a tentative, preparatory stage in life, not as a final one. It is final only in the sense that it possesses its own kind of completeness and thus, ideally, should be recoverable at all stages in one's life. For it develops to perfection one stage in the confronting of a problem, the stage where one steps aside as thoroughly as possible and attempts, in the spirit of absolute linguistic skepticism, to meditate upon the tangle of symbolism in which all men are by their very nature caught.

The corresponding methods of interpreting man's entanglements have been sloganized by us elsewhere as the "socioanagogic," since a primary aim here is to discover in what respects the objects of this world are enigmatic emblems of man's relation to the social order (that is, in what respects they may possess for man a "symbolic" character, over and above their nature as sheer *things*). Since language, however manipulated by the individual user, is essentially a collective or social product, the powers of the social order will inevitably be manifested in it, quite as these powers can only be developed by the use of linguistic resources. A social philosophy, as so conceived, would be built about four orders: the verbal or linguistic; the sociopolitical; the natural; the supernatural. And we shall end this section by briefly indicating the relation we think they bear to one another.

The verbal pyramid is most clearly revealed in the design of Platonist and Neo-Platonist dialectic, the upward way from particulars to higher and higher orders of abstraction, matched by a corresponding downward way from the one to the many which are imbued with the substance of its oneness. Such resources become interwoven with whatever social order happens to prevail, or to have prevailed when the symbolic traditions were taking form. Such order has its more or less clearly defined pyramidal structure, with criteria for distinguishing the direction socially up from the direction socially down. Here we would look for the situations which gave form to the terminology for familial relationships, and to the great persecutional words that grandly sum up the principle of negativity inherent in the nature of property.

Third, there is the natural order, whether conceived along Aristotelian lines (as in the medieval concern with the "great chain of being,") or along Darwinian lines, charting an evolutionary "descent" from "lower" kinds of entities to "higher" kinds. This is the order that, in the dramatistic terminology, is most fittingly discussed in terms of motion.

And finally, there are terms for a supernatural order, a terminology constructed after the analogy of the other three, since there can be no empirically literal vocabulary for the description of a realm that by definition transcends the conditionality of human language and human experience. That is, if the ultimate scene, or "ground of all possibility" is called a "lord," a supernatural relationship is being named metaphorically, in terms of what is, so far as our institutions are concerned, an obsolete social relationship. And the description of God as "simple" is in accordance with certain dialectical resources that permit of progress toward an over-all "term of terms" that will sum up complexity much as the title of a novel could be said to simplify the myriad details by one word that stood for the single spirit infusing them all. And terms referring to God as a body would be borrowed from the natural order.

But there is a paradox upon which a dramatist philosophy of social motivations lays great emphasis: Whereas we are by the nature of the case compelled to see the part that the other three orders of terms play in the terminology of the supernatural order, and whereas we are familiar with the transcendentalist dialectic of a writer, say, like Emerson, who contrives to interpret the many agencies of the everyday world as all variously embodying a single supernatural purpose, it is much harder to detect the ways in which the linguistic and social orders affect our ideas of the natural order. And this is the enigma, above all others, with which dramatism, as a social philosophy, is engrossed.

By the socioanagogic emphasis in linguistic criticism, we refer to a concern with the ways in which the structure of the social and linguistic orders affects the metaphors men use for the supernatural order and colors the "empirical reality" which men think they perceive in the natural order. We believe that the natural order is profoundly infused with symbolism, "mystery," and "divinity" of a purely secular and social sort, however transcendent its gleam may sometimes seem to be. Here, we believe, is a major source of man's exorbitant goads and false exaltations. We believe it to be a major source of the scramble so incessantly plaguing great nations that most persons seem to take it as "the norm," sometimes assuring us that man is "naturally predatory," and sometimes in unconscious sacrilege interpreting such worldly struggle as an evidence of man's "divine discontent."

An educational policy constructed in accordance with this principle would ground its techniques in a social philosophy that looked upon such inquiry as the ultimate end of secular study. But one could not know what the actual "alignments" in such a project would be, what social forces would be for it and what against it, unless it were actually attempted on a considerable scale.

The School and the Individual

But our zeal for the negative or admonitory in education should not seem to prevail over its counterpart, the lore of "positive" appreciation. With regard to the three major aims of education as so conceived, training in skills, moral admonition, and aesthetic appreciation (note that they are secular or technical analogues of the trinitarian three: "power," "wisdom," and "love"): Here would be an excellent point at which to remember the claims of the third.

Skills, we might say, are like the metal of a coin. On its reverse side is stamped the negativistic, admonitory social or moral philosophy of language. But on its obverse there are markings of a wholly different sort, to signalize the realm of aesthetic delight.

In so far as the suffering of man's hierarchal burdens is to be as growing old, the aesthetic affirming of the resources natural to such conditions is like being born anew, as with the "equations" of Goethe's *Faust*. (And perhaps if we accept a pedagogically "mortifying" device that makes us theoretically old while we are still physically young, we may get "as a bonus" a compensatory device that can keep us theoretically young when we are physically old.)

When we are under the sign of appreciation, the very same things that we had considered "droopingly" can now be viewed with almost the expectant air of a young puppy, that seems always brightly ready for some astounding thing to happen. Here is our chance for an Emersonian recovery, an aesthetic "compensation."

The negatives we would impose upon the individual (or rather, the negatives we would have him recognize as having already been imposed upon him by the combination of the social and linguistic orders, as re-enforced by the mechanical necessities of the natural order) are "collective," bearing upon his obligations to the tribe, and to himself as member of the tribe. Here would be a secular variant of "original sin."

But in contrast, his positive, aesthetic enjoyments can be received by him as an individual (though the public nature of the symbolic medium, through which he aesthetically receives, makes it unlikely that individual delights of this sort can be merely "solipsistic"), and the zeal with which we tell others of our enjoyments indicates how eager we are to "socialize" everything, a tendency which the social nature of language would help impose upon us, but which cannot overweigh the fact that when you enjoy the taste of a particular orange, it is being enjoyed by you and none other.

So, although the tribal negatives are uniquely translated into the decisions of each individual "conscience," and although aesthetic enjoyment, too, has its "tribal" aspects (as with the distinctive exaltations that can affect public gatherings), we would treat the aesthetically positive under the head of "the school and the individual," whereas the moralistically negative seems to have fitted best under the head of "school and society."

As regards this relation between moralistic admonition and aesthetic appreciation, once you "get the idea" of the pattern, you see how readily all ethical misgivings can become transformed into aesthetic promises, thus:

Have we proposed a distrust of ambition? Then see, on the other hand, what great tragic assertions have been made of this distrust, as with the grotesqueries of *Macbeth*, or the stateliness of murder in *Julius Caesar*. Do we discern how the motives of sheer ownership figure in relations between husband and wife? Then note how these are made almost exultant in *Othello*.

Does a writer seem to suggest that he despises all *people*, either in particular or in general? Then note how, by the very scrupulousness of his work, he shows that he most earnestly respects an *audience*. And no matter how questionable the scramble, there is a gallantry, an essential cult of the compliment, implicit in the earnestness with which a good artist will bring the best he has to market, even though he suspects that, by not making it worse, he may sell it for less.

Is there an overriding fear of death? Then see how the poet exploits this attitude to the ends of pomp, in the hope of infusing his work with a funereal, corpse-like dignity.

Is there a need of victimage, to relieve ourselves by thoughts of a vicarious sacrifice? Must we look for a goat? Then see how such impulses are made grand by the devices of tragedy.

Does the weight of a social order oppress us grievously, driving us within ourselves, imposing upon us the involuntary vows of psychogenic illness, making us prone to fantasies of sexual perversion that represent, in terms of erotic appetite, the jealousies and malice and self-punishments typical of the "hierarchal psychosis"? All this may, by the "alchemy of the word," be transformed into an aesthetic "remembrance of things past," that loves to contemplate the pageantry of corruption. And the tangled social motives may come to take the form that Stanley Hyman has called the "Albertine strategy" (having in mind Proust's resources whereby a heterosexual love is imagined not directly, but roundabout, by the aesthetic perverting of an experience that, in the real moral realm, had been *homosexual*).

Have we questioned the entire modern cult of gadgetry by which the wheels of industry are largely kept going, over and above production for war goods? Then note how this same gadgetry becomes the pleasant movement and glitter of a spectacular Hollywood revue, in which woman plays a leading role, as the gadget of gadgets. Well-groomed, specious flesh clothing the skeleton.

There is no tangle so hopeless that it cannot, with the symbol-using species, become the basis for a new ingenious assertion that transcends it, by the very nature of linguistic assertion. No way of life can be so wretched, corrupt, or even boring that some expert symbol user or other can't make it the subject matter of a good book. Wherever you might moralistically exclaim, "How awful!" there is the opportunity for the aesthetic to answer spiritedly, "But how *delightfully* awful!"

In sum, there is the transcendence in expression as such (the point emphasized in the Crocean aesthetic). Atop that, there is the transcendence implicit in the processes whereby the work "purifies itself" in the course of its unfolding. And beyond that, there is transcendence by the various ways whereby we feel ourselves similarly purified while undergoing the imaginary discipline of the story's action and passion (undergoing such either as spontaneous spectators or as students, or both). And so, each time we inspect a great work of human thought (that is, a great symbolic exercising), we can be delighted by the manifestations of its genius, a skill whereby even the accents of lamentation can be transformed into the pleasurable.

Here is a glorious realm of *solutions*. Here is easy going, atop hard going. But such expression is at the same time fearsome by reason of its very felicity, in so far as the availability of such cunning resources may tempt us to perpetuate an underlying moral ill by cultivating the happy exercise that makes it beautiful. A familiar example appears in the popular art patronized by commercial advertisers which helps make insatiable in real life the very appetites which it symbolically gratifies in the world of make-believe. In any case, by dodging between aesthetic positives and moralistic negatives, one seeks to improvise the "good life." Such an attempt is always complicated, as Aristotle's *Ethics* reminds us, by the fact that, before one can live *well*, one must contrive to *live*.

However, when we attempt charting the good life, we must be linguistically shrewd about our own statement, too. There is always the invitation to express such matters in terms more or less flatly opposed (polar terms, they have often been called), with some variant of the thought that what we want is a middle road between the two extremes. A variant is the discovery that, where two opposed principles are being considered, each of which has the "defects of its qualities," what we want is something that avoids the typical vices of either and combines the typical virtues of both. Or, dialectical resources being what they are, we can readily propose that any troublesome *either-or* be transformed into a *both-and*. Thus, when thinking of "authority, control, and discipline" on the one hand, and of "freedom and initiative" on the other, most people are likely to opt for a moderate mixing of the two. "There should be both respect for the individual and subordination of the individual to the group; there should be both patriotism and internationalism, in happy balance; education, as the projecting of traditions into new situations, must combine conservative and progressive tendencies; student interest must not be stifled by overly authoritative guidance, yet the student should not be deprived of such guidance where he requires it," etc. Such linguistic resources suggest why even excessively one-sided educators might tend to think of themselves as serving under the sign of the golden mean.

And there can be further very good reasons for such a view. As regards the relation between authority and freedom, for instance, the investigating of symbolic action is still in a highly problematical stage, while many teachable principles and rules of thumb have already been formulated; and this situation of itself almost compels one to ask of the student a kind of discipline not distinguishable from pronounced personal initiative.

And there is always the aura of *promise* in education, a promise implied when it is not made explicit. This promissory motive came to the aid of the various fly-by-night outfits that quickly cooked up likely looking courses to profit by the situation of the returning soldiers, with funds at their disposal under the G.I. educational bill of rights. Courses in vocational training draw especially on such hopefulness, on the willingness of the student-customer to be assured that, if he takes the course, he will somehow have a much better chance to hit the "jack pot" and thereby to experience the deliciously immoral thrill that occurs when a slight gesture, made accidentally at the right time, disproportionately calls forth an abrupt unloosening, an indecent downpour, of revenue.

Thus, the promise will be there to some extent, even when it's false. And it should never be wholly false, so far as a linguistic approach to education is concerned. For the analysis of symbolic action should not only sharpen kinds of perception that are competitively useful to the manipulating of symbols, it should also contribute to our lore of human foibles in general, and so make for much sheer shrewdness as regards the ways of the scramble. This should be particularly the case if the study of linguistic tactics is extended to a "post-Machiavellian" kind of inquiry in a realm where purely rhetorical devices overlap upon a realm of nonverbal materiality, as with the pronouncements of promoters, politicians, diplomats, editors, and the like, whose use of purely symbolic resources is backed by a tie-in with organizational or bureaucratic forces.

But, ideally at least, viewed in "the absolute," an educational program of this sort would come closer to such promises as were once called the *consolatio philosophiae*. Admonition would make of education a watching and waiting, appreciation would seek out the positive attitudes that corrected such negatives. Its great stress upon linguistic skepticism would imply that it is not designed to make up the student's mind for him. For it could not arrogate to itself the right (or assume that it had the ability) to anticipate the *particularity* that characterizes an individual's decisions. In fact, it cannot even deny its knowledge of paradoxical cases where training can be a sheer handicap to a man, as when the sudden introduction of new technological methods required that the former experts be discharged, since their very fitness for the old ways made them less fit for the new ways. It can, however, make such considerations an important part of its teaching, in accordance with the particular kinds of quizzicality in which it would become at home.

Education, as so conceived, would be willing to give full recognition to every important favorable and unfavorable factor in a given situation. If it failed to meet such tests, the failure would be caused by lack of knowledge or perception, not by any categorical claims to individual, professional, national, or universal rights or dignities, except the right and dignity of doing all in its power to study the lore of such rights and dignities.

Such, then, is what we take to be the nature of education as "preparation for adult life." The obligations of order hang over us, even if we would revolt against order. Out of such predicaments, ingenious fellows rise up and sing; thus promptly have all our liabilities been by symbol-using converted into assets. Similarly aesthetic, from this point of view, is any way of analytically *enjoying* the ways of rising up and singing. These ways may be "diagnostic," as all education in one sense is. And so we are led back to the realm of the admonitory.

And finally, and above all, in keeping with our "socioanagogic" search for the ways in which the magic of the social order infuses men's judgments of the beautiful (quite as it infuses their ethics and their perception of even "natural" things) we watch everywhere for the manifestations of the "hierarchal" motive, what Ulysses, in *Troilus and Cressida*, calls "degree." It is only "by degree," he declaims, that communities, schools, brotherhoods, businesses, inheritance, the prerogatives of age and office, even the regularities of nature, "stand in authentic place." Accordingly, "Take but degree away, untune that string, / And, hark! what discord follows; each thing meets / In mere oppugnancy." And later, with a strange imagistic paralleling of *Othello*, he sums up: "Chaos, when degree is suffocate, / Follows the choking." We cite from this long passage, not exactly to reaffirm the Shakespearean answer, but to recall how vast, in the perspective of Shakespearean drama, was the scope of the question.

School and Religion

The study of religion fits perfectly with the approach to education in terms of symbolic action. What more thorough examples of symbolic action can be found than in a religious service? What is more dramatistic than the religious terminology of action, passion, and personality? What terminology is more comprehensive than the dialectic of a theologian? What is linguistically more paradoxical than the ways wherein the mystic, seeking to express the transcendently ineffable, clothes theological ideas in the positive imagery of sheer animal sensation? Where, more perfectly than in versions of the heavenly hierarchy, can we find the paradigms of hierarchal terminology? And, as regards the principle of negativity, where does it figure more ultimately than in the dialectical subtleties of negative theology?

The great depth and scope of religious terminologies; the range of personalities and problems that have found accommodation within the religious framework; the kind of "inner freedom" that goes with the cult of ultimate praise made possible by the religious rationale; the religious placement of beauty and the practical; the ways in which religious scruples can sharpen even purely secular kinds of sympathy and awareness—to think of such matters is to realize that the long tradition of religion provides us with a field of study as vital and as sweeping as the over-all history of human culture itself.

Thus we could state unequivocally that the language of religion is the most central subject matter for the study of human relations in terms of symbolic action. Or perhaps we should make the claim even more specifically, in saying that the central concern would be not just religion, but *theology*, that is, the strict realm of dogma, and of a church's symbolic practices (its rites and rituals) as placed in terms of its dogmas.

But though ideally the dramatistic approach heads in the study of religious forms, the social obstacles are obvious. First, in a nation of many faiths, there would be embarrassment in the mere singling out of any one doctrine for special study, in a secular school. Second, dramatism would also require a systematic concern with the *misuses* to which a religious terminology can be put, as when its spirituality becomes a sheer rhetorical shield for the least spiritual of special interests. And though, if nothing else were involved, a truly religious person might be expected to welcome any teachings, from whatever source, that help admonish against the misuse of religion, there are many kinds of susceptibility here that make such considerations unadvisable.

Consider, for instance, the frenzy with which Molière was attacked for his comedy, *Tartuffe*, his enemies proclaiming that religion itself had been slandered in his portrait of a religious hypocrite. And even though a dramatistic analysis of such matters would be much milder, since it would but "study" temptations that Molière sought to make dramatically salient, it could not go far without raising resentments that would militate against its own purposes, by intensifying the very passions it would assuage.

Fortunately, the main concern in a dramatistic treatment of religious language (and of the rites rationalized by such a language) resides elsewhere. There are broad principles of theological placement that can be studied, for instance, when one is studying modes of placement in general. Thus, when considering the formal relationship that prevails between "scene" and "act" in a systematic terminology dealing with such matters, one can include various theological pronouncements in a list that also includes various secular treatments of the same problem. And by such means, theological considerations can be introduced relevantly, without much risk of the embarrassments that might result if a class of secular students were to "index" any one religious terminology as thoroughly as they might index a novel or drama.

A dramatistic stress could not simply omit such subjects, however. For the position is based on the awareness that religious terminologies have charted with especial urgency and thoroughness the problems of "sin" and "redemption" as these take form against a background of hierarchal order. Here, then, are the grandest terminologies for the locating of the attitudes that, by our interpretation, arc grounded in the feeling for negativity, the "idea of no," a symbolistic genius that makes itself felt in a variety of manifestations. Examples of such manifestations are sacrifice, mortification, penance, vicarious atonement, conversion, rebirth, original sin, submission, humility, purgation, in brief, "conscience"; thence secondarily in rejections, revolts, impatiences; and so with intermediate realms like indifference, betrayal, psychogenic illness, attempts to resolve social antitheses; and finally in the purely technical realm, as with the ability to know that the words for things are not the things, that ironic statements are to be interpreted in reverse of their surface meaning, and that the range of language can be extended metaphorically without error only if we know how to "discount" a metaphorical term.

There is a crucial paradox in the dramatistic approach to religion, however. For whereas it leads to an almost minute interest in the *letter* of the faith, requiring a particular stress upon the terms that specify *doctrine, dogma,* its approach to such elements is not doctrinal, but formal. That is, it does not ask: "Is such a doctrine literally *true* or *false?*" Rather, it asks, "what are the relationships prevailing among the key terms of this doctrine?" And: "Can we adapt the terminology to other terminologies, at least somewhat?" For instance, one might ask whether theological statements about "original sin" could fit with a purely secular notion that there is a kind of *categorical guilt* implicit in the nature of all sociopolitical order, with the malaise of its "degrees," a malaise sharpened by the feeling for negativity, as embodied in the "rights and wrongs" or "yeses and noes," of man's linguistically heightened conscientiousness.

Such a secularly formal (or, if you will, "aesthetic") approach to the literal particularities of dogma must be insufficient, as judged by the tests of advocates who would proclaim one doctrine and no other as the whole and only truth. But though educators, being concerned with preparations rather than fulfilments, might for their pains be classed among those "trimmers" who after death were denied even entrance into hell, since they could not wholly die through never having wholly lived, yet as regards the needs of education for the "global" conditions that technology is imposing upon us, precisely such a deflection seems particularly needed at this time. For it would seem to go as far as humanly possible toward the forming of such attitudes as are required if men of many different faiths are to participate in a common parliament of all nations and are to confront one another in an attitude better than mere armed neutrality, or in a diplomatic silence whereby all sorts of very important things are left unsaid. For though any specific measure can be debated in such a spirit, a world organization can flourish "positively" only in so far as all its members can work toward a frame of reference common to all.

It is the thesis of this essay that, since all divergent doctrines must necessarily confront one another as doctrinal "idioms," a framework for the lot could be provided only by the perfecting of some terminology for the study of idioms in general. A terminology as so conceived must necessarily adopt some point of view in which all could share. And a formalistic view is such a one, at least in principle. We say "in principle," since there are still valid points of disagreement as to whether a "dramatistic" species of formalism should be the kind to opt for. And Professor Benne, in this "dramatism," would prefer a "tragic" to a "comic" one, for reasons he has explained in his article on "Education for Tragedy." We only contend that a *generally* linguistic approach to the problem would be the proper counterpart of the purely pragmatic arrangements for having addresses at the United Nations translated into several languages and having choices among these translations made quickly available to the various delegates, with the help of machines.

The same considerations apply, of course, to purely "secular religions," notably such political philosophies as capitalism or dialectical materialism. These, too, are terminologies of action, hence essentially "dramatistic" in structure—and whatever their vast disagreements, they can at least meet in terms of their nature as terminologies of action. Admittedly, such an approach is not enough to resolve specific issues that lead to blunt, head-on collisions. One cannot ask an educational method to do the impossible. But one can ask that it provide a positive equivalent for the area of commonalty which even opponents must share, if they are to join the same battle.

Where the various "persuasions" are brought together, what topic surely transcends them all but the question of persuasion itself? If one particular persuasion among the lot could triumph, then we'll concede, however grudgingly, that such a result might be all to the good, though at the very least we'd want to suggest: The differences among the various areas of the world would soon give rise to new local emphases that, to many, would look like outright heresy, whereat the squabbles would begin anew. For such are the temptations to which the symbol-using species is prone, by reason of the nature of symbols. And, for these reasons, at least so far as the linguistic approach to educational problems is concerned, we believe that, *faute de mieux*, the nearest man will ever get to a state of practical peace among the many persuasions is by theoretical study of the forms in all persuasion.

It is regrettable that the author of the greatest rhetoric wrote his tract before the data on the great world persuasions were available to him. So, while Aristotle's formal treatment of the subject remains, to this day, the greatest of its kind, regrettably he had but comparatively trivial examples of verbal wrestling to analyze (trivial, that is, as compared with the symbolic ways of the great world religions, both worldly and other-worldly, that took form since his time, or since the awarenesses available to him). But the principles remain intact; and they are in their very essence dramatistic; and a search for the *forms* of persuasion, as exemplified in later materials, might very profitably abide by the suggestions which his treatise provides. Nor should we forget that, elsewhere in his own work, he supplies the further forms needed for a most ingenious locating of the hierarchal motive, the motive grandly essential to the modes of submission ("Islam") that characterize the world religions.

All such persuasive powers, the heights of symbol-using genius as embodied in definition, expression, and exhortation, we would with fearsomeness appreciate. Such is the dramatistic variant of the linguistic approach to education, an approach now often called "semanticist."

Epilogue

But suppose that all did turn out as we would have it, so far as educational programs went? What next? What might be the results?

First: In seeing beyond the limitations of language, many might attain a piety now available to but a few. Many might come closer to a true fear of God, through getting more glimpses into the ultimate reality that stretches somehow beyond the fogs of language and its sloganizing.

Or, on the contrary: There might descend upon mankind a boredom such as never before cursed symbol-using creatures. For all men might come to so distrust the motives of secular ambition, as clamorously established by all who help make secular aims "glamorous," that the entire pageantry of empire would seem as unreal as a stage set.

But those are the absolute alternatives: the alternatives of absolute piety (or "loyalty to the sources of our being"), and of absolute drought (be it mystic "accidie" or Baudelairean "spleen").

But here, in parting, once again we would "settle for less," holding out the hope of only this much: That such an approach should help some of the rawness to abate, by including a much wider range of man's symbolic prowess under the head of the fearsomely appreciated, and thereby providing less incentives to be overprompt at feeling exalted with moral indignation.

In the educational situation, characteristically, the instructor and his class would be on good terms. They would preferably be under the sign of goodwill. And is not education ideally an effort to maintain such an attitude as thoroughly and extensively as possible without loss of one's own integrity? If, where we cannot "love" our neighbor's ways, we might at least "fearsomely *appreciate*" their form, and in methods that bring our own ways within the orbit of the "*fearsomely* appreciated," would we not then be at least headed in the right direction? And is not this direction most urgent, in view of the new weapons that threaten not only our chances of living well but even our chances of living at all?

Bibliographical Note

There is a general sense in which *any* book could figure in a "dramatistic" bibliography, since any book is by definition an instance of "symbolic action." More narrowly, we should include here works that are built about the featuring of some term for "action," ranging all the way from theories of economic or commercial "transactions" to theologies that view God as "pure act." Spinoza's *Ethics* is a good example of the type, because of the symmetry with which it explicitly works out a balance of actives and passives.

All writers who have figured in the shift of emphasis from philosophy to the critique of language could be listed here, as with the traditional battles over "universals" (with nominalists and realists throwing equally important light upon the normal resources of language, and upon our language-ridden views of extralinguistic "reality"). In this regard, even the most positivistic or "scientific" of semantical theories could properly be included in our bibliography.

And though the empiricist stress of Locke, Berkeley, and Hume would be inferior to the scholastic tradition, when judged as philosophy, in admonitions as regards a critique of language are nearly perfect for our purposes. Our main shift of emphasis would be in the direction of a greater concern with the ways in which sociopolitical motives infuse men's views of their so-called "sensory" perceptions. Similarly, psychoanalytic and psychosomatic speculations fit well with the dramatistic emphasis, because of their great stress upon forms of symbolic action, though as with empiricism, the overly psychologistic stress usually somewhat deflects attention from the sociopolitical realm of motives.

Specifically, by "dramatism" is meant a linguistic theory expressly built about terms as "action," "passion," and "substance," and designed to consider language in the light of the logic, resources, and embarrassments of such terms. It would be more likely to stress *verbs* than *nouns* as the way-in, though for this very reason it finds itself paradoxically quite friendly to Jeremy Bentham's search for ideal definition in terms of nouns (with his "theory of fictions" designed to take account of the respects in which strongly verb-like and negatively tinged nouns would not lend themselves to his materially positive ideal). Likewise this approach finds much to its purposes in works as different as James Harris's *Hermes* and the redoubtable Home Tooke's *Diversions of Purley* (with its stress upon the nature of "abbreviations" in language).

In this specific sense, a systematically self-conscious statement of the dramatistic perspective is offered in *A Grammar of Motives* and *A Rhetoric of Motives*, by Kenneth Burke (Prentice-Hall, Inc., 1945 and 1950, respectively). The *Grammar* considers the logic of "substance" in general, the *Rhetoric* considers its place in personal and social "identifications." Also, both books offer many examples of the way in which works by other writers can be interpreted as implicit contributions to the dramatistic perspective.

As regards the ethical dimension in language, see particularly "A Dramatistic View of the Origins of Language" (*Quarterly Journal of Speech*, October and December, 1952, February, 1953) and "Postscripts on the Negative" (same publication, April, 1953).

A work now in preparation, *A Symbolic of Motives*, will deal with poetics and the technique of "indexing" literary works. Meanwhile, among articles by the present author already published on this subject are: "The Vegetal Radicalism of Theodore Roethke" (*Sewanee Review*, Winter, 1950); "Three Definitions" (*Kenyon Review*, Spring, 1951); "Othello: An Essay to Illustrate a Method" (*Hudson Review*, Summer, 1951); "Form and Persecution in the Oresteia" (*Sewanee Review*, Summer, 1952); "Imitation" (*Accent*, Autumn, 1952); "Comments on Eighteen Poems by Howard Nemerov" (*Sewanee Review*, Winter, 1952); "Ethan Brand: A Preparatory Investigation" (*Hopkins Review*, Winter, 1952); "Mysticism as a Solution to the Poet's Dilemma," in collaboration with Stanley Romaine Hopper (*Spiritual Problems in Contemporary Literature*, edited by Stanley Romaine Hopper, published by Institute for Religious and Social Studies, distributed by Harper & Bros., 1952); "Fact, Inference, and Proof in the Analysis of Literary Symbolism," (paper presented at Thirteenth Conference on Science, Philosophy, and Religion, and published in a volume distributed by Harper & Bros., 1954).

The author's first book of literary criticism, *Counter-Statement* (originally published, 1931; republished with new Preface and Epilogue, 1953, by Hermes Publications, Los Altos, California) is relevant to these inquiries because it treats of literary form in terms of audience appeal. His *Permanence and Change: An Analysis of Purpose* (originally published, 1935, revised edition published, May, 1954 Hermes Publications), centers about problems of interpretation, communication, and "new meanings," though the perspective is there called not "dramatic," but "poetic." An out-of-print work, *At-*

titudes toward History (New Republic, 1937) deals largely with problems of bureaucracy (now often called "organizational behavior"). Another out-of-print work, *The Philosophy of Literary Form* (Louisiana State University Press, 1941) considers many problems of "indexing," and outlines the theories of "symbolic action" that he behind such analysis.

Miscellaneous items: *Nous Autres Matérialistes* (*Esprit*, November, 1946). analyzing the motives in the "higher standard of living"; "Rhetoric Old and New" (*Journal of General Education*, April 1951); "Ideology and Myth" (*Accent*, Summer, 1947); "Thanatopsis for Critics: A Brief Thesaurus of Deaths and Dyings" (*Essays in Criticism*, October, 1952), a study of motives involved in the imagery of death; "Freedom and Authority in the Realm of the Poetic Imagination" (*Freedom and Authority in Our Time*, Twelfth Symposium of the Conference on Science, Philosophy and Religion, edited by Lyman Bryson, Louis Finkelstein, R. M. MacIver, Richard P. McKeon, distributed by Harper & Bros., 1953). In a symposium on "The New Criticism" (*American Scholar*, Winter, Spring, 1951), Burke at several points discusses what he means by the "socioanagogic" approach to literary forms.

For an authoritative summary of the "dramatistic" position, see "Kenneth Burke and the 'New Rhetoric'" (Marie Hochmuth, *Quarterly Journal of Speech*, April, 1952).

Kenneth D. Renne's article, "Education for Tragedy" (*Educational Theory*, November and December, 1951) while agreeing with Burke's general emphasis, offers grounds for a "tragic" species of such, in contrast with Burke's "comic" view. See also Kenneth D. Benne's essay-review, "Toward a Grammar of Educational Motives" (*Educational Forum*, January, 1947) for his evaluation of Burke's *Grammar of Motives*, from the standpoint of educators who arrived at the dramatist position by a somewhat different route. And see also, in this regard: *The Improvement of Practical Intelligence: The Central Task of Education*, by R. Bruce Raup, George E. Axtelle, Kenneth D. Benne, B. Othanel Smith (Harper & Bros., 1950).

While concerned with the sociology of literature in ways that only partly coincide with Burke's emphasis, Hugh Dalziel Duncan's *Language and Literature in Society* (University of Chicago Press, 1953) offers a thorough analysis of ways whereby the dramatistic perspective can be applied to problems of sociology. Donald E. Hayden's *After Conflict, Quiet; A Study of Wordsworth's Poetry in Relation to His Life and Letters* (Exposition Press, New York, 1951) is constructed in accordance with a dialectic pattern quite relevant to the dramatistic view of symbolic unfoldings. And among those many excellent volumes in the *International Encyclopedia of Unified Science*, particular attention should be called to "The Development of Rationalism and Empiricism" by George De Santillana and Edgar Zilsel (University of Chicago Press, 1941).

Works such as Francis Fergusson's *The Idea of the Theater* (Princeton University Press, 1949) and Herbert Weisinger's *Tragedy and the Paradox of the Fortunate Fall* (Michigan State College Press, 1953) almost inevitably fall within the "dramatist" orbit, because of their great stress upon dramatic forms. Fergusson's more recent book, *Dante's Drama of the Mind* (Princeton, New Jersey: Princeton University Press, 1953), is strongly dramatistic in its treatment of the *Purgatorio;* and it is particularly relevant to our purposes if, as we read it, we see it as implicitly concerned with the "hierarchal psychosis."

NOTES

1. Our views represent "semanticism" mainly in the sense that the emphasis is *linguistic*. But this essay does not propose to be a survey of the field. And, in one most notable respect, it runs directly counter to typical "semanticist" procedures. The late Korzybski's teachings, for instance, centered about an attack upon what he called "elementalism." Another word for it would be "substance-thinking." While sharing his distrust of such thinking (political "racist" theories are drastic enough grounds for such distrust), we take it that the principle of substance (and consubstantiality) cannot be eliminated from language; accordingly, we would seek rather for terms designed to make its presence as obvious as possible. Kant treated "substance" as a universal form or the *mind;* correspondingly, we would at least treat "substance-thinking" as a universal motive of *language*.

2. From the "dramatistic" point of view, for instance, experiments with animals would be categorically suspect, since animals are not typically linguistic; and experiments with children would be categorically suspect, since children are not sufficiently mature. Such material might serve suggestively, but it could not possibly have all the "dimensions" needed for the analysis of any complete linguistic performance. And we work on the assumption that our test cases should intrinsically possess such a range.

3. As for the importance of such an emphasis, consider the difference between the equation "reason equals respect for authority" aid the equation "reason equals distrust of authority." Such equations are studied, first of all, in a nonnormative, nonpreferential way, the assumption being that the best function of education is in giving us a free approach to such linkages, which otherwise tend to call forth automatic responses, making us in effect somnambulists.

4. In sum: So far as the curriculum is concerned, its specialties would be left pretty much as they are, the biggest division being a variant of the "Cartesian split," in this case involving the distinction between "natural motion" and "symbolic action." But, as with semantics generally, dramatism would place special stress upon the purely terministic elements that might otherwise be mistaken for sheer "objective fact" in the nonlinguistic sense. For instance, laboratory equipment being linguistically guided in its construction, one should expect even the most objective of instruments to reveal a measure of sheerly "symbolic" genius. When considering acts in life, one may have to cut across the special realms of curriculum specialization, in so far as such acts themselves cut across these realms.

2 Kenneth Burke as Teacher: Pedagogy, Materialism, and Power

Andrew King

Kenneth Burke thought of teaching as the practice of criticism. Because he thought of the practice of criticism as an intellectual way of life, he attempted to embody that way of life in his teaching. Burke's mission was to practice his creed in public, to show his students the power of rhetorical analysis and to let them engage in its exercises. His practice resembled that of Seneca, drawing alternate conclusions from case histories. While Seneca's mission was to make technically competent Roman bureaucrats, Burke's objective was individual and societal transformation. Burke wanted his students to transcend what he saw as the farcically empty careerism of the modern university in favor of a mythopoeic community.

Accordingly this chapter will spend considerable time talking about Burke's classroom manner as well as his ideas about teaching. But this chapter is about more than ideas and personal style. Burke wanted to unite theory and practice. Thus this chapter will also be about his teaching strategies. Burke used the analytical critical insights he developed for critiquing manuscripts as generative methods for creative writing. Out of the postmortem of literary criticism Burke birthed a heuristic method that allowed students to go beyond the canonical works and to create their own world of discourse. Accordingly each topic of Burke's teaching philosophy will be capped with an example of a specific teaching practice that arose from it.

BURKE'S SPECIAL CONTRIBUTION TO TEACHING

In contrast to the heavily structured classroom procedures in the literary classrooms of the 1940s, 1950s, and 1960s, Burke practiced what we now call lateral thinking. At a time when dominant Neo-Aristotelians and New Critics celebrated structural methods, he often eschewed logical, linear methods. He taught that each profession had its own argot, its own logical and characteristic perspective, and he lamented what he often called "the trained incapacity" of the dedicated professional. Long before split-brained research emerged, Burke combined logical and lateral thinking in a kind of one-two punch. Margaret Cox who sat in two of Burke's classes in the late 1950s at Bennington describes Burkes teaching as both "critical and creative."

She told me that Burke generally began each classroom period with some standard textual criticism executed in the stock manner of the New Critic in full bloom. She wrote: "We spent at least twenty five minutes talking about the formal organization of a poem." She remembered that Burke was "also interested in poetry writing and after eliciting a set of counter interpretations he might suggest an alternative version of the same subject matter" (personal communication, March 17, 1991). Thus, after the critic had finished his destructive analysis, the constructive thinker and composer arose to make a new and potentially better version. We teachers all know that this is very risky business, but if we can make our students active collaborators in a creative endeavor we will have fulfilled our fondest hopes and attained our loftiest pedagogical ideals.

Teaching Criticism as a Guide to Social Practice

Between my first encounter with Burke in 1970 and his death in 1993, I must have heard him teach a class or give a public lecture more than a dozen times. My two enduring impressions of his classroom manner are his sense of humor and his instant context with questioners. Burke taught with delight. He seemed terribly glad to be with us. He once told me: "I just love mucking around with students and professors" (personal communication, October 28, 1971). When he lectured his face was one high noon of happiness. He laughed wildly at his own jokes and complimented students for asking what he liked to call "big questions," questions about great literature, world survival, and the nature of the good life. In the 1970s he was still at the height of his powers in the classroom and in public lectures On one or two occasions he appeared to get lost in digression or to assume his audience possessed the same frame of reference as his long time colleagues, but when was at his best he was fluent, charming, passionate.

Of course he always wanted us to remember him at his best, and the best image I can recall is his performance at the William Harvest Lectures on Minneapolis in March 1976. A small compact man, five feet four inches tall and one hundred and thirty pounds, standing squarely in the center of a 50-foot stage, Burke entertained an audience of five hundred in the manner of an old fashioned Borscht Belt comedian. I see him now in my mind's eye, with one hand planted on the podium and the other waiving above his head as he compared Walt Whitman's prose to that of the early Sears Roebuck catalog. He performed a mini eulogy for ex-president Richard Nixon (whom he referred to as Milhous). He presented Nixon as a sad victim of presidential speech writer William Safire's love of prepositional phrases (i.e., the lift of a driving dream, the dawn of a new era, the birth of a new concept of government). Despite our reverence for the Gettysburg address, we believed Burke when he told us that such phrases sapped the power of the most vital message. For ninety minutes his speech bristled with puns, Sancho Panza-like aphorisms, and a kind of hipster baby talk delivered in comic book Brooklynese. But Burke was also in dead earnest that night for he also told us that literature was still of central importance and that the critic had a crucial role to play in making the deep and complex insights of art available to the rising generation.

His analysis that afternoon illustrated a technique that Burke taught to generations of his students. Through the strategy of "perspective shifting" Burke invited his audience to imagine what sort of writer Walt Whitman might have been had he lived in Britain. He speculated that Whitman might have turned out to be an observer of the inner spaces of the soul rather than the vast expanses of the North American Continent. During the same lecture he fantasized about the kind of propaganda Ezra Pound might have mounted had he turned against the Italian dictator, Benito Mussolini, instead of becoming the Duce's most enchanted listener.

We aging scholars who were privileged to have heard him so often and over a span of years unblushingly rank Burke as one of the great teachers of the century just passed. His manner appeared so spontaneous that we tend to overlook the way in which he labored over his craft. For Burke was far more than an entertaining lecturer; he was a wordsmith who struggled to make his best thoughts seem unexpected, inspirational, charismatic. His most "spontaneous" lectures were generally based on problems about which he had written one or more articles about in the past. He spoke about questions that he had been "harrowing" (he used the farm term for turning over the soil) for decades. On the other hand, even Burke newest material was usually anchored in a repertoire of stock phrases and ideas that he had polished over many decades. He could inflect an old Burkeism to cover a new situation so artfully that it seemed unexpected. He took these considerable oratorical pains for a reason. He was on a mission from which he neither flagged nor faltered. That mission was to demonstrate the power of criticism as a way of life. Much as he loved public performance, Burke was not at the podium to dazzle us with clever method or brilliant insight. He understood that he was embodying a model of what the dedicated literary life looked like. He was living out a practice. This concern with criticism as a fluid intellectual practice seemed incredibly daring during the 1970s, a time when so much academic criticism had been reduced to the construction of a technical jargon reserved for specialists. Unlike the technicians who embalmed and dissected their texts, Burke's criticism demonstrated an art of living, a practice of wisdom. Burke saw the academy and the public auditorium as a moral arena. He entered the arena as a fighter. Often a tiny sixteen by ten foot stage was the ring in which he would address, engage and conquer moral dilemmas.

Decades after Burke's justification of the practice of criticism as equipment for living and poetical understanding as a path to a more humane way of life, he continued to live out his creed that theory cannot be detached from practice. The 1970s saw a vast proliferation of methodology and technical vocabulary. In the academy criticism has been reduced to critical discourse. The graduate students of that day joked that the machinery of criticism had crushed literature Burke's free-wheeling practice highlighted the fact that modern literary criticism was no longer a developing life form but had become what Pierre Hadot might call a modern form of "scholasticism." Criticism like scholasticism can no longer directed toward people who were to be educated with a view of becoming fully developed human beings, but to specialists in order that they might learn how to train other specialists" (Hadot, p. 270). Burke came to the overheated literary classroom like a breath of healthy weather. While we academic bureaucrats were grading specimens of literature as if we were dealing with coal or vegetables or pig iron, burke still exuded a romantic view of literature, and he boasted a couple of simple flexible methods. Compared to Burke, even the giants of criticism like Steinmann and Blackmur seemed like labored practitioners of an esoteric cult.

Origins of Burke's Teaching Philosophy

Burke did more than argue for the superiority of the poetic way of life; he enacted it before our eyes. He refused to meet the technocrats on their own ground, but insisted on arguing on his turf. Numbers, graphs, mathematical models and charts did not sustain his eco-criticism. His appeals looked back to Emerson and Thoreau, hoping to reach liberal-arts educated students through a mythopoeic view of nature. For all of his clever parsing and verbal pyrotechnics, Burke's feelings came through. The city boy and literary scholar had been dipped in the earthy argot of the North Jersey poultry farmer.

Burke often joked that he had no formal teacher training but that most of his students had found him to be an incandescent teacher. He also noted that he had no training as a farmer either, yet he dared to plant vegetables and other things with modest success, and while he had been given no training as public lecturer, he still managed to give confounded good lectures. He once observed to me that Socrates had neither modern teaching machines and nor an extensive staff of support personnel, but that if he were to appear now, he would probably out teach all but a few of our best teachers today (K. Burke, personal communication, March 1976). People who heard Burke talk that way assumed that he was some sort of natural who taught from a single manila folder or that he was a savant who taught Burkeianism no matter what the assigned subject matter might be. Worse still some believed he was an indulgent eccentric who scraped up lectures from the seat of his pants. Nothing could be further from the truth. Burke taught out of a sense of mission and his courses and public lectures were structured by that mission. He thought the job of the critic was a very high calling, a job comparable to Aristotle's belief in the artist as the physician of society.

It is often asserted that people are most strongly branded by their life experiences of their early twenties and their mid-thirties. This was certainly true in Burke's case. Four things formed the granite foundations of his outlook. The first was the influence of Matthew Arnold's religion of aesthetics; the second was the Agrarian movement of the 1920s. Thirdly, the struggles of the Great Depression marked him deeply. Finally living under the sign of mutually assured destruction during the Cold War tied Burke's tongue and also honed it. Small wonder that the themes of transcendence, the power of aesthetics, the need for a grounded wisdom, and the utility of verbal self defense ran through his lectures

There seems to be a fifth influence: the two major figures whose ideas branded his soul, Marx and Freud. Like these masters of the great inner and outer worlds, Burke believed that ideas transformed individuals and societies. Freud had used language strategies to enlighten individual persons and to heal their relationships. Burke aspired to perform as similar service on for the society as a whole. Like Marx, the other Bad Bear thinker he admired, Burke believed in the vital role of the freelance intellectual. Like both Marx and Freud, Burke routinely challenged popular faith in conventional wisdom. As an artist and critic, Burke appreciated the complexity and contradictions of culture. As a farmer, Burke knew that conventional wisdom of agro technology vindicated itself through short-term gains in crop yields that were unsustainable over time and destructive the soils long-term fertility. A person who had lived drawing his own water and hewing his own wood until past the usual retirement age, Burke enjoyed comfort, but in his heart of hearts I suspected he found it a bit obscene. He believed that the American cultural obsession with products and services fostered by the advertising industry was a deliberate corporate strategy for avoiding accountability. Like C. Wright Mills, Burke reasoned that the emphasis on newness and novelty brought a sense of discontinuity that interfered with public memory (Mills, 1940, pp. 9–13). It prevented citizens from forming a coherent picture of the real costs of technological advance.

During the famous New Harmony Indiana 1990 Conference (the last he attended in person) Burke warned us that agency had usurped agent. In a somber voice Burke argued that to the extent we had put our intelligence in our own machines we have endowed them with a destiny independent of human wishes. He paraphrased Emerson's famous warning that "machines would soon be in the saddle and ride mankind." Burke decried the similar kind of fatalism in tin our surrender to the "judgment" of the marketplace. Here a mere mechanism had been the arbiter of business excellence. Success in the marketplace trumped the old fashioned virtues of justice, equity and sacrifice. The judgment of the marketplace was as implacable as that of the Juggernaut. Here we expected Burke to say something about the remedy, something about the fact that ordinary citizens were no longer capable of taking hold of their lives. Therefore the critic as strategically placed intellectual must take up the heavy burden of humanizing our basic institutions. Whether it was age or weariness or genuine disillusionment Burke did not say this. In his silence we felt sadness. Burke, the old hopeful teacher and critical guide, seemed to have lost the call. Later after a restorative of hot stew and buttered toast, Burke recovered his optimism. He regaled us with the salubrious effects of a neighbor saying no to a land developer, but somehow we knew that we were near the end of his long struggle for a better life.

Still, even to the end, Burke's model of social rescue still echoed the ideals of his early radical years. Covered with the honors of the profession Burke remained an outrider. He combined the power of a great critic with broad experience in the world of work. His marginal economic status as an editor of little magazines, as part-time farmer, as wandering teacher and as peripatetic lecturer gave him a breadth of perspective that is still met with but rarely. He communicated this outsiderliness to his students. He taught them to write by expanding and contracting frames of reference, or shifting perspectives from tragic to ironic through romantic, using reverse logic or by triangulating opposites. Textual criticism was not merely training for wisdom, but a practice that would result in the radical change in the way individuals lived in the world. Without directly seeming to do so, Burke communicated this sense to his students. Criticism was a strenuous exercise, a demanding "fitness" routine in the communal struggle for a "better life." Accordingly, the remainder of this chapter will discuss how Burke's three major themes guided his teaching. Particular emphasis will be given to the way in which they inform his instruction on social reform, power and materialism.

Burke on the Theme of Transcendence

Mid-Victorian literature had a late feverish bloom in *fin-de-siècle* America. The young Burke and his mates read *Tom Brown's School Days* fifty years after their English counterparts thrilled to Thomas Arnold's skill in transforming a juvenile carnival of brutality into a humane system. As Americans they were inclined to be sympathetic with his project of broadening a narrow classical curriculum to provide the new middle class soldiers, administrators and businessmen to man the far-flung empire. They were just in time for the late blooming American version of muscular Christianity. At nearly the same time they read Tom Brown's exploits at Rugby School, they encountered Thomas Arnold's apostate son, Matthew. Like Walter Pater, Matthew Arnold had called upon the arts to provide the social and moral capital once provided by religious faith. Despite the disillusionment of the Great War, Arnold's belief in the civilizing power of aesthetics captivated Burke, Cowley and Bishop. His post Christian idealism fitted well with the artistic ferment of resolutely secular Greenwich Village.

Americans came late to Matthew Arnold's ideas of aesthetic redemption. Arnold's doctrine of the uplifting powers of great literature inspired the linguistic project of Ogden and Richards, the lending library and book mobile movement, the arts and crafts efforts of the Roycroft Press; it cast a bright glow over the American literary scene of the 1920s. The horror of the trenches had diminished Arnoldian optimism in England, but not in America. The Victorian poetic idiom proved inadequate for the soldier-poets of the trenches. In the United States and Canada, Arnolds's ideas about the redemptive power of great art enjoyed an Indian summer. Arnold remained a major figure in university English departments and in the book and magazine culture of the East Coast. Richards echoed Arnold's message from his book, *Culture and Anarchy*, and told us that the new mass culture thrust upon millions of people the duty to make decisions that were once the purview of the few. They must do this by acquiring a heightened sense of the powers of language and the seductive powers of art (Russo, p. 113).

Many members of Burke's class and generation felt that a dominant capitalism had gotten brutal. There was more than a bit of nostalgia in their fascination with Arnold's vision of a restoration of crafts, of the power of literary education for the masses, of a belief that a more beautiful environment made people more civil and community-minded. The Arts and Crafts movement had been strong in the Pittsburgh of Burke's boyhood and until his fourth decade he was a consumer of Arnold and Agrarian inspired books on subjects such returning to the land or the use of greenhouses to make a living on a five acre farm or specialty crops for the comfortable farm family. Burke's friendships among the Southern agrarians like Tate, Brooks, Warren and Bishop strengthened his interest in Arnold's doctrines. Burke's vision of literature as equipment for living is simply a variant of Arnold's faith in the redemptive and civilizing power of good literature. It adds the idea of building a strong agrarian community as a species of action or as a way of acting together (Burke, 1950, p. 21).

Burke was not a dilettante like Warren or a dabbler like Tate. Lacking the familial support of the Southern agrarians or a set blindly doting relatives (like Alan Tate) he went to his seventy acre North Jersey truck farm on a long term loan secured by his father and working there in temperate seasons and commuting to New York to do magazine work. In agriculture Burke undertook to build symbolic bridges with those of his generation. But the shared commitment to the environment and the shared knowledge of agriculture proved elusive as nearly all of the agrarians except those at Richlands and a very few other places left the countryside within five years. Decades after his move to the farm and his embrace of the agro-bohemian profession, Burke attempted to carry out his program of literature as a guide to a better life in the classroom and on the lecture circuit.

Burke argued that literature is the ideal tool for social transformation. He had grown up in a time when the novel was first hailed as a major art form in America and his Greenwich Village years had put him in close proximity with the giants of American literature. He met all the great novelists, poets, editors and critics. He always resented students who seemed to think of literature as entertainment. Despite his bitter attacks on Eliot he became angry with a student who told him that he thought Eliot was really just a minor poet. Edmund Wilson might savage F. Scott Fitzgerald as an intellectual lightweight but not Burke (personal communication, November 4, 1971). Burke was an aspiring writer first. He became a critic by default. He would have been a novelist had he been gifted in that way. But if a great writer was the best thing, to be a critic was the second best thing. He was angry with people who thought writers were just freaks and savants. He was equally angry with people who thought of critics as pompous and parasitic.

Over an exchange of letters on Arnold in 1971 he wrote, "Good criticism of Poetry is more philosophical than philosophy" (personal communication, November 28, 1971). He noted that both criticism and philosophy rely on the exegesis of texts, but modern philosophy ends there. Criticism must go on because poetry is about a higher matter, "the perception of the unsayable." Burke noted that poetry takes the "unsayable and renders it visible, maybe dimly visible but at least accessible to us in way that prose can never achieve" (personal communication, March 1976). Like Milton, Burke believed that literary images disclosed a kind of higher meaning, a deeper degree of truth. Criticism made these truths more available to us by opening the work.

Transcendence became a humble teaching aid for his students. He used it to expand and contract narratives and literary images and to break the timid frames of his student's imaginative conceptions. Margaret Cox who sat in two of Burke's classes in the late 1950s at Bennington describes Burke's practice as "both critical and creative" and Burke as "an old gamester." She noted that he would "guide us to make opposite and conflicting interpretations of a short story or a poem. The he would help us construct what he called "a transcendent model" that might combine the apparent contradictions in a larger story. Jane Splinter, another Burke student from 1958 recalls that "we did not really rewrite the poems and short stories we studied, but sometimes Burke would have us imagine different endings of a single narrative." She also remembered that Burke talked about how a writer might overcome problems by taking "an upward path or a downward path" as he felt John Milton had done by "diving down to Hell and rising up to Heaven" (personal communication, May 12, 2000).

Teaching as a Transformative Practice

How did Burke practice this in the classroom? Great literature is a literature of power in part because it is a literature of complexity. As Burke was fond of telling his audiences, a play is a collection of stories, and "some of them are slugging it out." In Tragedy there are usually two main stories, and whichever story wins causes a train wreck. For example, Burke taught *Antigone* at Bennington as an example of "a story that ought to have had its ending rewritten." Creon tried to live out a story of his mastery in Thebes, a story in which communal and familial order were one. Antigone lived her story as well. She pursued the stubborn piety of her father. Even if the culture "arms" her father with superior force because it tells us that the well being of the polis is more important than the dignity of the individual, Antigone honors familial duty and public decency by burying her brother against Creon's orders. Both narratives are realized; each protagonist could claim a pyrrhic victory (personal communication, January 29, 1972). In the "war of words and nerves" (Blakesley, 2001, pp. 16–17) Burke reveals a more complex truth than that contained in any single perspective. Indeed, his method of dramatism emerged as a way of transcending single perspectives. A provisional truth can be found through the collaboration of two or more competing narratives. Thus knowledge is never the result of a mere consensus of critics, but the product of struggle, the idea of competitive cooperation that he featured in *Counter Statement*. As Blakesley tells it, "Burke believed that we could only gain understanding by constantly "introducing distinctions and contrary ideas" a process that we must use "to avoid becoming too hopelessly ourselves" (Blakesley, 2001, p. 17).

Burke had read (but as far as I know had never seen) *Streetcar Named Desire*. He was a text-bound critic who visualized the words in his head, and as far as I know never discussed any director's staging or theatrical choreography. In his criticism everything referred to the text and, at Bennington, as a struggle between conflicting narratives, much as Brooks and Warren might have done at the height of their New Critical orthodoxy. For Burke the play was about two irreconcilable tales of the American South. Blanche, a dispossessed aristocrat, lives in the hope that Southern Knights are not yet extinct and that one will deliver her from the wreckage of the Old South myth. Instead she finds Mitch, who represents the empty and joyless carnality of the New South, a place of rusting automobile factories and relocated Northern factories fleeing the specter of unionized labor. Tennessee Williams begins a third story at the intersection of these two quests, a parable of the "union of elegance and brutality" that is the New South. Burke challenged his students to write a different story or at least a different ending. This challenge fulfilled his belief that the critic must be as creative as the artist since all aesthetic understanding is collaboration between the artist and the viewer (K. Burke, personal communication, January 29, 1972).

"But which of these stories are true?" This was a question Burke was often asked by his students. They were not satisfied with the Burkeian doctrine that our links to the nonverbal are "inevitably inadequate abstraction." I recall that at the 1996 Burke Conference in Pittsburgh, Wayne Booth delighted in finding eight voices in Burke and that he repeated Burke's constant joke that "By God, I have a whole Parliament in my head again today." The students Burke encountered felt an odd disconnect between Burke's constant "heuristic joycing" and his foundational mission to make the world a better place. Reading about Burke did not disabuse them, for his commentators have often assumed a relativism that Burke himself did not believe in. A contemporary example notes that: "Burke recognizes the historicity and temporality of interpretation, meaning always being codetermined, the reader's horizon of expectation attempting to fuse with the author. Burke was a practitioner of hermeneutics whose textual horizon is a set of culturally and historically conditioned assumptions" (Henderson & Williams, 2001 p. 130). Henderson and Williams described this notion of transcendence in Hegelian terms, arguing that Burke's penchant for abstraction was a symbolic mortification of the flesh and a rejection of the concrete world. These kinds of observations are far truer of Burke's early and middle writing than of his ecological period, the more grounded Burke of the 1970s and 1980s.

I well recall the shock that greeted Jim Chesebro's critique of a panel that featured Burke's postmodern anticipations. Chesebro told the panel and an angry audience of Burkeians that they had mistaken Burke completely in talking about his decentered play and his levels of irony. Chesebro reminded them of Burke's agro-bohemian past. He told us that despite superficial resemblances, Burke's ecology was not the postmodern ecology of urban intellectuals. Although not as "versed in country things" as Robert Frost, Burke laughed at fools who dug shallow wells downhill from waste pits, and otherwise ignored the brutal laws of nature for aesthetic and ideological reasons. Everyone likes to speak about his early championing of Rachel Carson's *The Silent Spring*, the book that banned DDT from much of the planet. Many of us recall that Burke did indeed boast about being "a Carson man," but a later Burke, sobered by the data, was no longer Carson man after he read that banning DDT had been a first world luxury and that forbidding its use in Third World countries was being blamed for a recrudescence of malaria resulting in the deaths of millions. Burke noted that the First World was a world of choice. If we did not eat beef, we ate pork, and if we banned one substance, we could employ another (K. Burke, personal communication, October 7, 1984). He recalled his discussion of the limits of necessity or the term *ananke* (necessity) that originally meant "force" in the purely physical sense the opposite of persuasion (Burke, 1966, p. 319). He noted that in a world without choice, the persuasion associated with free action and vast resources is either meaningless or brutally destructive.

Burke's "groundedness" was a state that his larger public and his students discovered belatedly. He did not often talk about "country things" but mostly about literature. But he believed that a real and brutal world existed outside the wishes of those who talked about man's transformation of himself. He knew that if rain does not appear, the corn will wither; that even an agrarian intellectual must be alert and wide awake. He railed against the monoculture of American agriculture, of its reliance on limited seed stocks, its over-fertilization of the soil that threatened ground water and delivered unsustainable yields, its greedy field culture that resulted in massive topsoil loss sacrificing long-term fertility for quick fix production. Burke railed because he knew that he lived in a brutally real and finite world, and not a fantasy world of infinite growth, infinite resources and infinite personal options.

During his 1970s lecture junkets he was increasingly conscious of the urbanization of America. He knew his college audiences, students and professors both, were almost completely separated from America's rural past and once asked that if came to Minnesota he might bypass the main campus and address the farmers, foresters and fishermen on the Agricultural campus in St. Paul. He felt they might have some understanding of the sterner facts of the environment that he believed the romantic urban and suburbanites utterly lacked.

Burke's discomfort with postmodernism was deeply rooted. He felt that postmodernists had a dirty secret, and they were not his allies in the struggle to preserve nature. He believed that their outlook was our technological counter-nature in full bloom and that their secret agenda was to transcend nature in their desire to remake human beings and their surroundings. Despite their talk of ecology, they secretly wished to destroy nature and to create a totally human environment. They believed in the plasticity and malleability of human nature while Burke believed in its recalcitrance, a belief that always stunned them. Despite close reading of his works, Burke's followers were slow to realize that dramatism was not merely a literary convention. It was not a metaphor taken from the theatre; on the contrary the theatre was a projection of dramatism. The structure of drama was not an arbitrary invention, but something rooted in our germ plasma. It was a deep as the roots of the human race, perhaps deeper. Pentadic form is analogous with Kant's categories of the mind; it is how we make sense out of our experience. The drama is not metaphor; it is reality. It is our sense making apparatus. Some students as well as scholars have noted that Burke never "analyzes an actual play production or television ram but an imaged staging of it" (Henderson & Williams, 2001, p. 103).

Those of us schooled in the idea of the well-made play were always a little put off that Burke was not interested in improving the craft of drama. For him it was a giant storehouse of knowledge and power, analyzing its complex aesthetic provided insight in to better ways of living. He once illustrated Lord Kames's dictum that every sentence should contain an idea, a sentiment, and an image by having his students compose a series of such sentences. He cared less about the aesthetic excellence of these sentences than in the transformative growth for the imaginations of his students and their enhanced ability to defend ideas that mattered to them. He believed that the ordinary exercise of writing was salubrious and that it not only slowed down the buzzing in our heads, but helped us to discover what we really thought about the world and our place in it.

Burke often spoke to students who had been trained in debate. They were adept at exposing contradictions in an argument in order to refute of overthrows it. Burke found this orientation a "trained incapacity" that tended to interfere with deep analysis. When he spoke of frames of acceptance and frames of rejection, he was often talking about a frame of acceptance toward contradictions (Burke, 1984b, p. 18). Burke routinely introduced audiences to "the genius of the contradictory" (personal communication, October 28, 1971). Culture, myth, and the most banal routines thrive on contradictions. In an ideal world of abstract syntax and rigorous logic, contradictions are to be exposed and rooted out. In a grounded world of social praxis, contradictions are inevitable. This dictum was more than his doctrine of a perspective of perspectives or master perspective. In seeing one thousand different images of Jupiter from different positions in the solar system, one gets a perspective of perspectives on the giant planet, but it is a view without irony or ambivalence. One merely sees a fuller Jupiter.

Burke's "genius of the contradictory" is a perspective that embraces its opposite and its unintended consequences. For example, Burke notes that reformers often wind up saving the system they had intended to abolish (Burke, 1973, p. 211). Burke was amused that socialists in Britain ended up scouting Tory managers to make the ailing steel industry more competitive and thus de-nationalized it in everything but name. Burke found in Eisenhower a sterling example of the warrior who brings peace by putting the nation on a permanent wartime footing, (i.e., The Cold War). Burke once compared the "big idea" to a CIA double agent. It calls forth its opposition and then engages it to bring forth a result that neither side imagined. Burke's delight in this dialogue of contradictions was often on display in his public lectures in truncated form. In my judgment he did a better job with it in his delightful letters. This delight in contradictions was shared by the otherwise ponderously serious Edmund Wilson, who noted the higher literacy both sustains complex commercial society with its many roles and yet provides the critical tools to construct alternative imaginative worlds that undermine it.

Burke's delight in contradictions was an invitation for the free creative play of his students. He had always been fascinated by the dissociation technique of De Gourmont and urged his students to use it as a means of invention or "atom cracking." I well recall his delight with contradiction as when at New Harmony, Indiana, he described the conference weather as "somewhere between scalding cold and freezing heat" It reminded me of his dictum that students needed to court contradictions in order to attain what people like Wilhelm Dilthey and Max Weber have named "*teif verstehen*" or a deep understanding of life.

Beverly Thurston, also a former Pennington student, told me that "he played tricks like a mad little boy. The very last class I took from him was full of digressions about religion." Thurston noted that Burke had his students interpret the same events from religious and secular perspectives. "My best friend, Amy, was then very devout. I think Mr. Burke's methods were offensive to her and maybe to a couple of the others in the class. She used to frown very hard at him, but he never seemed to notice." She told me that Burke spent several class periods analyzing Andrew Marvel's famous poem about love and decay, contrasting the spiritual and sensual pairs of images. Years later she speculated that Burke was trying to construct, a colloquial Americanized version of the poem (B. Thurston, personal communication, June 9, 1998). In other words, Burke was teaching his students to use poetry as an inventional resource.

One must remember that Burke was at the height of his powers during and after World War II. The Cold War haunted his lectures like a specter. He continually brought home the serous role of the critic in desperate times and the fragility of civilization. He once remarked to me that German university professors of the late nineteenth and early twentieth century thought of civilization as a solid thing, a massive material and spiritual apparatus moving inexorably toward the millennium. The thought of German-speaking lands nearly dominated the world with Einstein, Freud, Jung, Nietzsche, Stefan George, Thomas Mann, and Max Weber. How dazed they must have been to see the ease with which the twin hammers of a worldwide depression and Adolph Hitler crushed the proud façade of the high culture of Central Europe. Thus, when Burke's students professed to be shocked by the sheer level of violence in so-called great literature, he told them the great works of the West merely reflected the human penchant for violent conflict; the ferocity of the tank battles of the World Wars were mere extensions of the violent struggles of classical times.

He was fond of reminding us that Western Literature begins with a celebration of Achilles's wrath. Burke would go on to tell them that many of our greatest poets have celebrated the hero, a human type who either undermines social order or saves us by bringing devastation to our so-called foes. Yet he would caution us not to despair. Praxis was our guide. When a religious student asked him why Christ as the ultimate scapegoat, or the perfect victim, did not free humankind from needing other scapegoats, he quoted George Bernard Shaw on the persistence of the old Adam. If Burke was cynical about continuity, he was idealistic about change. He held forth the idea of a benign scapegoat (i.e., symbolic abuse rather than physical), the comic scapegoat (the ambiguous victim) or the ironic scapegoat (i.e., a double or triple agent), and other modes of encompassing the manifold difficulties of the human barnyard (K. Burke, personal communication, January 29, 1972).

MATERIALISM AND DISCOURSE

Burke was less orthodox than McGee on the materiality of discourse. He lacked the gimlet-eyed orthodoxy of Neo-Marxist critics. As a utopian, he ignored the rational elements of Marxism as "science" in favor of its power as social drama. By materialism, Burke simply meant that that discourse has effects in the world. Burke scorned vulgar Marxism. Mind was more "than body in diffuse form (Burke, 1970, p. 78). He constantly pointed out that orthodox materialism involved the reduction of action to motion; Burke's version of materialism is more like that of the Creator in Longinus's *On the Sublime*, in which the act of utterance, the word itself authorizes the material and invests it with meaning . . . Burke noted that dialectical materialism came out of Hegel's Philosophy of the Spirit and still retained its idealism. He noted that materialism might explain the power of special interests, but only idealism could explain human loyalty, sacrifice and transcendence. He was at great pains to make these awkward distinctions, and in *A Grammar of Motives* wrote a tortured defense of Marxist dialectical materialism.

Burke insisted that Marxists, however, are not "vulgar materialist" or even "mechanical materialists" but dialectical materialists. We might well translate this term as "'idealistic materialist' . . . . dialectical materialism, in its constant call upon human agents, and above all its futuristic stress coupon kinds of social unification is intensely idealistic" (1970a, pp. 208–209). Throughout Burke's works he contrasts the idealism of Marxist materialism with that of scientistic idealism.

Burke cautioned his students (and his readers) against materialistic reductionism. A part of our drive toward perfectionism was a search for the simple motive, the reductionistic search for a perfect villain. Literature showed us that pure materialism was self-defeating, that such naked attempts to satisfy greed or to accumulate power are self-defeating. This was as true in the drama of communism's thrust for a new world as it was in art; Burke believed that Stalin's brutal land consolidation policies in which four million kulaks died, hastened the reaction that finally sabotaged and reversed his agricultural policies. The irony of these contradictions Burke noted should not bring about an attitude of superiority, but one of humility. Margaret Cox remembered that he called such moments "little acts of transcendence" (personal communication, March 17, 1991).

Power as an Issue in the Classroom

Burke seldom addressed the issue of power directly. As George Cheney, Kathy Garvin-Doxas, and Kathleen Torrens (1999) and others point out, Burke's entire program or "rescue operation," as Dillip Gaonkar calls it, is an attempt to construct a model of communications in which people share power (power-with) rather than have power over one another (hierarchy) (pp. 138-139). Although Burke felt hierarchy was inevitable, he felt its worst abuses could be mitigated. He believed that in the very instability of any particular order one could find powerful counter-resources. Burke's vocabulary bristled with surrogate power words, such as order, hierarchy. transcendence, entelechy, domination, frames of acceptance, identification, power of the negative. Burke found the power of the teacher an acceptable or legitimate form of power. It was legitimate because teachers labored to make their students their equals. Thus, their power was only temporary. It was exercised on behalf of the student and as soon as the student equaled or surpassed the teacher, the teacher's power was liquidated.

Jim Klumpp (1999) pointed out that Burke, like Martin Luther King, Jr., realized that unjust hierarchies could only be brought low by the use of countervailing power. He believed that one could not get outside of power. Burke reminded his students that their own writing would reflect the power arrangements of the times in which they wrote. For him it was an obvious truism that we unconsciously write about things in a hierarchical form: bosses and workers, science and art, humans and animals. Both the verbal and the nonverbal world contained huge reservoirs of power (Klumpp, 1999, p. 236) as Cheney, Garvin-Doxas, and Torrens (1999) note the "domain of power is simply bigger than the domain of Rhetoric" (p. 147). And rhetoric is shot through with power.

Burke taught that every vocabulary has an entelechy. He warns us against the "human desire for totality" (Burke, 1984b, p. 118). We have a drive for perfection, embracing one idea or system and driving all others to the wall. His greatest service in this regard was a constant preaching that we unmask or discover the covert motives of public messages. Burke's "motives" named the acts of domination (power-over) masked by the masking rhetoric of cooperation and community. Burke was especially keen on exposing the public-spirited language of land developers who spoke in terms of community service while arguing for the "right" of homebuilders and sellers to appropriate land for private gain. Blakesley (1999) found Burke especially able to unmask the rhetoric of the powerful because "at play . . . is always a tenuous dialectic between purposeful, directed discourse and an unconscious, spontaneous free play of signifiers (p. 73). Burke's technique of perspective by ambiguity alerted him to strategic nature of language that masqueraded as straight exposition. Burke once told me that during the late 1930s he heard a fanatic defender of Stalin excuse the dictator's murder of millions of kulaks on ideological grounds. Then Burke said he reminded himself that the fellow's defense was probably not sincere, but strategic (personal communication, March 1976). It was done precisely to get his goat and put him off his guard.

Burke felt that good rhetoric, like good cooking materials, had to be treated rather roughly. Thus Burke lectured characteristically treated words in realms beyond their traditional scope. Like his friends, C. Wright Mills and Hans Gerth, he had a genius for seeing patterns (Mills, 1940). Like Mills and Gerth, he was able to see whole professional vocabularies and the way, in which they inscribe group identities, defined and ordered communal values, and subverted or prevented rival identities, strategies and values. Burke long anticipated Lakoff and Johnson in presenting metaphor making as an act of willful assertion. In a letter written to me in 1971 he compared figuration to Nietzsche's will to power (personal communication, 1971). In the William Harvest Lecture, he called image making an attempt to gain control of the world even if we had to do it retroactively as historians (William Harvest Lecture, 1976).

One of the reasons Burke was leery of technology is that he felt it gravitated toward money and power. In Burke's mind technology produced a world that had two basic flaws. He used to say that technology was turning the world into a very comfortable hotel, and that such a world was a boring world empty of the old elemental human struggle. The seal hunter waiting the edge of an ice hole was never bored during his lonely vigil. The Laplander following his herd did not stare at the margins of ennui; the Amazonian forest dweller was not bored as he made his way through burning croplands. But the party wall between us and nature (what Burke called a system of counter-nature) had robbed our lives of adventure and grounded wisdom. The second difficulty is that technology tended to gravitate toward power. Burke felt that the sheer size and scale of the technological landscape was devouring the landscape. "We can't go on this way," he once wrote to me after describing the way in which a formerly rural highway had become lined with businesses in New Jersey (personal communication, May 18, 1977).

Burke did not think of the typewriter, the steam engine or the bicycle as technology. Like many persons he was comfortable with the level technology had reached in his youth. Hence, in Burke's mind it was only the decade of the 1920s when technology had begun to drain meaning from our lives. After all, his generation lived through an axial period of change in human society. Planes and automobiles only got rolling in his early manhood. He saw the last Belgian plough horses go in the 1940s. He saw the doubling and tripling of the size of tractors and other farm machines, and the mechanization of poultry farms. Burke was a teacher and scholar who simply added layers.

I shall always think of him as I saw him sitting on the stage waiting for a lecture to begin at Northwestern University. His well-fitting, dark suit contrasted with his brogans. He wore the old-fashioned high-top shoes with metal brads and puffed toe pieces that used to be called Li'l Abner shoes. One hand (I forget which) looked a good deal larger than the other, the mark of a man who had done more than a little manual labor in his twenties and thirties. Most of all I remember the look of eager anticipation on his face. All during the introduction he beamed impishly at his old friends and new listeners. He was at least as excited as we were. Burke could not wait to tell us what he had been up to. Those of us who had heard him before could not wait to hear. When he came to the microphone he began without introduction or preamble and went right to the red meat of his discovery. That was Burke the teacher at the very top of his game.

Conclusion

Burke's idea of the teacher's job was a large one. He saw himself as a wandering scholar who was an agent of social change, a light bringer in the charismatic sense.

As Burke made clear in his discussion of Augustine, inner transformation preceded social transformation. That inner transformation (Burke, 1970b, p.

61) was the work of the teacher. Thus his delight in Augustine's famous metaphor, "the fertile deserts of the wilderness." Although he may have scorned Eliot as a man, he admired the stark utopianism in "The Wasteland" and once confided to me "out of the stony rubble of 'The Wasteland,' a saner, greener world might be born" (personal communication, November 8, 1973). During the 1980s Burke lost much of his hardihood and depended upon the network of Burke scholars to continue his work of beating back the darkness. We owe an enormous debt of gratitude to Jim Chesebro, Trevor Melia, and Richard Thames for keeping Burke's flame burning bright and encouraging young scholars to embrace his genius. Thanks to them and to others, Burke remained an important figure and finally became a central figure in literary and rhetorical scholarship.

For practicing teachers, Burke's classroom techniques remain productive and viable. He practiced what Edward De Bono later named "lateral thinking" (De Bono, 1970). His methods of perspective shifting and frame breaking and of oxymoronic substitution are methods that teach creative writing as well as criticism of the prose of others. His idea of changing elements of a narrative or of writing several different versions of the same story are sure fire ways to get a student off and running in a burst of creativity. His use of dissociation or reversal of conventions (supply and demand becomes demand and supply) and his ability to reverse engineer and move across patterns show us how to energy to a classroom. For Burke was not interested in mere evaluation of a text, but in building one's own text. Burke's mode of instruction was too clever and antic for any sustained ideology of teaching. He believed in cooperative and coordinated thinking rather than mere adversarial fencing. He used the techniques of analysis and evaluation in an exceedingly inventive and creative way. Down deep Burke always admired the creative artist more than the critic. No matter how renowned he became as a critic, his classroom work pointed the student toward becoming the writer of joyous, energetic and original prose.

References

Anderson, F. D., & Prelli, L. J. (2001). Pentadic cartography: Mapping the universe of discourse. *Quarterly Journal of Speech, 87* (2001), 73–92.
Appel, E. C. (1993). Implications and importance of the negative in Burke's dramatistic philosophy of language. *Communication Quarterly, 41*, 51–65.
Blakesley, D. (2001). *The elements of dramatism*. Boston: Longman.
Blakesley, D. (1999). Kenneth Burke's pragmatism--old and new. In B. L. Brock (Ed.), *Kenneth Burke and the 21st century* (pp. 71-95). Albany, NY: State University of New York Press.
Burke, K. (1931). *Counter-statement*. Los Altos, CA: Hermes Publications.

Burke, K. (1950). *A rhetoric of motives*. Berkeley, CA: University of California Press.
Burke, K. (1966). *Language as symbolic action: Essays of life, Literature, and method.*. Berkeley, CA: University of California Press.
Burke, K. (1970a). *A grammar of motives*. Berkeley, CA: University of California Press. (Original work published 1945)
Burke, K. (1970b). *Rhetoric of religion: Studies in logology*. Berkeley, CA: University of California Press. (Original work published 1961)
Burke, K. (1973) *The philosophy of literary form* Berkeley, CA: University of California Press. (Original work published 1941)
Burke, K. (1976). "Dramatism." In J. E. Combs & M. W. Mansfield (Eds.), *Drama in life: The uses of communication* in *society* (pp. 7–17). New York: Hastings House.
Burke, K. (1984a). *Attitudes toward history* (3rd ed.). Berkeley, CA: University of California Press.
Burke, K. (1984b). *Permanence and change* (3rd ed.). Berkeley, CA: University of California Press. (Original work published 1935)
Burke, K. (1995). Dramatism and logology. *Communication Quarterly, 33*, 89–93.
Carter, C. A. (1996). *Kenneth Burke and the scapegoat process*. Norman, OK: University of Oklahoma University Press.
Cheney, G., Garvin-Doxas, K., & Torrens, K. (1999). Kenneth Burke's implicit theory of power. In B. L. Brock (Ed.), *Kenneth Burke and the 21st century* (pp. 133-150). Albany, NY: State University of New York Press.
De Bono, E. (1970). *Lateral thinking*. London: Penguin Books.
Henderson, G., & Williams, D. C. (Eds.) (2001). *Unending conversations: New writings by and about Kenneth Burke*. Carbondale, IL: Southern Illinois University Press,
Hadot, P. (1995) *Philosophy as a way of life*. London: Blackwell.
King, A. (2001) Burkean theory reborn: How Burkean studies assimilated its postmodern critics. *Rhetoric Review,, 20*, 32–37.
Klumpp, J. F. (1999). Burkean social hierarchy and the ironic investment of Martin Luther King. In B. L. Brock (Ed.), *Kenneth Burke and the 21st century* (pp. 207-241). Albany, NY: State University of New York Press.
Mills, C. W. (1940). Situated Actions and Vocabularies of Motive, *American Sociological Review, 13*, 904–913.
Peterson, T. R. (1986) The will to conservation: A Burekian analysis of dust bowl rhetoric and American farming motives. *Southern Communication Journal, 52*, 1–21
Rountree III, J. C. (2005). Coming to Terms with Kenneth Burke's Pentad. *American Communication Journal, 3*, 1–6.
Russo, J. P. (1989) *I. A. Richards: His life and work*. Baltimore: Johns Hopkins Press.

3 The Both-And of Undergraduate Education: Burke's "Linguistic" Approach

Elvera Berry

This chapter proposes a framework within which to examine education and a heuristic by which to generate educational agendas and shape curricula. Kenneth Burke, who defied traditional academic credentialing and whose use of language flies in the face of pedagogical accessibility, nevertheless speaks eloquently to many of today's educational challenges. Rooted in dramatism but influenced as well by his later logology, the chapter yields not only an analytic tool, but also a generative model uniquely suited to the examination of education in a democratic society. Burke's dramatistic approach becomes a methodological link between aesthetically conceived symbolic action and sociologically derived symbolic interaction. His extensive analysis of human beings, as defined by their linguistic capacity and activity, and his observations concerning education in a democracy, especially as laid out in his "Linguistic Approach to the Problems of Education," are incorporated in a trans-disciplinary perspective as "equipment" for learning.

Burke's linguistic metastructure provides a terminological screen that transcends both individual myopia and disciplinary nomenclature. At the intersection of his three aims of education ("the pragmatic, the admonitory, and the appreciative"), lies his simultaneous concern for both skillful preparation and "preparatory withdrawal." The chapter's inquiry yields insight into the inherently linguistic project of teaching and learning, particularly of undergraduate education; no longer conceived as a reified teaching Agent, education is envisioned here as reuniting teacher and students as participatory Joint-Agents engaged in the symbolic Act of learning on a Burkeian "voyage of discovery together."

Embarking on a Burkeian voyage immediately presents its own set of challenges. Is not "Kenneth Burke and education for the undergraduate," for example, a bit of an oxymoron? Kenneth Burke is hardly a welcome challenge for many graduate students (or faculty) in rhetoric-related disciplines, let alone an attraction for those more typically conditioned by the comfort of empirically concrete information and clearly identifiable "outcomes." Indeed, the image of concrete or cement may not be far off the mark. If Burke does anything at all, he takes a chisel to the cement of our concretized knowledge and forces us to reconsider educational content, goals, and methods.

My intent in the analysis that follows is to introduce a Burkeian conceptualization of undergraduate higher education by explicating, applying, and integrating the many pieces of Burke's own educational puzzle, especially as presented in his 1955 essay. Following a contextual overview of the history of American higher education, I will identify Burkeian notions of human and democratic identity; explore alternative models of the symbol-related "Self"; recommend an integrative linguistic approach to education, including specific pentad-driven educational agenda; and, finally, offer a way of thinking about undergraduate education that reflects a Burkeian understanding for twenty-first century undergraduate education.

Historical Context: American Higher Education and the Threat of Pragmatism

When one looks at the history of higher education, one discovers an uneasy truce between general and specialized education. General education, that aspect of undergraduate education intended to preserve and foster commonality of educational experience, has persisted as an ill-defined distinctive of American higher education. Consistently reactive rather than proactive, general education has remained a "public servant," changing in concert with the prevailing educational perspectives as well as with dominant social forces. Inasmuch as proponents of general education have held differing views of its substance and functions, no single perspective has dominated. Yet, despite ambiguity of purpose and terminology, general education has served to insure a kind of stabilizing compromise, if not stable motion, in undergraduate education. Indeed, one can trace the "stabilization" of the term "general education," along with its forms and functions, to the early decades of the twentieth century. By then, the American university, rooted in the American colonial and ante-bellum colleges, had yielded to the competition and compromise representative of the latter half of the nineteenth century.

The late-eighteenth and early-nineteenth-century ante-bellum reforms grounded in scientific inquiry, inductive empiricism, and intuitive reason grew out of colonial goals "to advance learning and perpetuate it," that is, to produce "a learned clergy and a lettered people" (Rudolph, 1962, p. 2).

Reason could be combined with scientific investigation and religious principles to serve tripartite functions: expansion of knowledge, relevance to society, and moral judgment (Duryea, 1982, p. 26). The Yale Report of 1828 epitomized a modified "collegiate way" dedicated to the "discipline and furniture of the mind," that is, to a "common foundation" in literature and science (cf. later "arts and sciences"). Representing Jeffersonian values of reason and virtue (40), Yale's undergraduate education was seen as in-depth general preparation for specialized professional study (Hofstadter & Smith, 1961, p. 284). However, whereas Jefferson's eighteenth-century conception had been "the right of every person to an equitable chance in the world, to his [sic] innate human dignity, and his fair station before the law" (Nevins, 1962, p. 21), the rising Jacksonian nineteenth-century egalitarianism focused on individualism and free enterprise in a context of anti-intellectualism, encouraged "learning by doing," and paved the way for practical electives and specialization resonating with faith in democracy's "inevitable progress" (Rudolph, 1962, p. 10). General education's cultivation of intellect and character underlay the "privilege" attendant to Jeffersonian perspectives but offered little to Jackson's popular cause.

The second half of the nineteenth century, fraught with socio-cultural and political upheaval, yielded equally significant change in higher education. With the passage of the Land Grant College Act (Morrill Act) in 1862, the government could ensure expansion of knowledge consonant with national interests as well as extension of opportunities in response to societal demands. With the publication of Darwin's *The Origin of Species by Means of Natural Selection, or the Preservation of Favoured Races in the Struggle for Life* in 1859, the college curriculum reflected compromise between belief in revealed truth and subscription to reasoned knowledge. Revelation and empiricism could now co-exist in an ordered universe under the umbrella of "intuitive reason" (Russett, 1976), paving the way for what Veysey calls "the investigative temper" (p. 133) and reinforcing the competition among "practical," "scientific," and "cultural" emphases in higher education. The result was an uneasy truce among experts, scholars, and liberal culturalists in increasingly fragmented and specialized academic departments.

However, each of the three conceptions represented an aspect that has remained integral to American higher education, and each was justified rationally: America needed knowledgeable workers who could build and sustain a free nation; America needed scholars and researchers who could create and maintain great universities; America needed citizens of culture and leisure who could perpetuate its legacy and civilization. One specialized in application of knowledge, another in extension of knowledge, and the third in the preservation and transmission of knowledge. Compromise was effected primarily through the elective system, yielding structures to accommodate debate, and through universities that could house and support all three.

Since the early twentieth century, higher education has, apart from technological developments, undergone remarkably little change vis-à-vis changes in the world. Two "world wars" and widespread regional warfare, scientific advances leading to new frontiers in space and medicine, and dramatic changes in transportation and communication have not altered basic higher education structures and curricula. More high school graduates and "older" students attend colleges or universities, more students are enrolled in non-traditional delivery systems, and more colleges and universities are tied through grants and financial aid to more external sources of funding. Nevertheless, students still accumulate credits within disciplinary categories and receive specified degrees through accreditation processes, faculty still debate the relative merits of the "liberal arts" versus professional training, and administrators still attend to current marketability in their decision making. Moreover, utility and research functions still rest, to some extent, on general education's foundational "services."

The specific details of higher education conversations may have changed, especially in light of technological advancements, but fundamental issues of concern and debate remain eerily consistent. Faced with "what to do" to ensure employment and success, many high school graduates enter a collegiate environment of fragmented academic programs and profession-driven courses where they are encouraged to *read* in order to identify "the point," to *study* in order to accumulate facts, and to *practice* in order to master technique and technology. Reading to "clothe oneself in wonder and insight," studying to become "steeped in relevant questions," and practicing to "perfect the imperfectable" are anathema to much of the current world of higher education. In a credential-driven society, inter-, cross-, and trans-disciplinary thinking is foreign to most student and faculty daily rituals. "Conversation" is often relegated to hurried consideration of credit-hour requirements and course offerings; numbers of hours, courses, loans, students, and publications; and tensions among conflicting demands, personalities, and academic departments. The resultant tension between pragmatic goals and liberal-education concerns, remains and permeates higher education.

Dramatism in the Service of Humanity and Democracy

As early as 1935 (in *Permanence and Change*), Burke described the "occupational psychosis" that develops from trained tunnel vision, that is, from any exclusionary preoccupation. Today, we cannot ignore ever-increasing specialization and a kind of "technological psychosis" that permeates academe. god-terms of education and culture, "specialization" and "technology," cut two ways: the very route to advancement becomes the path to retreat. The more we practice *one* way of thinking, the less likely we are to recognize the value of *other* ways of thinking; the more narrow our vision, the less we are able to see; and the more we converse with those "just like *us*," the less we can contribute to the broader conversation. How are we to execute an effective "dialectical dance?" What does Kenneth Burke offer us as we approach the end of the first decade in the twenty-first century?

Burke's contribution to ways of framing undergraduate education, of general education, in particular, can be organized around his understanding of the centrality of human language and the responsibilities attendant to higher education in a democracy. We look first at his "linguistic" foundation, especially in terms of dramatism, the guiding principle for "unifying the curriculum" (1955, p. 274).

Burke perceives the capacity for linguistic discriminations to be the differentiating characteristic of the *human* animal, and language to be central to human identity and development. His own adherence to the centrality of language is epitomized in his definition of man [sic], that is, of the human being. Not decrying the Aristotelian "political animal," the anthropological "culture-bearing animal," the psychological "social animal," *et cetera*, Burke (1966, ch.1) seeks to subsume such perspectives under a linguistic umbrella containing five clauses, each of which is "like a chapter head, under which appropriate observations might be assembled, as though derived from it" (3). Addressing human "physicality, animality, and symbolicity" (24), this definition is a precursor to Burke's ultimate reduction: "We are bodies that learn language" (Brock, et al., 1985, pp. 31–32) while at the same time explicating his earlier reference to "the political, word-using, tool-making animal" (Burke, 1961, p. 370).

> Man is
> the symbol-using (symbol-making, symbol-misusing) animal
> inventor of the negative (or moralized by the negative)
> separated from his natural condition by instruments of his own making
> goaded by the spirit of hierarchy (or moved by the sense of order)
> and rotten with perfection. (1966, p. 16)

This summary definition may be likened to a work of art. While its statement is complete, its artistry lies not in that which is stated, but in that which is released. It is language, that is, "symbolic action," that enables both statement and release. "Symbol-using," for example, takes on new significance in the presence of "symbol-misusing." As "inventor of the negative," which also "moralizes," one becomes a victim of personally created dilemmas. Finally, the subtle juxtaposition of being "goaded by . . . hierarchy" and "moved by . . . order" explodes in the equation of "rotten" with "perfection." Thus, Burke perceives humanity in its element: dialectic embedded in individual and collective symbolic action.

Although grounded in dialectic, however, Burke transcends the usual limitations of polarization. Lifelong friend Malcolm Cowley (1969) observed of Burke: "He is a dialectician who is always trying to recognize opposites by finding that they have a common source" (p. 250); his is a both-and dialectic of "reconciliation" in which "words are a mediatory realm, that joins us with wordless nature while at the same time standing between us and wordless nature (Burke, 1961, p. 373). Words reflect both *homo faber* and *homo sapiens*; the former uses old symbols to generate new words while the latter uses new words to explicate old symbols. In either case, language serves to define and to join, as well as to come between. Moreover, both individuals and society function by means of, as well as in terms of, language; inseparable from one's universe of discourse, one must be understood within that socializing linguistic universe. Burke reminds us that one moves "by and through language, beyond language. *Per linguam, praeter linguam*" (1955, p. 263)—particularly in the "socio-political hierarchy which is the most immediate of all man's [sic] concerns" (Rueckert, 1963, p. 230). Language, the mediating link between individual and society, is thereby elevated to the transcendent realm of moral choice and "motive," rather than relegated to the level of a mechanistic, pseudo-neutral "vehicle" of discourse.

Consonant with sociologist Hugh Dalziel Duncan's admonition that, "we must return the study of man [sic] in society to a study of communication, for how we communicate determines how we relate as human beings" (1962, p. 438), Burke provides a means of apprehending such a study in his "Linguistic Approach to Problems of Education." Here, Burke addresses our use of symbols both to establish and maintain the hierarchies we deem necessary for social order, and reinforces Duncan's conclusion that "hierarchal relations are sustained through persuasion because superiors, inferiors, and equals must court each other . . . in love . . . in hate . . . in irony" (p. 254). Mediating mutually dependent individual and society, language provides communicative channels as well as transcendent symbols of communion requisite to the persuasive "courtship" that is particularly important in a democratic society where equals revere the principle behind authority, and "obedience is a freely given act of will" (p. 326).

Formal education, the systematic preparation of the citizenry for such democratic participation, rests on the one approach that can transcend the particularities of all other perspectives: the linguistic. While Burke examines that foundational approach implicitly throughout much of his writing, he addresses it explicitly in his 1955 essay. Emphasizing, above all, an incipient linguistic "attitude" that should cast its shadow across all three "aims" of education: "the *pragmatic*, the *admonitory*, and the *appreciative*" (p. 273), Burke dances into, around, and through layers of terminological complexity: disciplinary substances, educational values and hierarchies, linguistic rankings, methodological perspectives, verbal orders, and the like. However, his characteristically endless connections both across and within separate categories lead always to fundamental questions regarding purposes and implications: To what end do we educate? And with what consequences?

For example, most would concur that in some sense, we attempt to educate for necessary "pragmatic skills," tacitly understood "moral admonition," and higher-level "aesthetic appreciation." Burke, however, extends his overall "aims" of education to dramatistic analogues of "motive" as he pairs skills with "power," admonition with "wisdom," and appreciation with "love" (p. 291). In so doing, he forces us to think beyond the ticket-granting activities of pragmatic training, beyond rule-imposed ethical boundaries, and beyond art for art's sake. Thus, while he does not offer definitive answers regarding educational content or form, he does introduce a dramatistic perspective on education with sufficient detail to enable one to extrapolate a "linguistic agency"—that is, a vision of the "dramatistic" leading to perspectival imperatives.

Mediation Model: Symbol-Bound Self

Even if one considers only the most basic variables of influence on individuals-in-society, one is confronted with myriad reflections of a symbol-bound self (as illustrated in Figure 1). The Mediation Model depicts a Self defined and governed by symbolic action. Representing both product and producer of societal forces, the Symbol-Bound Self is found at the complex interface of interrelated, mediating variables (Individual, Society, Communication) and agents (family, peers, education). The *Individual's* heritability, motivations, and environment interact with *Society's* political ideology and cultural norms; these interact, in turn, with *Communication's* systems and symbolic functions. Commonly perceived "agents" of socialization are seen in relation to the primary variables: *family*, with its secular and religious traditions and interpersonal patterns, links Individual with Society; *peers* represent potential mirrors of the individual, communicated through sub-cultures; and *education* is society's means of communicating multiple cultural and political agenda.

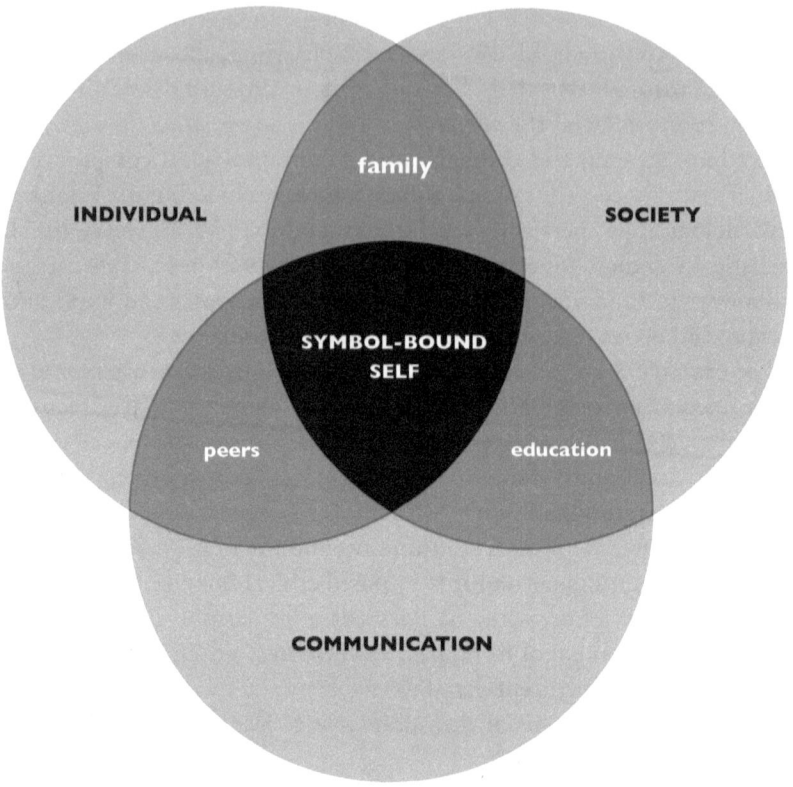

Figure 1. Mediation Model: Symbol-Bound Self

Despite its integrative nature, however, the Mediation Model does not explicate language-oriented and symbol-directed human action. Inherent in the "action of persons" are questions of decision making and moral choice which remain only inferential in this model. Burke's dramatistic conception, on the other hand, rests overtly on a philosophy of rhetoric that promotes a "choosing" Self who is both unique and "consubstantial" with others. Rhetoric constitutes the activity of the Self; the linguistic constitutes the embodiment of human *act*ion, *re*action and *trans*action. In short, mechanistically, one can move only as a symbol-bound animal; dramatistically, on the other hand, one is freed to exercise moral choice.

By way of quick review, dramatism's "generating principle" is the pentad which becomes a mediating, methodological bridge between aesthetically conceived symbolic action and sociologically derived symbolic interaction. Act, scene, agent, agency, and purpose function collectively as a terministic screen, a heuristic, for answering the question: "What is involved when we say what people are doing and why they are doing it?" (Burke, 1962, p. xv). Not merely a collective screen, the pentad concerns "the basic forms of thought . . . exemplified in the attributing of motives" (p. xvi), and "can be used to analyze symbolic expressions work, *both as symbolic expressions, and as charters for action in society*" (Duncan, 1971, p. 149). Each pentadic term performs a unique function but is, at the same time, inseparable from the other four terms; implying the "idea" of all other terms, as well as that of itself, each influences and is affected by the others. In addition, each stands in primary "ratio-relationship" with the others (scene-act, scene-agent, scene-agency, scene-purpose, act-purpose, act-agent, act-agency, agent-purpose, agent-agency, agency-purpose) yet carries its own essence that contributes to the methodological character of the whole. Conceptualized as a linguistic "screen of all screens," the pentadic paradigm fosters examination of both individual and collective symbolic action, yielding a "rounded statement about motives" by offering "some kind of answers to these five questions: what was done (act), when or where it was done (scene), who did it (agent), how he [sic] did it (agency), and why (purpose)?" (Burke, 1962, p. xv).

Burke's essay of 1955 does not include detailed explication of the pentad and its ratios as found, for example, in *A Grammar of Motives* (1945, 1962), but dramatism with its "five key terms" and their implications is foundational to Burke's "linguistic" take on education, as well as central to a Burkeian conceptualization of undergraduate higher education. From the outset, the dialectician sets forth the alternatives (whether to be *more* or *less* "thoroughgoing" in promoting a dramatistic—versus idealistic, *ontological*—versus *epistemological*, "approach to problems of education"). Then, having at once "center[ed] upon the *substantiality* of the *act*" (1955, p. 259), he casts the dramatistic die: substance as *act*, with "consubstantiality" as consummate *acting together*, becomes the linchpin of Burke's treatment of the verbal "act" as a "terministic center" (1969, p. 21).

One of the challenges in using the pentad is that it may appear, at first, to be merely a substitute for traditional "guiding questions." Just as journalists find questions of *Who? What? When? Where? How?* and *Why?* helpful in focusing on and examining data, so, also, do critics find Burke's investigative pentad informative. However, the pentad is far more than a clarifying "semantic" tool for data-sorting; grounded in "poetic meaning," it rests on implication-filled assumptions about the nature of human beings as creatures of both "symbolic action" and "non-symbolic motion," and about the nature of the ongoing "drama of human relations" (Rueckert, 1963). In Benard Brock's words, "The pentad becomes an instrument designed to understand the nature of reality—human symbolic reality" (1985, p. 98).

A second challenge is that Burke (1962, pp. 29–35) links the pentad not only to four "substances" (geometric, familial, directional, dialectical) but also (p. 129) to corresponding "philosophic terminologies" (materialism, idealism, pragmatism, mysticism, realism), both of which add analytic complexity as well as welcome insight into human ways of being. The following synthesis of pentad-substance correspondences and emphases, including a proposed "substance" vis-à-vis Act, is useful for analytic/exploratory purposes:

Scene: Geometric substance echoes participation in a context;
Agent: Familial substance echoes common heritage or associates;
Agency: Directional substance echoes motivational tendencies;
Purpose: Dialectical substance echoes verbal action.
Act: (proposed Dramatistic substance echoes identification and consubstantiation.)

Similarly, the "primary philosophic languages" that Burke identifies as "the kinds of assertion which the different schools would exemplify in a hypothetical state of purity" (1962, p. 131) can be summarized pentadically:

Scene: Materialism emphasizes the immediate context;
Agent: Idealism seeks to embody the universal;
Agency: Pragmatism concentrates on available means;
Purpose: Mysticism pursues contemplation;
Act: Realism emphasizes objectivity.

Immediately, we recognize that inasmuch as perspectival changes affect the interaction among players, any changes in perspective entail recreation of the drama. Dramatizing the pentad itself serves to illustrate the power of perspectives. For example, subtle yet dynamic shifts in relationship among substance, philosophic terminology, and the pentad demonstrate the impact of one's frame of reference.

Given first in Sociological Terms:

Geometric materialism creates the scene;
Familial idealism moves the agent;
Directional pragmatism orders the agency;
Dialectical mysticism determines the purpose;
Dramatistic realism guards the act.

Recreated as a Political Motive:

Materialistic geometric scene encourages

Idealistic familial agent to court
Pragmatic directional agency in order to persuade
Mystical dialectical purpose to participate in a
Realistic dramatistic act.

Pentadic Model: Dramatistic Self

Clearly, one's overriding Motive effects perspectival change in personal action; likewise, pentadic alignments effect perspectival change in one's view of education. Pentadic exploration of the "Mediation Model: Symbol-Bound Self" (Figure 1) yields, instead, a "Dramatistic Self" emerging out of the interplay of mediating variables and socializing agents (see Figure 2). Still within the confines of the same socio-political milieu, the Self is now surrounded, supported, and freed by a pentad of potentialities out of which to construct a *Weltanschauung*—that is, one's own ideology which, according to Burke, "is like a spirit taking up its abode in a body: it makes that body hop around in certain ways; and that same body would have hopped around in different ways had a different ideology happened to inhabit it" (1966, p. 6).

Although models and categorizations are necessarily arbitrary, and cannot portray adequately human interaction, independence, and inter-dependence, the "Pentadic Model: Dramatistic Self" does encourage a multi-dimensional conceptualization. It is a fluid model. Elements of the pentad relate directly to specific variables, but those variables are neither fixed nor static. For example, the scene in which an individual agent's act takes place is Society, itself a product of many interacting agents and scenes. Since whatever we do is rife with both personal implications and social consequences, the agent is the Individual, but one's act cannot be divorced from the scene in which action occurs, from the intentions (purpose) of the act, or from the medium (agency) of action.

In the context of the pentad, relationships among all variables and socializing agents are dynamic. Just as each pentadic element shares in the "idea" of the other elements, so each mediating variable (individual, society, communication) and each social agent (family, peers, education) shares in the "idea" of other variables and agents. The world of the dramatistic self is a Burkeian world of both-and: self and other, knowledge and ethics, motion and action, division and identification, constraint and freedom, the semantic and the poetic. The self is conceived in terms of dialogic interaction: one who was symbol-bound is symbolically, or rhetorically, released; intentional choice is effected within the constraints of symbols and the freedom of pentadic possibilities.

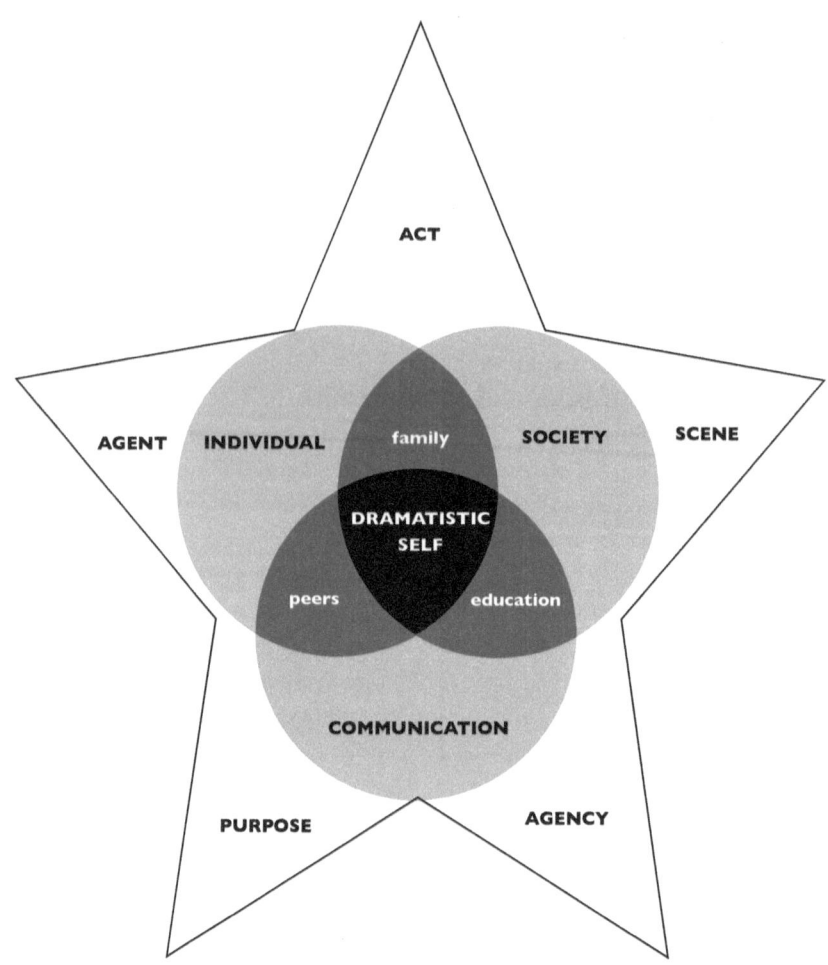

Figure 2. Pentadic Model: Dramatistic Self

The Pentadic Model may be idealistic in its attempt to conceptualize the ongoing drama of human relations, but it is ideal in its reflection of the Self in linguistic complexity. The following dramatic rhetorical moment, transforming the socio-political, symbol-bound self into a dialogic, dramatistic self, illustrates Burke's penchant for understanding through integration.

> Scene: plays the role of society ("rotten with perfection");
> Agent: poses as moral Individualist ("goaded by the spirit of hierarchy");
> Agency: speaks Society's language ("separated. . . . by instruments of [one's] own making");

Purpose: addresses the Individual on Individual's own terms ("inventor of . . . moralized by the negative");
Act: cooperates in forms of sacred ritual and comic art, only to succumb to victimage; and
Attitude: (implicit in the Act) moves from "symbol-misusing" rejection, to "symbol-making" doubt, to "symbol-using" acceptance.

"And thus to study a movement is to study the progress of a killing; which is to say, to study rhetoric" (Griffin, 1969, p. 61). The rhetorical/linguistic self, conceived dramatistically, becomes a sacrificial lamb . . . a secular scapegoat . . . a tragicomic clown.

Pentadic Approach to Education

Inquiry into a linguistic perspective began with a reminder that language is the characteristic human activity and that communication is the mediating link between individual and society, and led to a dramatistic perspective on typical socializing variables and agencies. The pentadic lens turns, now to the critical "agency of education," as explicated in Burke's "Linguistic Approach to Problems of Education." The intent is to move from a basic pentadic statement, through dramatistic inquiry, to a statement that incorporates Burke's multifaceted understanding of education and that yields, ultimately, a Burkeian conceptualization of undergraduate education.

On the simplest level, a straight-forward pentadic statement reads:

Education (agent) teaches (act) individuals
through theory and practice (agency)
to function as equals (purpose)
in a democratic society (scene).

The agent here is education, which functions both as external stimulus and internalized guide to action within the community, offers vocational choice and appropriate preparation, and translates common ends into personal means. The act is teaching, the individualization of social and academic norms as well as the necessary interference with learners' pre-established meanings in order to initiate new meanings. The agency is the curriculum, which is a conceptual ordering of disciplinary, multidisciplinary, and experiential opportunities subscribed to by social agents reflecting academic norms and standards. The purpose is citizenship, which involves responsible judgment in light of what one knows and cooperation in spite of specialized interests, goals, and experiences. The scene is democracy, which is "nearest to being the institutionalized equivalent of dialectical processes" (Burke, 1955, p. 285), and of all systems of governance, resting most directly on the recognition of alternatives and the ability to reconcile differences cooperatively.

Despite the apparent reasonableness of such an ideal, however, the statement lacks sufficient complexity. Perceived as a socializing agent, education is assigned moral qualities of action inherently reserved for *human* agents who are capable of integrating diverse agenda and of transcending their own limitations. The linear, rather than interactive, model portrays persons primarily as either products or recipients of action—the action of characterless embodiments of human constructs, which readily become scapegoats for their inventors. Such reification ensures dichotomized tensions between disconnected "doing" and personal "being," between narrowly defined academic specialization and broadly conceived liberal learning, and between conditioned social function and enlightened private autonomy.

A Dramatistic Approach to Education

A dramatistic approach, on the other hand, is inherently integrative and appropriately tentative. Built around the merger of the *pragmatic*, the *admonitory*, and the *appreciative*, wherein

> the admonitory (the "negative") is to be treated as "foremost among the equal": . . . Education must not be thought of merely as a means of preparing students for market, though that's what much of it now is. Education must be thought of as a *technique of preparatory withdrawal*, the institutionalizing of an attitude that one should be able to *recover at crucial moments*, all along the subsequent way. . . . a kind of smiling hypochondriasis. (Burke, 1955, p. 273)

While not discrediting tangible preparation, Burke treats preparation paradoxically: one prepares in order to withdraw and stands aside in order to act; one appreciates and admonishes simultaneously; one accepts, but never indubitably. Education, itself, is perceived "as a tentative preparatory stage in life, not as a final one. It is final only in the sense that it possesses its own kind of completeness and thus, ideally should be recoverable at all stages in one's life" (p. 287).

How might the relatively simple initial pentadic statement be re-framed to embrace a more comprehensive Burkeian stance? Dramatistically, education, itself, must reflect and foster *"tentative" preparatory purposes*. Burke advocates a "universal attitude" toward education—an attitude that calls into question and modifies the typically competitive looking ahead merely in order to "get ahead" (pp. 271–272). Wrestling with educational purposes and "motives of world order" that might accommodate and guide the mid-twentieth-century global technological scene, (1959, Appendix to *Attitudes Toward History*), he asks two questions: "What do people do for one another?" and "What kinds of motives help or hinder such (ideally) 'fraternal' services?" (p. 358). His response consists of a fully developed essay devoted to "The Seven Offices," or "categories for an 'official' terminology of motives," in which he concludes, "The basic offices (their number still tentative) that people perform in their relations to one another, are: Govern, serve (provide for materially), defend, teach, entertain, cure, pontificate (minister in terms of a 'beyond')" (1959, pp. 358–359). These offices move beyond the linguistic to the administrative and attitudinal functions that unite and separate the "talking animals."

Referring to *Philosophies and Education*, a book (edited by Nelson B. Henry) that Burke used in teaching his own course "in the theory of language (trade name for the course: 'Language as Symbolic Action')," Burke (1959) introduces his "seven offices" around distinctions between the "grand" motive of universal talk and the *particularized* "global" view (pp. 354–357). Though separate offices, they are not mutually exclusive; each may imply and incorporate the others. In particular, since people are political (at least to the extent to which they seek to "govern," or control, and define themselves in relations to hierarchal exigencies), all offices may be seen as "governing" agents. This is not to suggest that all individual acts are so motivated, but that each office is potentially "governmental" and should be examined accordingly. For example, "teaching," which Burke views as paramount (cf., Cicero's "first office of an orator" [p. 359]), "has an implied function of government insofar as it inculcates values and attitudes that lead to corresponding modes of conduct" (p. 361). Indeed, teaching, with its own logical functions of "formal education," "purveying of information," theoretical speculation, critical examination of assumptions and presuppositions, and the like, plays a significant role in every other office.

Burke (1959) concludes his discussion of offices and their educational implications with two challenges:

1. The overall aim of secular education would be to discover just what it means to be a symbol-using animal. (Such would be the "grand" aim of education.);

2. The basic educational problem at this stage of history would be: How best adapt the symbol-using animal to the conditions of world empire that are being forced upon us by the irresistible "progress" of technology? (Such would be the "global" aim of education.) (p. 375)

While specific details of Burke's late-1950s context may not obtain half a century later, his fundamental challenge of "grand" and "global" aims remains acute in relation to education's *"governing" curricular agency.*

The curriculum reflects not only disciplinary content but also the linguistic means of apprehending the various disciplines and, additionally, the interaction of Burke's "offices." Distinctions among epistemological perspectives enable us to classify the curriculum into traditional arts and sciences, along with their subdivisions. Nevertheless, whether we use typical distinctions (e.g., behavioral sciences, fine arts, humanities, natural sciences, and the like), or Burke's broader categories of "sciences of motion," "biological sciences," and "symbolic action proper" which may be of either a practical or symbolic nature (see 1955, pp. 278–282), we confront the arbitrariness of all divisions. "Natural motion" and "symbolic action" merge, regardless of their content, as soon as one begins to analyze and organize materials, for such activity requires human judgment.

To comprehend the content and methodology of an academic discipline, students must internalize its unique symbol system. At the same time, in order to make collective sense of the disciplinary samplings that yield possible approaches to the world and experience, students must rely on the linguistic common denominator. It is as if "language" were stamped indelibly upon all matters of human interest and concern. In that sense, highly symbolic rhetorical action may be the most "practical" of all actions, providing a means of ordering experiences in relation to one another. It is, therefore, utterly reasonable for Burke to speak of "'unifying the curriculum' by asking the students themselves to think of their various courses in terms of a single distinctive human trait (the linguistic) that imposes its genius upon all particular studies" (1955, p. 274).

The *act of "teaching"* personalizes and translates theoretical persuasions and curricular design through motive-laden communication. Burke's "linguistic ladder" for education functions as an especially instructive composite screen, a linguistic metastructure, which subsumes all other terministic screens and transcends disciplinary structures. The cluster of implication-laden terms contains both interdependent and hierarchal rungs: the "logical," or indicative, serves as the basis of the "rhetorical," or persuasive, which leads to the "poetic" and, finally, to the "ethical," or personal (p. 267). Teaching, itself a trans-disciplinary linguistic act, is grounded in judgments both motion-based ("It *is* not") and dramatistic ("Thou *shalt* not"). Moreover, the act of teaching calls for interactive judgment that is language-dependent. In short, the Act of teaching is conceived as a "joint enterprise," in which, ideally, "teacher and class are on a voyage of discovery together" (Burke, 1955, p. 276).

As navigators, *primary teaching agents* chart the course, thereby determining in large measure what will be discovered and by what means. Their interpretations of democratic ideals pilot the educational ship, their perceptions of the skills of the crew and of the needs of the passengers give form to the curriculum, and their own characters play a vital role in determining the nature of the voyage. Nevertheless, although they are granted administrative powers, their real power lies in their ability to engage all aboard in the joint process of discovery. Educator-agents choose among alternative models of education. Their judgments confirm the perspective they select and constitute behavioral evidence of personal and educational ethics. Consciously or unconsciously, they exemplify attitudes which either thwart or encourage dialogic interaction. They may perceive students as I-Thou "subjects" or as I-It "objects" (Buber, 1955); they may interpret persons as other selves engaged in symbolic action, or judge them as products of societal motion; they may behold each Self as the epitome of interrelated complexities, or strictly as a dichotomized creature (rational *or* emotional, materialistic *or* idealistic, mechanistic *or* dramatistic, etc.); they may advise others by providing ethical means for decision making, or exploit and coerce by making decisions *for* others.

Embodying the ideology their education reflects, teaching-Agents replace the reified "agent" of education as the link between the communal past and the communal future. Agents teaching in the *democratic scene*, in and for which education exists, are responsible for nurturing equally free agents who are capable of symbolic "dodging" between personal values and the communal rules that are part of the office of "governance." A democratic education dedicated to free and responsible equals is bound by both individual and collective ideas, as well as by their accompanying "thou shalt not's [sic]." Duncan (1962) observes that, "For Burke, rhetoric promotes social cohesion by making it possible [for individuals] to act 'rhetorically upon themselves and others'" (p. 154). In order to stimulate critical thought and interactive discourse, they must respect selves as well as ideas; in order to cultivate responsible decision makers, they must appreciate others' freedom to differ; in order to foster integration of knowledge, skills, and attitudes, they must provide models of integration and encourage, but not force, their adoption. In the drama of democracy, therefore, rules are symbols of hierarchal struggle rather than of authoritative command, in that "rules define *how* we can struggle. They are a social sanction for rivalry" (Duncan, 1962, p. 343), as well as the means to democratic cooperation.

The pentadic statement, as originally proposed, was a descriptive statement: Education (agent) teaches (act) individuals through theory and practice (agency) to function as equals (purpose) in a democratic society (scene).

Further examination of that statement in light of pentad-related "substances" (geometric, familial, directional, dialectical, and proposed dramatistic) and "philosophical terminologies" (materialism, idealism, pragmatism, mysticism, and realism) yielded fruitful analysis. Incorporation of Burke's "seven offices" and "linguistic ladder generated educational perspectives that can now be explored within the ten primary pentadic ratios. It is within the dynamism of the ratios that Burke's various categories can be synthesized and democratic aims of education be particularized.

Drawing on Burke's explicit suggestions, implicit recommendations, and inferred commitments, I propose the following ratio-based educational agenda:

Scene-Act = education for *order*

Scene-Agent = education for *community*

Scene-Agency = education for *adequacy*

Scene-Purpose = education for *power*

Act-Agent = education for *character*

Act-Agency = education for *method*

Act-Purpose = education for *cooperation*

Agent-Agency = education for *interaction*

Agent-Purpose = education for *identification/consubstantiation*

Agency-Purpose = education for *technical preparation*

These ratios and corresponding agenda are neither discrete nor unrelated, but understood in the context of Burke's linguistic ladder ("logical," "rhetorical," "poetic," and "ethical"), they can be infused with judgment and translated into "steps" in pyramidal ascent (Figure 3 illustrates the hierarchy of "Pentadic Ratios and Educational Agenda.") However arbitrary the distinctions, they serve to ameliorate destructive competitive ambition and, instead, to encourage balance among Burke's *pragmatic*, *admonitory*, and *appreciative* concerns.

The final addition to the overall schema is Burke's own "educational ladder" (1955, pp. 283–284) composed of four rungs. For convenience, these "emphases" may be identified as: Partisanship Indoctrination, Partisan Defense/Offense, Humanitarian Appreciation, and Dialogic Interaction. Education includes all four, but dramatistically conceived education would seek to promote the highest rung, "dialogic interaction," as closest to the ideal of learning-among-equals—and of democratic education for citizenship.

On a continuum between motion and action, the lowest rung of the education ladder, "partisan indoctrination," is closer to educational motion than

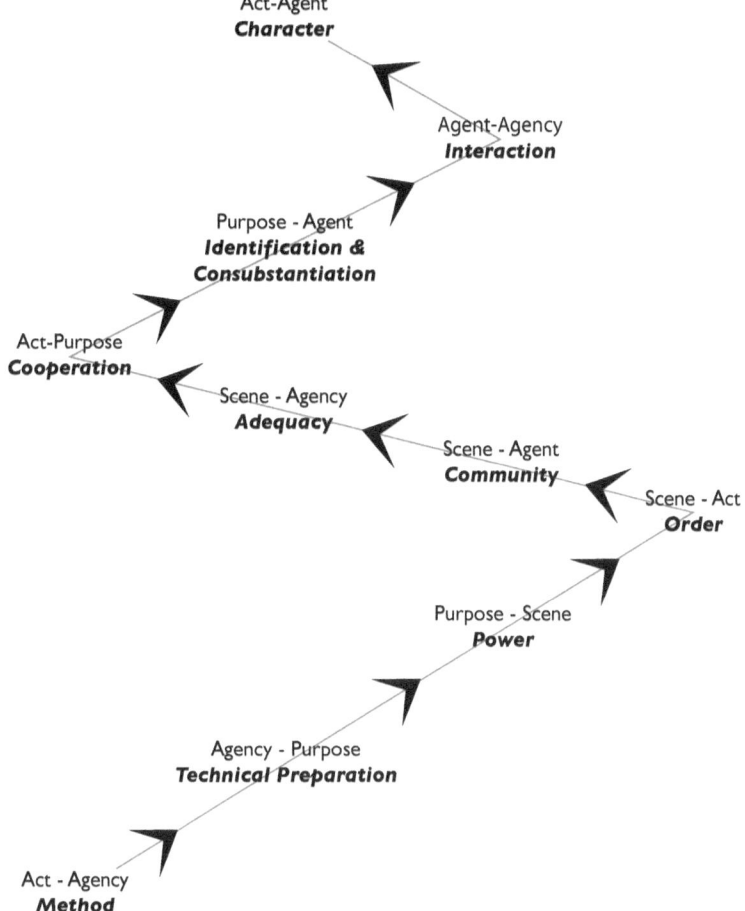

Figure 3. Pentadic Ratios and Educational Agenda

to personal action. Its goal is acquisition of skills useful for immediate performance in an environment governed by superiors. In this context, Burke's "offices" of governing, teaching, defending, serving and entertaining reflect the power of indoctrination, emphasizing knowledge and practical action in keeping with hierarchal dictates.

As depicted in Figure 3, the first four pentadic ratios (act-agency, agency-purpose, purpose-scene, scene-act) yield educational agenda that are especially supportive of "partisan indoctrination":

- Act-agency elevates means to an ultimate position and emphasizes educational *method*, where the future is imagined in terms of present methodology.

- Agency-purpose concentrates on techniques and views *technical preparation* as the end of education; one is taught how to perform and equates that performance with "being."
- Purpose-scene risks circularity: good citizenship depends on democratic scene's fostering an informed citizenry; *power* is gained through promissory education and preserved by patriotic defense.
- Scene-act explains action in light of environmental motion; governed by cause-effect determinism, one is implicitly admonished to act in accordance with past conditions, following an established *order*.

Thus, lacking a significant Agent, the first four educational outcomes are prescriptive and reinforce dependence on what *is*, rather than consideration of alternatives.

The second rung, "partisan defense/offense," calls for judgment and awareness. Since its goal is "winning" the linguistic battle, it must encourage knowledge of opposing perspectives as well as awareness of its own. Acquisition of singular skills is coupled with wisdom in judgment, and governed by moral admonition. Governing, teaching, defending, serving (a variety of ends), and curing (for multiple purposes) remain part of this "combat model," in which practical performance determines the victor and the vanquished, the superior and the inferior. "Partisan defense/offense" speaks directly to three ratios: scene-agent, scene-agency, and act-purpose. While separable only conceptually from each other and from the rest of the ladder, the distinctions are nevertheless informative.

- Scene-agent defends the present as depicted in its leaders; as good and evil become polarized, agents govern either by inculcations of "appropriate" values or through mystical "pontification." Education is designed to move people to action that will ensure the desired *community*.
- Scene-agency preserves traditional means as well as material ends. Appropriateness is determined by strict adherence to shared norms, and educational methods are measured by the criterion of *adequacy*.
- Act-purpose moves from practical action to symbolic action. Still performance-oriented, this ratio entails commitment beyond oneself. Seeking to cure dichotomized conflict, it translates "symbolic adequacy" into *cooperation*.

Thus, education moves from dominance of the established Scene, and the struggle to outwit the opponent, to the challenge of understanding another citizen—another *Self*.

The third rung, "humanitarian appreciation," replaces *practical* action with *symbolic* action. Prevailing descriptivism leads to recognition, appreciation, and acceptance of "objectified" difference while "offices" of governing, teaching, entertaining, and curing are re-framed to humanitarian ends. Two ratios, in particular, address "humanitarian appreciation": purpose-agent and agent-agency.

- Purpose-agent provides a leader whose wisdom and acts represent and define the community; citizenship and patriotism are taught through education based on *identification and consubstantiation*.
- Agent-agency acts not in terms of a declared leader, but in alliance with personal or collective character. The cure for partisanship is the study of disparate motives, leading to symbolic *interaction* requisite to learning.

The highest rung, the apex of the pyramid of pentadic ratios, generates "dialogic interaction." This rung regards interaction, and its accompanying doubt and confrontation, as the mark of personhood. Equals engage in dialogue in order to internalize each other's perspectives. The ultimate in aesthetic appreciation, "dialogic interaction," may be equated with the remaining act-agent ratio as well as primarily with Burke's "offices" of governing, teaching, and pontification. True learning inheres in Pontification grounded in respect for personal integrity, in humbling appreciation of symbolic acts, and in love for humankind.

- Agent-act transcends social conflict by valuing individuals engaged in conflict and by seeking means to mutual growth. Desired learning occurs when promissory preparation gives way to appreciation of significant variables, when the tentative replaces the absolute, and when the rhetorically perfect is subsumed under the perfectly rhetorical; that is, true learning demands reflective education for *character*.

Finally, succession from the motion of *method* and *technical preparation* ("partisan indoctrination") to the action of personal *character* (the epitome of "dialogic interaction"), yields a revised statement reflecting Burke's educational motives and linguistic approach:

Teachers and students are participatory "joint Agents"
who engage in learning (a symbolic "act")
through the "Agency" of identification, interaction,
and conflict
for the "Purpose" of cooperation
despite misunderstandings
in a communal, democratic, and universal "Scene."

The permeating "linguistic point of view," a screen for human acts and constructs, promotes dialogue requisite to education in and for a democracy. Pointing out that "the word transcends the thing it names," Burke calls his linguistic point of view "a step to one side" (Burke, 1955, p. 269). Especially in the context of education, it might also be conceived as "a step across," that is, a transcendent step. Here, language has become a metastructure by and through which education takes place: just as symbolic action transcends perspectival action, so a linguistic meta-screen transcends specialized terminological screens. Through such a linguistic screen, the educational agenda outlined above comprise a vision of education for AWARENESS and APPROPRIATENESS.

The first five agenda (method, technical preparation. power, order, community) emphasize AWARENESS, while the remainder (adequacy, cooperation, identification and consubstantiation, interaction, character) stress APPROPRIATENESS. "Awareness" of available materials, procedures, and modes of interaction is requisite to deliberate choice among alternatives. Moreover, conscious selection of the "appropriate" means to human ends depends on "awareness" of possible acts and motives. Thus, each transitional step involves awareness of alternatives (dialectic analysis) as well as appropriate choice (rhetorical selection). Understood linguistically, "symbolic adequacy" represents a bridge between two worlds: the world of technical hierarchy and the world of attitudinal commitment; that is, symbolic adequacy turns technical hierarchy into attitudinal commitment—and scientific Awareness into dramatistic Appropriateness. A "linguistic education" would, therefore, be measured not only by the degree of awareness, but also by the extent to which action and reaction were appropriate to the Self in relation to other Selves.

Higher Education for Personhood

We trace the resultant progression of, and interaction among, our educational agenda whose primary objective is *personhood grounded in deliberate choice*. Assimilation of method and technical preparation yield potential power, which determines social order and the nature of the community. One may automatically exercise available power (mechanism) or reflect on its ordering purposes and consequences for the community (dramatism). Whereas mechanistic "motion" emphasizes technique and information, dramatistic "action" responds to the community as a collection of equally human selves adequate to the task of cooperation. One may choose to identify and become consubstantial with others, acting on the awareness of the appropriate response, or to be content merely to recognize the potential for that choice.

By the same token, one may determine the appropriate kind and degree of symbolic interaction with other selves. Ultimately, one's character is demonstrated by the degree of consonance between awareness and appropriate choice. Education aimed at such personal accord in the face of social discord addresses selves potentially in conflict with one another but, instead, in harmony with themselves and in relationship with others.

Ideally, the entire undergraduate curriculum would be grounded in rhetorical studies as the way to educate for "preparatory withdrawal." Rhetoric would provide the means to both Awareness and Appropriateness, its end being "personhood"—that is, realization of human selves. Challenged by polarized possibilities and guided by the admonitory, one would examine and generate alternatives in the spirit of "smiling hypochondriasis." A linguistic metastructure would account for the comprehension of all systems as well as of their interrelationships. It would address Burke's educational concern that "when considering acts in life, one may have to cut across the special realms of curriculum specialization, in so far as such acts themselves cut across these realms" (Burke, 1955, p. 282).

More specifically, a linguistic metastructure would emphasize that both scientist and artist envision possibilities based on past results, present contingencies, and transcendent language. Although separated by content and nomenclature, all disciplines rely on the integrating language of reflection, imagination and choice. The laboratory may not demand ongoing dialogue with others, but it does entail discourse with self and detailed recording for others to question, validate, or use. The social sciences do not exist apart from selves in communication and community. Philosophical and mathematical abstractions become meaningful only when translated into identifiable terms and shared symbols. History is the human story preserved through language and adapted in light of those it serves. Literature presents models of interaction, both explicit human responses to circumstances and, more significantly, implicit alternative visions. The arts as a bridge between experience and inspiration constitute miniature socio-dramas. What is needed, therefore, is not a mere reordering of the curriculum, nor yet another restructuring of course content, but a linguistic re-conceptualizing of the entire educational enterprise.

If education is to ensure both individual and collective well-being, it must reflect a deliberate search for authentic personhood. Balance between external determinism and internal idealism occurs in the democratic arena of choice and uncoerced consensus, that is, in the arena of interacting, interdependent pentadic elements. Dramatism offers both the interactive context (a heuristic pentad) and a guiding perspective (the linguistic metastructure), thus providing a framework within which educational purposes may be examined and determined, as well as a potentially normative, integrating curricular approach that defines symbolic parameters and illustrates methodological procedures applicable to all substantive, philosophical, and rhetorical activity. A transcendent perspective superimposed on all disciplinary equations affirms the ability to translate the particular into the abstract—the capacity to see the nomenclatures of disciplinary methods through the eyes of a linguistic methodology. In contrast with fragmented disciplinary attitudes and selective interdisciplinary efforts, the proposed *personhood* approach assumes a *trans*disciplinary posture: not confined to the agenda of specializations, the linguistic metastructure encourages and enables exploration of relationships among all disciplines; not bound by competing philosophical perspectives, it fosters an attitude of cooperation; not polarized to dialectic ends, it acknowledges dialectic as a means to the rhetorical end of human choice.

Holding that all human beings, "as symbol-users, are of the same substance" (Burke, 1955, p. 286), Burke advocates "respect for the individual" based on shared powers of discrimination. This positive sense of the "discriminating animal" militates against negative personal judgment and its accompanying collective discriminations, that is, against prejudice. It militates, also, against the kind of "humanistic education" that "becomes the attempt to teach and to acquire the kind of 'insignia' that are thought to be proof of cultural election" (p. 271). Such "humanistic" education focuses on educational agenda aimed at Awareness (education for method, technical preparation, power, and order) to the neglect of agenda bespeaking Appropriateness (education for cooperation, identification and consubstantiation, interaction, and character). Emphasizing skills and partisanship, such an education promotes the instrumental nature of language (the "promissory" preparation for agency-purpose), rather than its ontological nature (the "consubstantial" character of agent-act).

Where language is perceived as the mediating variable among all human experiences, hence the common element permeating all of education, all four rungs of Burke's Linguistic Ladder obtain. The "logical," dominated by technique to the end of personal gain, gives way to "rhetorical" ends of community and cooperation, and to "poetic" identification and invention guided by the "ethical." These four rungs serve collectively as a linguistic umbrella—as a point of view that can translate preparatory knowledge into integrated action. Thus, the process of education involves initiation not only into the various academic disciplines but also into the nature and role of language. The recommended linguistic model is a participatory model in which teaching is not, in Skinner's terms, a "technology," that is, "simply the arrangement of contingencies of reinforcement" (Skinner, 1968, p. 5). Neither a spectator sport to be experienced vicariously, nor a controlled substance to be administered selectively for the duration of a four-year illness, undergraduate education calls for a process of commitment among co-learners.

Figure 4 provides a summarizing grid depicting essential Educational Agenda generated by pentadic Ratios in the context of Burke's educational ladder and offices, "linguistic ladder," and aims of education. All of these terminological perspectives are shown in relation to each other as well as in relation to fundamental education for Awareness and Appropriateness. Reflecting both a Burkeian perspective and the developmental nature of education, the hierarchal presentation in Figure 4 (read from the bottom) depicts how terminological integration reveals education for personhood.

Personhood Model: Undergraduate Education

What emerges is the potential for an undergraduate education that reflects both an overall linguistic approach and the goals implicit in the "terminological integration" of particularities identified in Figure 4. A skeletal schema of undergraduate education, shown in Figure 5, reminiscent of the "Mediation Model of the Symbol-Bound Self" (Figure 1) and "Pentadic Model of the Dramatisitc Self" (Figure 2), demonstrates a framework for the applicability of a Burkeian theoretical stance. Retaining a tripartite structure, the model places personhood at the center of interacting variables: the individual's specialized curriculum (or major), and society's general education curriculum are communicated in the context of the co-curriculum; selected concentrations (or minors), required core, and distributed electives complete the components of the typical undergraduate program. Although the components themselves are not unique to a Burkeian perspective, the interactive conceptualization, in which each component impinges on all others, reflects the dramatistic self as learner.

The typical undergraduate curriculum consists of purposive educational experiences traditionally realized in classroom courses and credit-hour requirements as well as in non-course-related learning. Heavily disciplinary in orientation, the formal undergraduate curriculum is supervised by teaching faculty assigned to academic departments and is typically divided into "liberal education" and "specialization." The former finds expression in the general education curriculum, and the latter in the specialized curriculum of majors and upper-level studies. the co-curriculum, or third primary variable in traditional undergraduate programs, represents a contextual composite of learning experiences—from dormitory life to involvement in student organizations, from campus employment to participation in social and cultural activities. In other words, the way students live out their lives in the learning

	Pentadic Ratios and Educational Agenda	Educational Ladder and Offices	Linguistic Ladder	Aims of Education

Appropriateness ↑	Act-Agent **Character**	Dialogic Intervention
		  Govern
		  Teach
		  Pontificate
			The Ethical	Aesthetic Appreciation

	Agent-Agency **Interaction**
	
	Agent-Purpose **Indentification and Consubstantiation**
		Humanitarian Appreciation
		  Govern
		  Teach
		  Entertain
		  Cure
			The Poetic	

	Act-Purpose **Cooperation**
	Scene-Agency **Adequacy**
	Scene-Agent **Community**
		Partisan Defense/ Offense
		  Govern
		  Teach
		  Defend
		  Serve
		  Cure
			The Rhetorical	Moral Admonition

Awareness	Scene-Act **Order**
	Scene-Purpose **Power**
	Agency-Purpose **Technical Preparation**
	Act-Agency **Method**
		Partisanship
		  Govern
		  Teach
		  Defend
		  Serve
		  Entertain
			The Logical	Skills

Figure 4. Terminological Integration: Education for Personhood

context is a significant variable in our "Personhood Model: Undergraduate Education" (Figure 5).

The personhood envisioned through dramatism is more than the sum of the parts of typical curricular compromise. Pragmatic concerns preclude deviation from a common vocabulary of generally accepted definitions and educational components, but these shared "symbols" take on new significance in the context of a linguistic metastructure. Burkeian personhood presupposes the possibility of human choice and depends on the Self as an acting agent. That self is perceived to be more than a finite biological system; it is a "body that learns language" and, in the process of learning language, learns to "know" knowing. The resultant awareness is the springboard for reflective discovery of self not only in relation to things, events and ideas, but also in relation to other selves. Indeed, appropriate action rests not on awareness, alone, but also on translation of awareness into decisions in light of interacting selves. Persons capable of individual action as well as social cooperation move from Burke's lower-order to higher-order aims and offices of education: that is, from the "pragmatic," through the "admonitory," to the "appreciative"—and from partisanship, through defense/offense, to humanitarian appreciation and dialogic interaction (as shown in Figure 4).

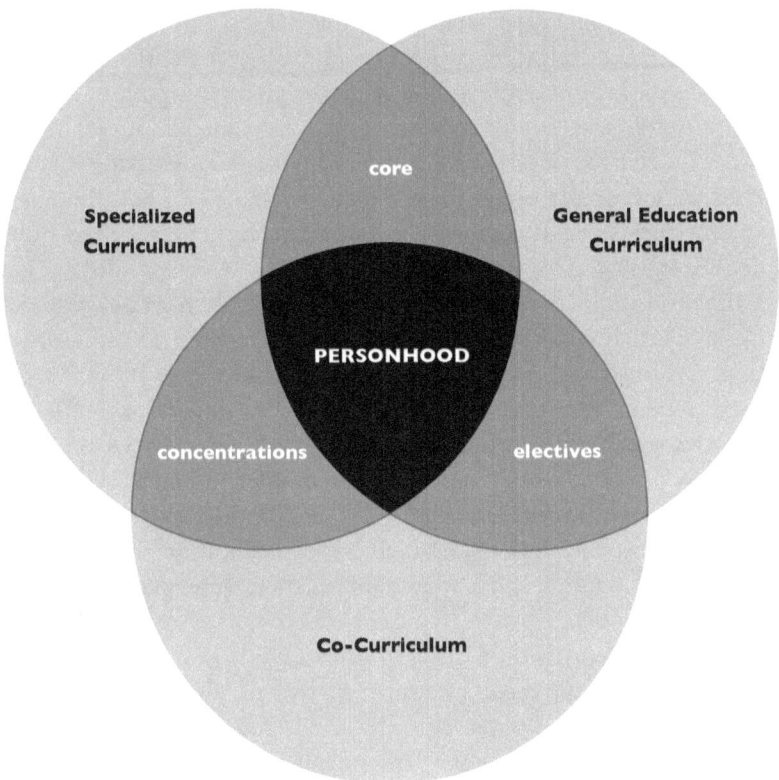

Figure 5. Personhood Model: Undergraduate Education

Representative Implications

The preceding observations suggest understandings which might inform policy and practice, were one to implement a Burkeian undergraduate program. Such a program would necessarily emphasize the interdependence of the three primary curricular components: general education curriculum, specialized curriculum, and co-curriculum. What follows is not an exhaustive list of specific ingredients but, rather, a representative sampling of implications within those three components, each of which would address Burke's "aims of education": skills, moral admonition, and aesthetic appreciation.

The general education curriculum, involving acculturation into the range and storehouse of human learnings, includes that set of academic experiences common to all—or most—undergraduates: core requirements, introductory courses in the liberal arts and sciences, skills-based foundational courses, etc. Whatever its vocabulary, structure, and requirements, it seeks to provide contact with the past and knowledge for the future in light of current individual and societal assessment. Typically lacking an overall integrating perspective, general education curricula tend to reflect carefully apportioned "slices of the pie," the political guarantee of disciplinary "exposure." Students are left to order lower-level, fragmented, and often diluted introductions to "strangers" they hope never again to encounter. Under a unifying linguistic umbrella, faculty would design general education curricula not through coercive inter-departmental compromise, but through cooperative cross-disciplinary dialogue aimed at Appropriateness as well as Awareness.

A Burkeian dramatistic-general-education curriculum would, therefore, engage students in both expansive and integrative ways of thinking and framing significant human questions as they move in and out of disciplinary conversational parlors. Pragmatic "skills" of discourse, critical reflection, and the like, would obtain across disciplinary divides; faculty would engage in cross-disciplinary teaching and learning in order to illustrate the neverending "voyage of discovery" in which they, too, continue to engage; and students would experience throughout their "general education" the interplay of skills, moral admonition, and aesthetic appreciation represented across traditional ways of knowing.

The specialized curriculum involves initiation into the nomenclature and attitude of an academic discipline. As a "major," or "depth component," it consists of that set of academic experiences selected by students in light of personal interests, abilities, and professional goals. Designed by departmental faculty, specialized curricula tend to reflect myriad internal and external concerns and constraints, and faculty are often called upon to make politicized decisions without benefit of a guiding educational perspective. Moreover, especially in response to perceived market demands, specialization may continue to focus on lower levels of information-awareness despite the coveted higher levels of interaction and appreciation. That is, students may encounter not merely a potpourri of introductory general-education samplers, but a barrage of "advanced" specialized samplers—a difference of degree, not of kind. Again, a linguistic point of view would guide curricular decision-making, suggesting that the specialized curriculum be understood within a trans-disciplinary context. Indeed, the salient issue may not be how disciplines are defined but, rather, what glue holds them together.

Under the linguistic umbrella of a *personhood model*, curricular specialization is contextual, and "integration of thought and action" transcends the bounds of specialization. Burke speaks of placing all specific documents "within the unending human dialogue as a whole" and warns that "education must not be thought of merely as a means of preparing students for market, though that's what much of it now is" (1955, p. 273). Placing all "documents of specialization" within a Burkeian dialogue would encourage understanding of both part and whole. Moreover, the skills, moral admonition, and aesthetic appreciation built into the general education curriculum from first-semester introductory courses through senior-level integrative seminars would find expression in each specialized curriculum, as well. Students would be encouraged to treat even the most technical aspects of science or psychology or literature as part of a greater whole—always thinking dialectically in terms of connectedness.

The co-curriculum involves socialization into the learning community of interacting selves. The least structured of the curricula, it includes that set of individual experiences, both planned and circumstantial, that augments formal learning. The co-curriculum does not belong to any one department, administrative office, or support service. Rather, it encompasses campus programs and opportunities that foster student personal and intellectual development. Although Burke does not address the co-curriculum per se, his inclusive "theory of human relations" embraces its functions. Given his "social philosophy" of language and our inferred linguistic guiding perspective, the co-curriculum is inseparable from the curriculum proper. Yet co-curricula lack an ordering conception that can guide both inquiry and experience, and goals of Awareness tend to outweigh Appropriateness; that is, questions of "what" and "how-to" overshadow "whether to" and "under what conditions." In pentadic terms, co-curricula tend, also, to be dominated by immediate scene, purpose, and agency in the form of lower-level practicality, rather than by considered act and agent in appreciative dialogue.

What better opportunity for traditional undergraduates to practice higher-level educational agenda of community, cooperation, identification, interaction, and character than the myriad programs typically orchestrated by the office of student affairs—yet often disconnected from the "curriculum": dormitory life, student government, social and cultural events, the arts, collegiate sports, and the like. Inasmuch as we know that whatever occurs throughout the student experience affects learning, and whatever is learned informs experience, the co-curriculum would afford an ideal contextual opportunity to bring together Awareness and Appropriateness. Here, skills, moral admonition, and aesthetic appreciation would merge in the ongoing "real" drama of student life.

The pivotal transitional educational agenda, that is, the building of community and practice of cooperation, rest finally on Burke's "institutionalizing of an attitude." Through mutually supportive curricular content and co-curricular context, students can be led by and through the tangle of compartmentalized symbolism, beyond the tangle. To this end, we would not disengage students from specialized studies, but would, with Burke, "allow for the traditional autonomy of the various disciplines," so conducting "our investigations that we might glimpse, brooding over the lot, a lore of the universal pageantry in which all . . . necessarily and somewhat somnambulistically [as in sleepwalking] take part, by reason of their symbol-using natures" (1955:282). To this end, the general education curriculum, the specialized curriculum, and the co-curriculum would converge—and personhood emerge.

References

Brock, B. L. (1985). Epistemology and Ontology in Kenneth Burke's Dramatism. *Communication Quarterly, 33*(2), 94–104.

Brock, B. L., et al. (1985). Dramatism as Ontology or Epistemology: A Symposium. *Communication Quarterly, 33*(1), 17–33.

Buber, M. (1955). *Between man and man*, Trans. R. G. Smith. Boston: Beacon.

Burke, K. (1954). *Permanence and change: An anatomy of purpose*. Los Altos, CA: Hermes. (Original work published 1935)

Burke, K. (1955). Linguistic approach to problems of education. In N. B. Henry (Ed.), *Modern philosophies and education, The fifty-fourth yearbook of the National Society for the Study of Education, Part 1 of 2* (pp. 259–303). Chicago: National Society for the Study of Education.

Burke, K. (1961). *Attitudes toward history*. Boston: Beacon Press. (Original work published 1937)

Burke, K. (1962). *A grammar of motives*. Cleveland, OH: Meridian. (Original work published 1945)

Burke, K. (1966). *Language as symbolic action: Essays of life, Literature, and method*. Berkeley, CA: University of California.

Burke, K. (1969). *A rhetoric of motives*. Berkeley, CA: University of California. (Original work published 1950)

Burke, K. (1970). *The rhetoric of religion: Studies in logology*. Berkeley, CA: University of California. (Original work published 1961)

Cowley, M. (1969). Prolegomena to Kenneth Burke. In W. Rueckert (Ed.), *Critical responses to Kenneth Burke: 1924–1966.* (pp. 247–251). Minneapolis: University of Minnesota.

Duncan, H. D. (1962). *Communication and social order*. New York: Bedminster.

Duryea, E. (1982). Prologue to the American system of hither education: Higher learning in Western culture. *Occasional papers series*. Buffalo, NY: SUNY at Buffalo.

Griffin, L. M. (1969). A dramatistic theory of the rhetoric of movements. In W. Rueckert (Ed.), *Critical responses to Kenneth Burke: 1924–1966* (pp. 456–478). Minneapolis, MN: University of Minnesota.

Hofstadter, R., & Smith, W. (1961). The Yale report of 1828. In R. Hofstadter & W. Smith (Eds.), *American Higher Education, Vol. I* (pp. 275–291). Chicago: University of Chicago.

Nevins, A. (1962). *The state universities and democracy.* Urbana: University of Illinois,.

Rueckert, W. H. (1963). *Kenneth Burke and the drama of human relations.* Minneapolis, MN: University of Minnesota.

Russett, C. E. (1976). *Darwin in America: The intellectual response, 1865–1912.* New York: W. H. Feeman.

Rudolph, F. (1962). *American college and university.* New York: Vintage.

Skinner, B. F. (1968). *The technology of teaching.* New York: Appleton-Century-Crofts.

Veysey, L. R. (1962). *The emergence of the American university.* Chicago: University of Chicago.

4 The Education of Citizen Critics: The Consubstantiality of Burke's Philosophy and Constructivist Pedagogy

Peter M. Smudde

The irony that Kenneth Burke sidestepped higher education, was largely self-taught in multiple fields of study, and expended considerable efforts in academe has not been lost on Burke scholars (cf. Foss et al., 2002, pp. 188–191). Indeed, Burke himself only published one treatise on education, "Linguistic Approach to Problems in Education," in 1955. In fact, in a letter to Malcolm Cowley dated August 9, 1945, Burke showed he was considering the role of his work in education and referred to the idea for such a treatise as "an unexpected quickie" after having completed his *A Grammar of Motives* (1945/1969a) and still deciding on "whether to plunge into the Rhetoric book" (Jay, 1988, p. 267). Certain critical reviews of the *Grammar* that centered on its applicability to education may have helped to spur Burke on to complete the treatise but only after finishing *A Rhetoric of Motives*. The question, then, is how does Burke's philosophy of education and his larger system befit the field of education? Furthermore, what consubstantiality does Burke have with any current pedagogical perspective? This chapter answers these questions by summarizing Burke's formal educational philosophy with respect to his broader system; establishing points of convergence between Burke and constructivist pedagogy, including problem-based learning; presenting a concise framework for a Burkeian "symbolic of education" that blends these orientations; and finally formulating a instructional design based on the "Burkeian constructivism" framework.

A Burkeian Pedagogical Perspective

A search of research on the application of Burke to specific or general areas of education reveals only a handful of work (see Appendix 1), and most of it was published sporadically within the last 30 years. The introduction of this book also showed the few sessions connecting Burke and education held at national conventions. Most of the published work focuses on how to teach Burke's ideas or how to use one or two of his tools to teach something, so they tend to be fairly tactical. In this vein the application of Burke's ideas to learning environments has focused almost exclusively on the dramatistic pentad, leaving the rest of Burke's method essentially untouched. Very few look at larger issues concerning teaching, but this approach is often done as part of a bigger framework about Burke's ideas about rhetoric and rarely focused solely on education writ large. What is important to do, then, is to move beyond these selective yet useful essays about Burke-based teaching tactics. This chapter begins this effort with an investigation of how Burke's larger perspective on education *and* his system combine as a philosophy of education, including particular methods or "tools" for enacting that philosophy.

Burke's Philosophy of Education in Brief

The core treatise for Burke's philosophy of education is his 1955 article, "Linguistic Approach to Problems of Education." This work is the focus of this chapter, and others of Burke's writing will be used as well. What is important to note is that Burke's notion of what defines humans is the starting point for his ideas on education. For example, beyond his core treatise on education, Burke makes a short and somewhat detailed reference to education eleven years later in "Definition of Man" (1966). Therein he wrote that his definition of man

> is surely normative [not merely descriptive] in the sense that its implications are strongly admonitory, suggesting the kind of foibles and crotchets which a "comic" theory of education would feature, in asking man to center his attention on the understanding of his "natural temptations" towards kinds of turbulence that, when reinforced with the powers of the new weapons, threaten to undo us.
>
> I'm not too sure that, in the present state of Big Technology's confusions, any educational policy, even if it were itself perfect and were adopted throughout the world, would be able to help much, when the world is so ardently beset by

> so much distress and malice. The dreary likelihood is that, if we do avoid the holocaust, we shall do so mainly by bits of political patchwork here and there, with alliances falling sufficiently on the bias across one another, and thus getting sufficiently in one another's road, so that there's no enough "symmetrical perfection" among the contestants to set up the "right" alignment and touch it off. (p. 20)

Burke's preoccupation with the literal and symbolic destructive capabilities of nuclear technology for war guides a large part of his thinking about many matters in human relations, including education. In this passage, education is a comic corrective to the tragic frame of "Big Technology" and its influence on everything, especially humanity's demise (cf. Enoch, 2004).

Even in his only writing of his formal perspective on education, Burke's concerns about the affect of "Big Technology" are apparent, but they are more subdued. Burke's formal philosophy of education is systematic, reflecting his work before and anticipating his work to come after the publishing of "Linguistic Approach to Problems of Education." Indeed, the locus of his educational philosophy in 1955 is a refined understanding of humans, which had not been articulated as a formal "definition of man" by this point but was certainly forming/formed in his mind, as it was first published six years later in *Rhetoric of Religion* (1961/1970, p. 40), re-examined in 1966 in "Definition of Man," stated more simply in the third edition of *Permanence and Change* as "Bodies That Learn Language" (1935/1984, p. 295), then revised in 1989 as "Poem." The bottom line for a Burkeian symbolic of education: humans are driven by symbols, which they create, use and misuse; and education is a particular realm of human relations that engages humans linguistically in the sharing and building of both practical and theoretical knowledge (cf. Burke, 1950/1969b, p. 77). In short, language structures thinking and is the locus of learning—education is symbolic action. The ultimate end of education is to produce *citizen critics* who, through dramatism, bridge the frames and methods of humanism *and* positivism to improve the human relations and the human condition. Figure 1 illustrates key aspects of Burke's philosophy of education.

The poles of positivism and humanism are traditional opposites that have real potential if they were to be bridged. The former's "main purpose is to perfect technical ability, to teach special skills"; the latter's focus is "the attempt to teach and to acquire the kind of 'insignia' that are thought to be proof of cultural election" (Burke, 1955, p. 271). Each pole alone has value on its own, but the greatest impact on learning is when the two are combined. So Burke's view of education is synthetic; that is, he sees education not as

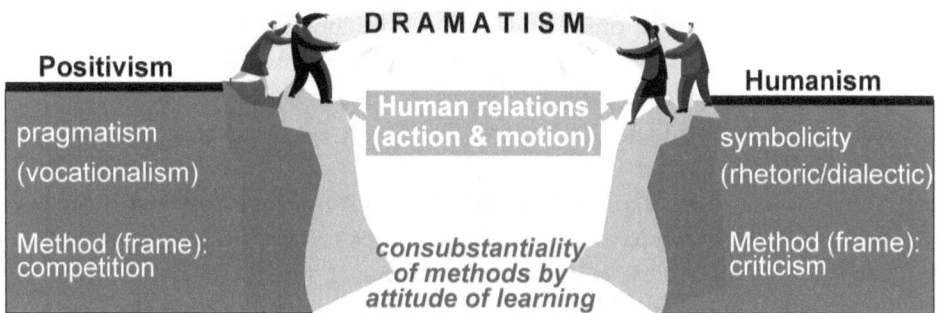

Figure 1. Model of major aspects to Burke's philosophy of education.

a venue for just pragmatic learning nor only study of human symbolicity. Burke sees clear benefit to the two combined as one into something better through dramatism, which "in a commingling of techniques and hypochondriasis, will 'appreciate' man's [sic] ways of thundering" (Burke, 1955, p. 271). Burke's view of education, then, establishes a comic corrective for a division of orientations that perpetuates a tragic vision that pits one view against another rather than establish common ground between them.

Education, in this way, is rhetorical—a particular realm of symbolic action about human needs (motion) and human knowledge-building (action). Education is symbolic action as it involves the "drama of human relations" with any and every aspect of living. The dramatistic approach to education involves an holistic approach that "is a critical or essayistic analysis of language, and thence of human relations generally, by the use of terms derived from the contemplation of drama" (Burke, 1955, p. 264). This critical dimension to education is key, as instructors engage in a kind of "courtship" of students about subjects (Burke, 1950/1969b, p. 229). As courtiers, educators are in a "special professional class" that "[initiate students] into the mysteries of their code" (Burke, 1950/1969b, p. 230). Education has "a mythic glow, as it would be a form of 'pure persuasion,' the rhetorical motive dialectically made ultimate" (Burke, 1950/1969b, p. 230).

That persuasion concerns the direct application of examples of human relations as the objects of learning. The nature of those objects, by virtue of their origin in human action, are symbolic acts—texts that command attention on multiple levels using particular methods, as there would be "no difference 'in principle' between textual analysis and social analysis" (Burke, 1955, p. 275). In Burke's view, education "seek[s] to become a sophisticated and methodized set of parables, or fables" (Burke, 1955, p. 271). These texts, then, are equipment for learning and living, "in the hope of learning something about the ways in which the 'personality' of the work relates to the 'personality' of a social order; and then . . . we look for ways whereby the work embodies, however assertively, even militantly, the *malaise* of a given property structure (with the goads, and 'mortifications,' and demands upon our 'patience,' and invitations to victimage, that are intrinsic to any such order)" (Burke, 1955, p. 275).

Education, then, is as much retrospective as it is prospective, and it perhaps places more emphasis on the latter than the former. The reason is that education is "a *technique of preparatory withdrawal*, the institutionalizing of an attitude that one should be able to *recover at crucial moments*, all along the subsequent way" (Burke, 1955, p. 273). The ultimate outcome of education would be citizen critics who have developed advanced practice-theory bridge building "into man's [sic] ways as symbol user" (Burke, 1955, p. 275). Indeed, the citizen critic is a "poetic humanist" (Brock, 1990, p. 7) who is expert in the study of human relations and the ways people make sense of and affect change in the world through symbolic action—"that we are 'poets all'" (Burke, 1955, p. 281). The question now is how would an educator achieve this outcome?

Burkeian Pedagogical Methods

Burke developed his ideas and grand system over time, and tracing the evolution of Burke's thinking is both doable and fruitful. Indeed, examining his early ideas in light of his later, more-refined articulations of them illuminates greater possibilities for understanding and, especially, application. This situation is the case when it comes to examining the Burkeian agencies that an educator could use in a dramatistic educational setting.

In his article, "Linguistic Approach to Problems of Education," Burke lays out a method and curriculum that operationalize his philosophy. His thoughts here, naturally, are at once based in the theoretical and the pragmatic. Education focuses on myriad aspects of human relations, and as such is linguistic in nature as language orders people's world and worldviews. This focus places emphasis on symbolic action (i.e., texts) about things, which means teaching is very much a matter of guiding students in the act of "indexing" texts for their formal characteristics and dramatistic dynamics (Burke, 1955, p. 276). Examples of Burkeian tools for enacting a dramatistic educational environment are given in Table 1; whereas, these tools are revealed variously in Burke's 1955 article and can be applied from his other, later works. Other Burkeian tools may be added and otherwise organized, but this repository will do as a start.

Table 1. A Basic Burkeian Teaching Toolbox.

Attitudes/Goals	Agencies/Tools	Purposes/Learning Outcomes
Facilitate learning and an effective learning environment	Dialectic	Engage in "courtship" of students by teacher and vice versa; challenge students through didactic discussion
	Identification	Help students bridge their own thinking with others,' including students, extant knowledge, theories, case examples, etc.
	Pentad/Hexad	Apply as a framework for the educational situation/lesson, including the selection of learning objects and the use of instructional media
	Trained incapacity	Determine limits to what's accomplishable (and what blinds us) in an educational setting and students' capabilities therein and possibly beyond
Stimulate inquiry	Representative anecdote	Employ one or more learning objects as illustrative of a particular point, concept, etc.
	Substance	Discover the philosophical and pragmatic foundation of a symbolic act
	Perspective by incongruity	Engage discussion about something by approaching it from an unanticipated, unusual and valuable vantage point
	Master tropes	Distill the "true" essence of something in new terms through metaphor, metonymy, synecdoche, and/or irony
	The negative	Recognize and/or employ the implications of the opposite of what's symbolized or not

Attitudes/Goals	Agencies/Tools	Purposes/Learning Outcomes
Become fluent in critical language and thinking	Naming	Apprehend the key terms and the conventions for creating key terms of a subject
	Terministic screens	Develop competence to appropriately apply a subject area's terms and "equations" to make sense of phenomena; awareness of "god terms," "devil terms" and "ultimate terms" (cluster agon)
	Framing	Be cognizant of one's orientation or attitude toward a term, concept, etc.; define the context for a term, concept, etc. for discussion (acceptance, rejection, passivity, comic, tragic, etc.)
Become fluent in critical discourse	Form	Understand the discourse conventions of particular types of symbolic action, both that which is studied and that which is created by the student
	Indexing symbolic structure	Establish hierarchy among particular conventions within a discourse genre to understand its intricacies
Employ micro- and macro-level analysis	Pentad/Hexad	Reveal the motives behind a given symbolic act/learning object; divine subsequent symbolic action through the pentad/hexad
	Terms for order	Illustrate the goad for perfection; trace the evolution of a series of related symbolic actions over time and how they led or lead to a new order

What is important to realize about the "basic Burkeian teaching toolbox" is that it employs a dramatistic structure. The toolbox also organizes Burke's various methods in clusters so we can have an idea about what may go with what for certain educational needs, including tool combinations with educational objects. The toolbox is organized (by columns) specifically along the elements of the hexad (Burke, 1968, p. 446); whereas, three are stated and three are unstated but assumed. The latter are assumed—or really left open—because certain educational dimensions (i.e., scenes/classes, acts/lessons, and actors/educators) vary too much to be effectively chronicled in Table 1. Like any toolbox, the tools therein may be used at one's discretion, much like a screwdriver may be used either on a screw or to open a paint can. The hexad is used to organize the toolbox over the pentad because the dimension of attitude is ever-present and important in the literal drama of educational human relations more holistically. Agency corresponds to pragmatism, and purpose corresponds to mysticism, thereby bridging practice and theory in the toolbox as well. The hexad (and the pentad, depending on an educator's preference) is used as a tool as well in two particular areas in the toolbox. The reason is that the hexad/pentad can be especially handy, as Table 1 shows, when creating a learning environment and engaging in focused analysis of human relations.

The other tools in the toolbox span a range of Burke's work, bringing together ideas and methods that can complement one another under particular circumstances displayed in Table 1. If anything is apparent in the toolbox, it is that one is not and should not be dependent on one aspect of Burke's system, because the whole of what Burke gave us is truly greater than the sum of its parts, even when any one part is employed individually, as extant scholarship using Burke to educational problems shows. Indeed, this kind of systematic understanding and application of Burke to education breaks new ground in Burkeology and pedagogy. What is missing, however, is a more defined, contemporary educational perspective with which Burke is consubstantial. Why is this matter important? Such consubstantiality may (at least) help make Burke more appealing and usable for research and practice in education, plus the common ground between them can provide greater explanatory power than either of them separately. One perspective that is consubstantial with Burke's is constructivism. After summarizing key tenets of constructivism, the matter of its common ground with Burke can be formally established as a further refined symbolic of education.

A Constructivist Pedagogical Approach

Many times we educators integrate real-world experiences into our courses when we introduce real/realistic symbolic action to address our classes, ask our students to review real/realistic symbolic action by others, or prepare realistic symbolic action discourse assignments. All are good things, and the kinds of realistic, hands-on work students involve help them learn about the substance of the subjects we teach. More pedagogically speaking, these examples of real/realistic symbolic action, like the discourse examples we use from companies, are "educational objects" (Friesen, 2001) that serve multiple uses and have great instructional value. We instructors invoke kinds of virtual experiences based on those objects (including related discussion and assignments) function at a constructivist level that require students to actively solve complex and realistic problems using multiple perspectives and be aware of their own stake in the knowledge-creation process (Reiser, 2001, p. 63). Such experiences could be part of authentic learning tasks that reflect the complex nature of real-world, real/realistic symbolic action in which students would eventually engage.

Theoretical Principles

A learner-centric bias is key to constructivistic education, whose principal proponent is Vygotsky (1978, 1986). According to Vygotsky and constructivist pedagogy, learning is based on human symbolic action—"language, mnemonic techniques, formulae, concepts, symbols, signs, and so on" (Karpov & Bransford, 1995, p. 61). Learning, then, precedes the development of students' skills, and an instructor's guidance is similar to a master-apprentice relationship (Karpov & Bransford, 1995, p. 61); whereas, "socially shared activities [transform] into internalized processes" (John-Stener & Mahn, 1996, p. 192). Such an approach is one that allows students to participate in knowledge building under the guidance of an instructor or other more-competent person (i.e., working within their "zone of proximal development") that is at once social and individual. Learning is social as students collaborate with one another and an instructor who guides students' learning through activities involving complex and realistic problems and discovery about constituent aspects or basic skills (i.e., top-down processing). Learning is individual as students, through their discoveries, foster a sense of ownership of their learning and can monitor their own knowledge growth. Students are intimately involved in the cocreation of knowledge in the problem-solving process, which is facilitated by "scaffolding." That is, students examine a problem in a real-life, authentic context; are given just enough instructional guidance to help them along in their tasks; then arrive at an appropriate solution on their own (cf. Slavin, 2003, pp. 259–263).

An ideal constructivistic learning environment (cf. Driscoll, 2000, pp. 382–391) in courses would take advantage of the complexity of educational objects to demonstrate realistic and relevant situations from which students can dive into and learn how to handle at an appropriate level (i.e., beginner, intermediate, and advanced). Class discussions or small-group work would facilitate a communal dimension for learning, as students' perspectives on theoretical and practical issues are wrestled with socially and collaboratively.

Students would be encouraged to entertain multiple perspectives to understand real/realistic symbolic action situations because multiple views of what can be done can stem from multiple models and research about what effective real/realistic symbolic action, and thereby be used to explain responses to assignments. Students also learn to take responsibility or "ownership" for their own development as knowledgeable real/realistic symbolic action folks and achieve the learning goals for the course. As a result, students become increasingly aware of their developing knowledge and can help themselves in constructing new "mental structures" about subjects and situations throughout their lives.

Old and new "mental structures" about subjects—especially in context—would be formed, explicated and tested until satisfactory ones emerge (cf. Driscoll 2000, p. 376). The ultimate goal is that students develop knowledge about human relations and symbolic action practice and theory that can be applied in congruent contexts. More-specific goals would focus on building students' abilities on matters like developing particular forms of discourse and analyzing specific case examples of human relations.

Instructors would give students direction and feedback about their thinking related to both the theoretical and the practical dimensions of real/realistic symbolic action as dramatized in educational objects. In this manner, an instructor fosters a constructivist learning environment, where students are actively involved in the process that is framed by prerequisite skills and knowledge, an assignment, class discussions and experience. With effective contextualization of real/realistic symbolic action into lessons plans, students can confront specific challenges that require them to understand and apply certain concepts. Research on this kind of approach has demonstrated significant student learning in math and science courses plus nonmath and nonscience courses (Bransford et al., 2000, pp. 208–209). Selected educational objects facilitate students' learning by capitalizing on varied learning styles, and video is one example that emphasizes visual and auditory dimensions for critical thinking and application. The focus of this critical thinking involves problem-based learning (Jarvis, 2002; Jarvis et al., 1998, pp. 117–118), especially in a constructivist approach about "real life" situations, affecting both teaching and learning outcomes.

Practical Method

The instructional method emphasizes student reasoning, critical thinking, concept understanding, cognitive flexibility in weighing multiple perspectives, ownership of one's learning development, and self-reflection about one's knowledge construction. This constructivistic approach allows students to bridge theory and practice in ways that empower them to—with the instructor's guidance—take charge of their own learning, achieve learning goals, "connect the dots" between what they have come to know and what they are coming to know, and construct effective ways of thinking about real/realistic symbolic action that will serve them in their work as real/realistic symbolic action professionals.

Stories and case examples from the broad realm of human relations that we share in our classes in video or any medium are beneficial in many ways, especially at a cognitive level (cf. Pauly & Hutchison, 2001). We engage our students in authentic problem solving that requires various levels of cognitive processing at different stages in our real/realistic symbolic action curricula. By the time our students graduate, they should be well-prepared to solve the complex, ill-structured real/realistic symbolic-action problems that may have many solutions. From individual writing assignments about situations, to the creation of particular real/realistic symbolic action discourses, to the analyses of case examples, the problems we give our students approximate the demands of human relations in the "real world." As Johassen and Hernandez-Serrano (2002) put it, "Novices in school are trained only to work on problems that are, by nature, decontextualized and well structured [sic], while problems in everyday and professional contexts are complex and ill structured [sic]" (p. 68).

Realizing that the choice of media used for instructional purposes has an effect on cognitive processing, Cobb (1997) argues that the most efficient instructional media are those that "do some of the learners' cognitive work for them" (p. 32). This idea means that the way information is presented through a chosen medium gives the learner some amount of data to work from beyond what is in memory, and the learner builds knowledge about the task and subject by working through the problem-solving process at increasingly deeper levels. This "cognitive efficiency" with which someone works with information in a given medium is based on the rationale that "while different media may not create different cognitive products, such as concepts, schemas, and mental models, . . . they clearly do create different cognitive processes at different levels of efficiency (with regard to speed, ease, effectiveness). In other words, the form in which information is presented can determine how it is processed in a mind, and hence how it can be learned" (Cobb, 1997, p. 27).

A Concise Framework for a Symbolic of Education for Citizen Critics

Having summarized Burke's philosophy of education and constructivist pedagogy, the next step is to address where the two converge. These two orientations come together at a fairly abstract level but with direct pragmatic implications, the combination I call "Burkeian constructivism," that I will address in the final section of this chapter. Key points of consubstantiality between Burke and constructivism, based on the discussion above, are shown in Table 2.

Table 2. Key areas of consubstantiality between Burke and Constructivism.

Burke	Constructivism
Humans use language to make sense of the world and experience	Humans use language to learn, then behaviors develop thereafter
Humans are goaded by hierarchy and seek to create order; critical/instructional methods and orientations to enable this are key (educational ladder)	Humans learn best when lessons build one upon the other using selected instructional objects (scaffolding)
Humans operate by both action and motion, where action is the locus of what gets done and a critic can engage his/her skills to particular matters or problems	Humans' best time to learn something is at the moment when they are most open to possibilities (zone of proximal development); problem-based, "authentic" learning facilitates creation of such zones
Human relations are grounded in the realm of action, and particularly symbolic action, and education is a specialized realm of symbolic action based on linguistic means	Human education is possible through communication between instructor and student, where the instructor enables students to assume ownership of his/her learning through discovery

The education of citizen critics is very much a matter of courtship between educator and student, involving a kind of mystery of order among all aspects of the educational situation. In this synthesis of Burkeian and constructivist pedagogy, educators employ authentic ideas and methods that are framed in a comic way to correct for the tragic or passive frames individuals and society has for aspects of human relations. From buying groceries to taking a position on public policy, citizen critics' education involves more than the internalization of mere recipes for the motions of survival. It involves a deeper understanding of the natural dynamics of humans' motion and action, and how that understanding is the foundation for symbolic action as a participant in society to any degree. To be a citizen critic is to be a creative problem solver who is interested, willing, able, and active in making things better, and to do so because one's education has established a solid foundation for action for such change. The values of such an education grow out of the dramatistic approach for instilling critical awareness, skills, and thinking about the prevailing social (i.e., democratic) milieu that perpetually provides both educators and students with examples from which to learn and grow. Literature and life are equipment for teaching, learning, and living.

Burkeian constructivism gives us a new, synthetic view of education that balances the rhetorical and the behavioral dimensions of this realm of human relations. Most important, we have a way to move beyond purely psychological motion by having a powerful approach to analyzing education as symbolic action. From theories of education, to preparations for learning environments, to enacting lessons, to giving feedback on students' work, we can view it all dramatistically as symbolic action and derive insights about them at their appropriate levels. Those levels of insight make up the stuff of the education of citizen critics—poetic humanists who are better prepared agents in and for society, for all its foibles and successes. With the threat (and the promise) of the technologizing of the world, positivistic values that privilege the secular and pragmatic must be counterbalanced with humanistic values of the spiritual and holistic. Citizen critics approach human relations and motives in dramatistic terms, emphasizing action. Education, then, spurs society's evolution from its present base primarily on science and technology to one that is principally humane, "treating humans as 'participants in action' rather than stressing competitive aspects" (Brock, 1990, p. 7). Education, as symbolic action, is "the dancing of an attitude" (Burke, 1941/1973, p. 9) for and about learning among all people involved.

An Application of the Framework

The preceding sections developed a philosophy of a "symbolic of education" for citizen critics, now we turn to a methodology. This final section presents a pragmatic side of the theory and answers the question, "How can Burkeian constructivism be applied to educational settings?" To answer this question this final section relies on two instrumental ideas: attitude toward education and instructional design.

Attitude Toward Education

To Burke, attitude shapes or modifies human action (1949/1969a, p. 237). Or as the old saying goes, "attitude is everything." These two views are consubstantial at least because attitude is linguistically constructed, central in human activity, and assumes guiding principles (e.g., orientation, world view, personal philosophy) are the foundation of an attitude that is behind an action. For educators, attitude and action begin with a philosophy of teaching and learning.

Anyone who goes into education has a view of teaching and learning. The question is, "What is that view?" A philosophy of teaching and learning is a personal statement about what education is/is not, does/does not do, involves/skips over, etc. Such a philosophy is personal and should be formalized in a document. The point of a personal philosophy of teaching and learning is not necessarily to crystallize principles in the theory and practice of education, although it can do that. A personal philosophy of teaching and learning also is not merely an exercise in theorizing, although it is theoretical in content. Leamnson (1999) argues that a philosophy of teaching and learning is necessary and should include at least statements about the nature of learning; the centrality of language; the importance of process toward learning goals; the background, readiness, and intellectual and emotional needs of students; the difference teaching makes; the value of active and attentive students; and the love of being an educator (pp. 7–8). A personal philosophy of teaching and learning is truly a practical matter of "knowing thyself." A philosophy of teaching and learning is something that liberates one's attitudes, knowledge, experiences, biases, and behaviors. It liberates these things for an educator because it allows someone to know her- or himself *first*, and this is important to understand before designing a lesson or course and delivering it to students. A personal philosophy of teaching and learning also is liberating for students because it reveals the same things to them and serves as a touchstone for discussions about teaching and learning in life.

Reflecting on teaching and learning in the context of Burkeian constructivism can ground an educator's symbolic action for her or his students. Some of the basic tenets of a personal philosophy of teaching and learning, then, would reflect principles shown in Figure 1 and, especially, Table 2. Technically speaking, the common ground between and practical usefulness of Burke and constructivism come together in particular themes or attitudes about education and the symbolic action involved in both teaching and learning. The following are selected principles from my own Burkeian constructivist philosophy:

- Education is rhetorical action, with instructors facilitating that action and students driving it in a kind of "courtship" and "coaching of attitudes."
- People are teachers and learners simultaneously.
- Instructor and students cocreate the learning environment.
- An instructor demonstrates values in his or her words and actions, lives as a moral example to students, and leads students and makes decisions on sound ethical grounds.
- An instructor serves best as a guide on a journey through extant knowledge and beyond, giving students (including the instructor) opportunities to discover what they know and are coming to know, especially through real-world/realistic learning objects and assignments.
- Students should feel a sense of ownership of their learning. Learning how best to learn is key to each person.
- Key to facilitating learning is cognitive problem solving, and degrees of cognitive dissonance are a good thing. Students experience learning, then, at intellectual and emotional levels, which spurs interest and inquiry.
- "Building bridges" or "connecting the dots" between theory and practice is important, as it links the "why" with the "what" and "how." These connections link what students know with what they need to know and are coming to know; they link new ideas, concepts, principles, skills, etc. with old ones, which builds competence.

A philosophy of teaching and learning is not just one about particular "truths." It is a formal codification of what an educator values, believes, and acts upon within learning environments, which could be anywhere with anyone. A philosophy of teaching and learning also can be specialized for specific learners and learning (e.g., first-year students; cf. Leamnson, 1999). The idea that learning is constructed linguistically is central to Burkeian constructivism, and a personal philosophy that establishes an educator's orientation toward teaching and learning goes a long way in her or his careful crafting of learning opportunities and the facilitation of learning among students who seek the instructor's guidance.

Instructional Design

Once one knows her or his attitude toward education through a personal philosophy of teaching and learning, the next step is to put that philosophy to work. Instructional design "is a discipline in which practitioners constantly look to the findings of other disciplines (e.g., cognitive psychology, communication) to study and improve methods of developing, delivering, and evaluating instruction and instructional processes" (Brown & Green, 2006, p. 7). At a personal and rhetorical level, instructional design also enables one to apply her or his personal philosophy toward effective teaching and learning about specific material. There are multiple models for instructional design, and educators choose to use the one that suits their needs best (Brown & Green, 2006, pp. 9–23). Because instructional design models vary in kind and in usability, I believe it is appropriate to account for the common ground among all models. This common ground is captured in the metamodel, "ADDIE," which stands for each of five phases of instructional design, which will be described below (Birchelmeyer, 2005; Brown & Green, 2006; McKeachie, 2002; Molenda, 2003, 2004; Peterson, 2003; Welty 2007).

The ADDIE metamodel is an apt one to use to apply to Burkeian constructivism because ADDIE "is actually a means for describing the essential components of *any* instructional design model" (Brown & Green, 2006, p. 12; cf. Molenda, 2003, 2004). Because of the limitations of this chapter, I will only briefly explain how the ADDIE metamodel helps enact Burkeian constructivism by tying it to an example—selected challenges to a college course in professional/technical writing. The example includes applications of tools from the Burkeian teaching toolbox in Table 1. Subsequent investigations can develop a more-detailed instructional design, and this treatment should be sufficient to help others apply this chapter's approach. The approach can be used for new and existing courses.

The first phase of the ADDIE metamodel is *analyze*. This phase "identifies a performance gap" between what students actually know and what they must or should know but do not (Welty, 2007, p. 41). The best way to begin thinking about closing the gap is to compare students' current competency in professional/technical writing to industry demands. Research on and resources for professional/technical writing abound, and an educator can lean on them, her or his own knowledge and experience, plus the counsel of industry professionals. Depending on where in a curriculum sequence a particular course fits, analysis should consider prior learning and experience students would have and not have coming into the course under development/revision. In terms of the Burkeian teaching toolbox, this phase can involve conjuring a dialectic learning environment where students and teacher are in an educational courtship, establishing identification between students and the subject matter plus each other and the teacher, determining the trained incapacities students have developed and should avoid in writing (especially in a career). A beginning technical writing course would address certain matters differently or instead of those in an advanced course. Specific data and colleagues' opinions about student performance in relevant courses (especially prerequisites) will be needed to gauge the span of the gap between students' competence and industry demands.

The second phase is *design*, and it involves "a planned approach to addressing the performance gap [that] is outlined and approved" because "the learning product [fits] into the larger curriculum" (Welty, 2007, p. 41). The best way to engage in this phase is to use the findings from the analysis phase to specify desired learning outcomes from the course in professional/technical writing and work backwards. Fink's (2005) approach to the design phase is especially useful. His "backward design" process includes five steps: (1) identify situational factors among the subject, students, teacher, and environment that can help or hurt learning, (2) establish goals for student learning by a course's end (i.e., addressing the six areas of foundational knowledge, application, integration, human dimensions, caring, and learning how to learn) so that the combination of these goals results in significant learning, (3) consider feedback and assessment procedures to guide students during their learning, (4) find appropriate teaching and learning activities that will move the students progressively and significantly toward fulfilling learning goals (i.e., the richer the learning the better), and (5) integrate all these components into a system that contribute to and support each other. One key result from this design phase should be a draft syllabus and schedule for the course that lays out the range of things that will be covered and completed. Tools from the Burkeian teaching toolbox that can be especially handy in the design phase may include using the pentad/hexad as a framework for specific lessons or examples about writing assignments and work situations, applying one or more perspectives by incongruity to reveal dimensions about the dynamics and demands of professional writing that may otherwise remain hidden (especially because of any trained incapacities), and illustrating the importance of a particular point or orientation about the roles of professional writing in today's organizations through a representative anecdote.

Develop is the third phase of the ADDIE metamodel, which includes all activity needed to bring a learning product (i.e., anything from a whole course to individual assignments) into being for an educational opportunity (Welty, 2007, p. 41). With the syllabus in hand the teacher devises the actual learning products/objects, from lectures and class activities to assignments and scoring rubrics. This phase can be lengthy because it involves the development or revision of the very material the teacher and students will use based on the results of the analysis and design phases. Certain revisions of the syllabus and course content may be necessary as the teacher considers situational constraints that may affect the course design and schedule. Tools from the Burkeian teaching toolbox can help in this phase. Naming can be key to helping students unlock the secrets of the writing process in nonacademic settings, and teministic screens can similarly help students become competent in analyzing the process as critics and participants. The essence of the writing process in organizations can be revealed through both substance and master tropes. The negative can also be used to address what professional/technical writing is or is not, and framing can help students understand their own and organizations' orientations toward writing and see how those orientations can be strengthened or corrected. Assignments must address matters of form so that students understand and apply the conventions for organizational discourse meant for various purposes and audiences.

The fourth phase is *implement*. This phase is the enactment of learning products—the literal symbolic action—between a teacher and students (Welty, 2007, p. 41). All the planning comes together and should pay off in learning that moves students closer to fulfilling one or more course goals. In a professional/technical writing class, lecture and class discussion or activities lead to new levels of knowing about industry expectations in process and people management, writing quality, text production and distribution, reader usability, and continuous improvement procedures for future texts. Assignments specifically challenge students to think about and solve specific problems in one or more of these areas, and each assignment builds in complexity and challenge from its predecessors. Particular Burkeian teaching tools from Table 1 that can help in this phase include those from the previous phase and others too. Assignments should require students to demonstrate their command of subject matter by using the key terms and concepts in context (i.e., substance, naming, terministic screens, and framing). Assignments should also challenge students to demonstrate their command of and problem-solving abilities for particular writing situations and how audiences would respond to the finished work (i.e., form, indexing symbolic structure, pentad/hexad, and terms for order).

The final phase is *evaluate*, and it involves measuring and analyzing the findings about both student learning and the effectiveness/appropriateness of a learning product (Welty, 2007, p. 41). Knowledge about how well students are learning is gained though various methods, such as direct/indirect, authentic, and embedded assessment techniques in courses and programs (cf. Allen, 2004; Huba & Freed, 2000; Maki, 2004; McKeachie, 2002; Shaughnessy, 1979; Walvoord, 2004; Weigle, 2002). Based on that knowledge, if things could be better, educators can make adjustments; and if things work well, educators know where to capitalize on success. Scoring rubrics can be used for all assignments to present assessment criteria, such as specific skill sets, effectiveness expectations, and other requirements with numerical values to indicate varied levels of successfulness in meeting learning expectations. When coupled with a teacher's written and oral comments, these rubrics are useful tools for showing students how well they are learning on assignment-specific dimensions and according to course-general learning goals. Such assessments of student proficiency should result in significant learning during and outside of class, giving students ways to improve their own work, discuss their performance with the teacher, and talk with their peers about the work they are doing. Burkeian teaching tools that are potentially helpful in this phase involve matters of form and indexing symbolic structure (i.e., how well students followed an assignment's requirements and discourse conventions) and terms for order (i.e., how well are students progressing in their mastery of course content through assignments, class participation, etc.). Although these tools are given here as examples of largely holistic assessments, other Burkeian teaching tools may be useful to measure students' performance on those specific dimensions.

Conclusion

Significant learning through symbolic action involving thinking, doing and sharing educational experiences among students and between students and their teacher is what Burkeian constructivism is all about. It is an alternative, humanistic response to the challenges of education at the turn of the millennium that parallels other changes in education. After digesting the criticism of his own philosophy and program for education early in the twentieth century, John Dewey commented on the wisdom of change in education:

> Mankind likes to think in terms of extreme opposites. It is given to formulating its beliefs in terms of *Either-Ors*, between which it recognizes no intermediate possibilities. When forced to recognize that the extremes cannot be acted upon, it is still inclined to hold that they are all right in theory but that when it comes to practical matters circumstances compel us to compromise. Educational philosophy is no exception. (1938/1997, p. 17).

This comment underscores the relevance for critiquing education writ large, proposing alternative approaches, and making revisions for the better. Education is not an *either-or* business; it is a *both-and* business, as Elvera Berry argues in Chapter 3. Accordingly, this chapter looked back on Burke's thinking about education, rhetoric, and human relations to look forward toward a more holistic Burkeian philosophy of education—an extension of his work that has scarcely ever been done and certainly not on a broad, systematic scale. Such a pedagogy has great promise, but it needs further development. This chapter also presented the author's initial thoughts on a Burkeian pedagogy that is a synthesis of his philosophy with constructivism and approaches for problem-based learning. When coupled with the other chapters of this volume and the handful of work that has been published or presented, we are on to something that surely can add value to the scholarship of teaching and learning—the symbolic nature of education for citizen critics.

Appendix 1: Works Applying Burke to Education

Benne, K. D. (1947). Toward a grammar of educational motives: An article review. *The Educational Forum, 11*(2), 233–239.

Benne, K. D. (1951). Education for tragedy. *Educational Theory, 1*(4), 199–210, 217.

Cheney, G. (1983). The rhetoric of identification and the study of organizational communication. *Quarterly Journal of Speech, 69*, 143–158.

Enoch, J. (2004). Becoming symbol-wise: Kenneth Burke's pedagogy of critical reflection. *College Composition and Communication, 56*(2), 272–296.

ey Selingo, S. M. (2001, 20 April). A puzzling figure in literary criticism is suddenly central. *Chronicle of Higher Education, 46*(32), A26. EBSCOhost.

Foss, K. A. (1983). Celluloid rhetoric: The use of documentary film to teach rhetorical theory. *Communication Education, 32*, 51–61.

Foss, S. K. (1982). Rhetoric and the visual image: A resource unit, *Communication Education, 31*, 55–66.

Jacobi, M. J. (1985). *Literature as equipment for writing: Applications of Kenneth Burke's dramatism to the teaching of composition.* Unpublished doctoral dissertation. University of Oregon, Eugene, Oregon.

McComiskey, B. (1995). Defining institutional problems: A heuristic procedure. *Business Communication Quarterly, 58*(4), 21–24.

Nelson, J. (1983). Using the Burkean pentad in the education of the basic speech student. *Communication Education, 32*, 63–68.

Quandahl, E. (1997). "It's essentially as though this were killing us": Kenneth Burke on mortification and pedagogy. *Rhetoric Society Quarterly* 27(1), 5–22.

Quandahl, E. (2001). "More than lessons in how to read": Burke, Freud, and the resources of symbolic transformation. *College English, 63*, 633–654.

Raup, R. B., Axtelle, G. E., Benne, K. D., & Smith, B. O. (1950, 1943). *The improvement of practical intelligence: The central task of education.* New York: Harper & Brothers.

Salibrici, M. M. (1999). Dissonance and rhetorical theory: A Burkean model for critical reading and writing. *Journal of Adolescent and Adult Literacy, 42*, 628–637.

Simons, H. W. (2004). The rhetorical legacy of Kenneth Burke. In W. Jost and W. Olmstead (Eds.), *A Companion to Rhetoric and Rhetorical Criticism* (pp. 152–168). Malden, MA: Blackwell Publishing.

Thompson, T. N., & Palmeri, A. J. (1993). Attitudes toward counterculture (with notes on nurturing a poetic psychosis). In J. W. Chesebro, (Ed.), *Extensions of the Burkean system* (pp. 269–283). Tuscaloosa, AL: University of Alabama Press.

REFERENCES

Allen, M. J. (2004). *Assessing academic programs in higher education*. Bolton, MA: Anker.

Bichelmeyer, B. A. (2005). "The ADDIE model"—A metaphor for the lack of clarity in the field of IDT. *IDT Record*. Retrieved October 4, 2008, from http://www.indiana.edu/~idt/shortpapers/documents/IDTf_Bic.pdf

Bransford, J. D., Brown, A. L., & Cocking, R. R. (Eds.) (2000). *How people learn: Brain, mind, experience, and school* (expanded edition). Washington, DC: National Research Council, National Academy Press.

Brock, B. L. (1990, April). Kenneth Burke and the 21st Century. *The Kenneth Burke Society Newsletter, 6*(1), 4–8.

Brown, A., & Green, T. D. (2006). *The essentials of instructional design: Connecting fundamental principles with process and practice*. Upper Saddle River, NJ: Pearson.

Burke, K. (1955). Linguistic approach to problems of education. In N. B. Henry (Ed.), *Modern philosophies and education: The fifty-fourth yearbook of the National Society for the Study of Education, Part 1 of 2* (pp. 259–303). Chicago: National Society for the Study of Education.

Burke, K. (1966). Definition of man. In *Language as symbolic action: Essays on life, literature and method* (pp. 3–24). Berkeley, CA: University of California Press.

Burke, K. (1968). Dramatism. In D. L. Sills (Ed.), *International encyclopedia of the social sciences* (Vol. 7, pp. 445–452). New York: Macmillan.

Burke, K. (1969a). *A grammar of motives*. Berkeley, CA: University of California Press. (Original work published 1945)

Burke, K. (1969b). *A rhetoric of motives*. Berkeley, CA: University of California Press. (Original work published 1950)

Burke, K. (1970). *Rhetoric of religion: Studies in logology*. Berkeley, CA: University of California Press. (Original work published 1961)

Burke, K. (1973). *The philosophy of literary form* (3rd ed.). Berkeley, CA: University of California Press. (Original work published 1941)

Burke, K. (1984). *Permanence and change* (3rd ed.). Berkeley, CA: University of California Press. (Original published 1935)

Burke, K. (1989). Poem. In H. W. Simons & T. Melia (Eds.), *The legacy of Kenneth Burke* (p. 263). Madison, WI: University of Wisconsin Press

Cobb, T. (1997). Cognitive efficiency: Toward a revised theory of media. *Educational Technology Research and Development, 45*(4), 21–35.

Dewey, J. (1997). *Experience and education*. New York: Touchstone. (Original work published 1938)

Douglas, A. (2000). Learning as participation in social practices: Interpreting, student perspectives on learning. *College English, 7*, 153–165.

Driscoll, M. P. (2000). *Psychology of learning for instruction* (2nd ed.). Boston: Allyn and Bacon.

Duncan, H. D. (1989). *Communication and social order*. New Brunswick, NJ: Transaction. (Original work published 1968)

Enoch, J. (2004). Becoming symbol-wise: Kenneth Burke's pedagogy of critical reflection. *College Composition and Communication, 56*(2), 272–296.

Fink, D. L. (2005). *A self-directed guide to designing courses for student learning.* Unpublished manuscript. [Based on his book, *Creating significant learning experiences: An integrated approach to designing college courses.* San Francisco: Jossey-Bass, 2003.]

Foss, S. K., Foss, K. A., & Trapp, R. (2002). *Contemporary perspectives on rhetoric* (3rd ed.). Prospect Heights, IL: Waveland.

Friesen, N. (2001). What are instructional objects? *Interactive Learning Environments, 9,* 219–230.

Gillen, J. (2000). Versions of Vygotsky. *British Journal of Educational Studies, 48*(2), 183–198.

Green, S. K., & Gredler, M. E. (2002). A review and analysis of constructivism for school-based practice. *School Psychology Review, 31,* 53–70.

Harlan, T. (2003). Vygotsky's zone of proximal development and problem-based learning: Linking a theoretical concept with practice through action research. *Teaching in Higher Education, 8*(2), 263–272.

Henson, K. T. (2003). Foundation for learner-centered education: A knowledge base. *Education, 124*(1), 5–16.

Huba, M. E., & Freed, J. E. (2000). *Learner-centered assessment on college campuses.* Boston: Allyn & Bacon.

Jarvis, P. (2002). Practice-based and problem-based learning. In P. Jarvis (Ed.), *The theory and practice of teaching* (pp. 123–131). London: Kogan Page.

Jarvis, P., Holford, J., & Griffin, C. (2000). *The theory and practice of learning.* London: Kogan Page.

Jay, P. (Ed.) (1988). *The selected correspondence of Kenneth Burke and Malcolm Cowley: 1915–1981.* New York: Viking Penguin.

Jonassen, D. H., & Hernandez-Serrano, J. (2002). Case-based reasoning and instructional design: Using stories to support problem solving. *Educational Technology Research and Development, 50,* 65–77.

John-Steiner, V., & Mahn, H. (1996). Sociocultural approaches to learning and development: A Vygotskian framework. *Educational Psychologist, 31,* 191–206.

Karpov, Y. V., & Bransford, J. D. (1995). L. S. Vygotsky and the doctrine of empirical and theoretical learning. *Educational Psychologist, 30*(2), 61–66.

Karpov, Y. V., & Haywood, H. C. (1998). Two ways to elaborate Vygotsky's concept of mediation: Implications for instruction. *American Psychologist, 53*(1), 27–36.

Leamnson, R. (1999). *Thinking about teaching & learning: Developing habits of learning with first year college and university students.* Sterling, VA: Stylus.

Maki, P. L. (2004). *Assessing for learning: Building a sustainable commitment across the institution.* Sterling, VA: Stylus.

McKeachie, W. J. (2002). *McKeachie's teaching tips: Strategies, research, and theory for college and university teachers* (11th ed.). Boston: Houghton Mifflin.

Molenda, M. (2003). In search of the elusive ADDIE model. *Performance Improvement, 42*(5), 34–35.

Molenda, M. (2004). ADDIE model. In A. Kovalchick & K. Dawson (Eds.), *Educational technology: An encyclopedia* (pp. 7–10). Santa Barbara, CA: ABC-CLIO.

Peterson, C. (2003). Bringing ADDIE to life: Instructional design at its best. *Journal of Educational Multimedia and Hypermedia, 12*(3), 227–241

Reiser, R. A. (2001). A history of instructional design and technology: Part II: A history of instructional design. *Educational Technology Research and Development, 49*(2), 57–67.

Scholes, R. (2003). Learning and teaching. *ADE Bulletin, 134–135,* 11–16.

Shaughnessy, M. P. (1979). *Errors & expectations: A Guide for the teacher of basic writing.* New York: Oxford.

Slavin, R. E. (2003). *Educational psychology: Theory and practice* (7th ed.). Boston: Allyn and Bacon, pp. 43–48; 257–269; 275–286.

Vygotsky, L. S. (1978). *Mind in society: The development of higher psychological processes.* Cambridge, MA: Harvard University Press.

Vygotsky, L. (1986). *Thought and language.* Cambridge, MA: MIT Press.

Walvoord, B. E. (2004). *Assessment clear and simple: A practical guide for institutions, departments, and general education.* San Francisco: Jossey-Bass.

Weigle, S. C. (2002). *Assessing writing.* Cambridge, MA: University Press.

Welty, G. (2007). The "design" phase of the ADDIE model. *Journal of GXP Compliance,* 11(4), 40–52.

Wertsch, J. V. (1988). L. S. Vygotsky's "new" theory of mind. *The American Scholar, 57*(1), 81–89.

5 Extending Kenneth Burke and Multicultural Education: Being Actively Revised by the Other

Mark E. Huglen and Rachel McCoppin

This essay contributes to the conversation and critique of liberal and multicultural education, arguing that the educational curriculum ought to place more emphasis upon being actively revised by the other, in other words actively seeking self revision. This position stems from and extends Kenneth Burke's articulation of four rungs of learning in "Linguistic Approach to Problems of Education," briefly: rung #1 is the narrow partisan position that seeks to defeat an opponent; rung #2 is another narrow partisan position that seeks to gain knowledge of other positions to equip better to defeat those other positions; rung #3 is the position that seeks to appreciate other positions; and rung #4 is the position that is willing to be revised by other positions.

When Burke's narrow partisan position leans more toward the animal world, imageries of survival emerge—imageries of the hunt for food and the cult of the kill. Just beyond the animal world, conditions of war compel soldiers and nations to enact survivalist positions: seeking to gain knowledge of the other and design strategies to defeat the other. Beyond war the civil world is characterized by the nature and competitions of games—ranging from professional sports competitions to community sport and recreation activities. The position that seeks to appreciate others, or tolerate others, is where most of the conversation and critique of liberal and multicultural education is today. However, stopping here is not good enough: Liberal and multicultural education must rise to another level, placing more emphasis upon being actively revised by the other.

LIBERAL EDUCATION

In *Philosophy and Social Hope*, Richard Rorty (1999) talks a lot about two dominant tensions at work in education today: truth versus freedom and socialization versus individuation (p. 114–126). Rorty contends traditional liberal education is usually concerned with the Truth that stands behind reality—the *essential* reality, which the political right is commonly associated with today. Rorty and others contend traditional liberal education stems from the essentialisms of Plato's *Republic* through Mathew Arnold's *Culture and Anarchy* to Alan Bloom's *The Closing of the American Mind*. The truth standing behind reality is assumed to represent the picture perfect reality.

An assumption for traditional humanism is that reason is a truth-tracking faculty. Starting with self-evident truths, the assumption is that rational moves similar to the $2 + 2 = 4$ equation will eventually follow the path to the universal Truth that stands behind reality. Therefore the further assumption is that once enough individuals and groups arrive at the truth, there will be at some future time one universal unity. However, the world is much more complex and messier than this utopian picture suggests, leaving too many individuals and groups out of the equation—what counts as unity? Who defines unity and therefore holds the power? Such questions call traditional humanism into question.

The questions about unity and its relation to essence and even divine presence can be understood as the outgrowths of the theological model for university curriculums. Peter Barry (1995) points out the Church of England once controlled the university, and "the teachers were ordained ministers, who had to be unmarried . . . the subjects were the classics (ancient Greek and Latin literature), divinity . . . and mathematics. . . . As far as higher education was concerned . . . right up to the 1820s, the organization of higher education had not changed since the Middle Ages" (p. 12). The questions being asked by the colleges and universities of the time were matching their missions, but the colleges and universities themselves were woefully restrictive in regard to race, class, and gender.

Rorty's answer to the search for the Truth that stands behind reality is to focus, instead, upon freedom and democracy. For Rorty and his mentor, John Dewey, the truth does not stand behind reality but emerges in human encounters, which means the uses of reason and rationalism have different meanings on the two sides of the opposition: On the side where the truth stands behind reality, which is usually associated with the political right, the search is like a participation in divine essence. On the side where the truth emerges in human encounters, which is usually associated with the left, the quest is a critique of the crusty and often oppressive set of social and political arrangements constructed throughout the years.

Another tension in *Philosophy and Social Hope* is between socialization and individuation. Rorty associates socialization with the political right and individuation with the left. When the political right sees itself succeeding, students are produced and reproduced in the wrappings of the ideological apparatuses of the society in which they live, including educational training, religious training, and economics-based training. However, when the political arrangements in society only serve particular individuals, or when the constructed conventions rid particular individuals and groups out of the picture, or when productions and reproductions fail to match changing circumstances: the political left sees itself succeeding by critiquing, enacting, and leading change. The critique helps to create fairer conventions and match forever-changing circumstances with new sets of arrangements.

David Burchell (2004) points out liberal education in the university curriculum can be traced to the Arnolds. In 1828 Thomas Arnold, father of Matthew Arnold, became the headmaster of Rugby School and cultivated a liberal humanist education system:

> [Arnold] saw his job as headmaster of a major public school as being to inculcate values of dutiful public service into his clientele, seen as potential custodians of the public weal, in expectation of the day (not too far off) when the people would break loose their historical shackles and claim the mantle of political authority for themselves. (Burchell, 2004, p. 252)

Arnold saw Britain moving toward full universal citizenship in the 1800s. He needed a system to educate the middle classes and others not only for traditional liberal education outcomes for the body, mind, and soul, but also for their occupations and civic responsibility. Arnold was among the first to see that the middle classes would eventually transform higher education (Burchell, 2004, p. 252).

The Reform Bill of 1832 enfranchised higher education for the middle classes, and this opened the way for the enfranchisement of higher education for all adults (Burchell, 2004, p. 252). In his *Culture and Anarchy*, Arnold called for a classical humanist education along with a pragmatic education (Burchell, 2004, p. 256). Students learned not only technical skills for their jobs but also moral and political knowledge for their lives. Arnold wanted the English public school to be a model of a self-governing society: He wanted to teach his students how to govern themselves (Burchell, 2004, p. 253).

Generally, liberal education consisted of a belief that the classics were timeless and somehow transcend the limitations of the age (Barry, 1995, p. 18). Liberal education maintained that "human nature is essentially unchanging. The same passions, emotions, and even situations are seen again and again throughout human history" (Barry, 1995, p. 18). According to Rorty, the political right sees success in the appropriate suppression of passions and emotions. On the other hand, the radical left sees such suppression as an alienation of the true self. For the right, the classics help students track fundamental truths to enhance life and disseminate human values. For the left in the tradition of John Dewey, Michel Foucault, Karl Marx, and Friedrich Nietzsche, the truth is not a fundamental essence but a discourse of power and therefore inculcating students with the classics is a disservice to the whole of humanity.

Arnold's liberal education produced variant models until the 1960s and 1970s. Old-fashioned liberal education essentially claimed that students simply needed to be introduced to a specified classical curriculum to reach a unified sense of self and community. However, the inadequacies of this model began to rear their ugly heads during the consciousness-raising era of the civil rights movement, women's movement, and Vietnam war because particular individuals and groups were not part of the prevailing unity picture; nor did many of those individuals and groups want to be remade and repackaged into the dressings of the imageries of those holding the power.

Ana M. Martinez Aleman and Katya Salkever (2003) comment that up until the 1970s most liberal arts colleges held a commitment to Christian morals, and the student body came from similar backgrounds (p. 565). Yet, "Despite the confidence in liberal education's ability to foster a democratic and pluralistic common culture on campus, the significant change in the student body since the 1970s proved alarming. With the inclusion of traditionally underrepresented groups and radicalized epistemologies in the academic disciplines, colleges struggled to retain the spirit of community borne of unified knowledge" (p. 566). Dissent on college and university campuses in regard to the unity picture ensued and continues to the present day, and it is this dissent in the form of critical thinking that feeds the focus on difference and diversity in multicultural education.

Multicultural Education

When Martinez Aleman and Salkever argue "multicultural forces present contradictions to liberal education's absolute, unified and objective knowledge traditions" (p. 566), we agree: Unified and objective knowledge traditions contradict multicultural forces. The alternative is to promote difference and diversity, and this is where most of the conversation about multicultural education is today. However, we also feel Rorty and Mark Lawrence McPhail (1996) have put their fingers on another problem by pointing out that the enterprise of multicultural education is now placing too much emphasis on difference.

Part of the conversation needs to move from the critique of liberal education to an extension of multicultural education. We agree with George D. Kuh and Paul D. Umbach's (2005) insight that "some of the educationally powerful features of liberal arts colleges could be constraints in a world that is becoming increasingly diverse in virtually every way" (p. 14). We also agree with Martinez Aleman and Salkever that the "nature of the challenge brought by multiculturalism to liberal education rests on the defense of liberal education as perennially applicable to the human condition . . . that it engenders a community of spirit via the democratic resolution of tension between individual rights and social responsibilities" (p. 567). However, we also feel the continuous circulations and recirculations of the unity/difference or unity/diversity oppositions create other challenges and incapacities for extending multicultural education.

In *Zen in the Art of Rhetoric: An Inquiry into Coherence*, McPhail (1996) calls the misplaced arguments in multicultural education "a rhetoric of negative difference." A rhetoric of negative difference is not so much being negative, but arguing for the essential Truth through the negation of oppositional forms. For example, if multicultural education were to say "unity," a rhetoric of negative difference would argue diversity; if multicultural education were to say "similarity," a rhetoric of negative difference would argue difference. A rhetoric of negative difference stems from a non-conscious or conscious assumption that reality is usually two-sided: either/or logic; bivalence; and the law of the excluded middle are ways McPhail describes this phrase.

McPhail promotes rhetoric as a martial art and explains the intricacies of argument should be learned to know how not to argue: he promotes an actively non-argumentative approach to knowing and being. His approach to multiculturalism recognizes but does not emphasize difference: it searches for similarity in a larger whole, much like Burke's concept of identification/division: division/identification. McPhail promotes the philosophy of coherence for his martial arts approach, which means the search for similarity never fully-realizes itself—*as essential Being*—but holds for a period of time.

Rorty's concern is the focus on difference can move too far, so far that community-building cannot occur. The fear is when similarities rise to essence and essential being, the problems of unity and uniformity emerge from the resonances of traditional liberal education. He explains the radical left is so fearful of the flow toward unity and nationalism that it ceases to participate in the political system, but when any group ceases to participate it becomes irrelevant in regard to effecting change. Rorty is an anti-essentialist, but he feels a healthy sense of community-building and nationalism would be good for the country and academic enterprise.

McPhail's philosophy of coherence and conceptualization of dialogical coherence provide a language for Rorty's position—mutual respect for fellow human beings in the conversation. The philosophy of coherence allows the Being to emerge, but it does not complete itself in any essential or foundational way. Dialogue calls for mutual respect among human beings, and coherence provides the philosophy to feel secure in constructing the healthy sense of community-building and nationalism Rorty desires. However, Rorty, McPhail, and the multicultural conversation can move even farther.

Extending Burke and Multicultural Education: Being Actively Revised by the Other

On Burke's educational ladder, rung #1 is the narrow partisan position that seeks to defeat an opponent; rung #2 is an equally partisan position and seeks to gain knowledge of other positions to equip better to defeat those other positions. Rung #3 is the position that seeks to appreciate other positions and can be thought of as a transition position: back down to #1 and #2 or up to #4. Here is what Burke says about #4:

> A fourth rung would be involved in a much more complicated set of maneuvers. Here, the kind of material assembled in investigations on the third rung would be treated as voices in a dialogue. One would try to decide how many positions one thinks are important enough to be represented by "voices," and then one would do all in one's power to let each voice state its position as ably as possible. No voice deemed relevant to the particular issue or controversy would be subjected to the quietus, and none would be inadequately represented (as were one to portray it by stating only its more vulnerable arguments). But although one would be as fair as possible in thus helping all positions to say their say, a mere cult of "fair play" would not be the reason. Rather, one hopes for ways whereby the various voices, in mutually correcting one another, will lead toward a position better than any one singly. That is, one does not merely want to outwit the opponent, or to study him, one wants to be affected by him, in some degree to incorporate him, to so act that his ways can help perfect one's own—in brief, to learn from him. (Burke, 1955, pp. 283–284)

In Burke's scenario voices are sought out and brought to the conversation: each voice needs to ably state its position. Listeners in Burke's scenario rise in importance. Burke states, "one does not merely want to outwit the opponent, or to study him, one wants to be affected by him, in some degree to incorporate him, to so act that his ways can help perfect one's own—in brief, to learn from him" (1955, p. 284). We interpret this to mean this position is willing to be revised by other positions and extend Burke even further: To incorporate an attitude of actively seeking self revision—being actively revised by the other.

There are not many clear-case examples of actively seeking self revision. In politics, the democrats and republicans maintain their divisions through argumentation and debate, which mostly function in Burke's second rung. To enact our position, each party would need to dissolve their division, cross over to the other side, and learn from the other. Partisan politics as known today in the United States would experience revolutionary change. In religion, parishioners enter churches, mosques, synagogues, and the like for the purpose of seeking forgiveness and revision in their lives, but the more powerful enactment of our position would be if the entity itself with its priests, cannons, and bureaucracies sought revision from its own parishioners, as well as from other churches, mosques, and synagogues. Such "turns" would be bold, radical moves that would improve human relationships throughout the world.

We also see potential examples of our position of actively seeking self revision peaking through in the area of service learning in academe and, of course, the overall importance of service learning is well documented in academe. Service learning projects often allow students the opportunity to interact with an "other," enabling understanding and acceptance of diverse groups of people: "Service-learning produces a number of positive effects on college students . . . includ[ing] a . . . reduction of stereotypes and better cultural understanding; and development of interpersonal skills, citizenship, [and] social responsibility" (Worrell-Carlisle, 2005, p. 198).

Michael D. McNally uses a service learning project to teach the value of American Indian traditions to students who have little or no background with this culture. He discusses his reason for conducting this project: "human encounters work against the grain of deeply rooted stereotypes concerning Indigenous peoples, and [are] more transforming because students emerge with a sense of both the beauty of Indigenous traditions and of what's at stake with Indigenous cultural survival" (McNally, 2004, pp. 603–4). McNally also relates that "Unlearning racism can seldom if ever happen through book learning and essay writing alone. Service projects of any sort consistently engineer jarring experiences that stir up the tidiness of categories carried deep within students' minds" (p. 606). All told his students were transformed by their interactions with the other.

Elaine Norris writes about a service learning project where her class interviewed elderly residents of a nursing home about issues relating to feminism. She states that "our service-learning experience transformed our relationships with people, the most fundamental feminist goal. We engaged in learning with our senior partners as interwoven subjects of knowledge.... Taking on perspectives of age and of each senior partner specifically prevented us from turning our service and learning into a self-serving patronizing experience that is ageist and inconsistent with feminist principles" (Norris, 2006, p. 79). Again, the students finished the project feeling as if their views on ageism and feminism had been changed because of their experiences with the other.

Undoubtedly service learning is an important tool for assisting awareness and acceptance of the other, but to truly reach our position of actively seeking self revision, the instructor would not be the one seeking revision for his or her students. For these examples to be true to our vision of actively seeking self revision the students themselves would need to be the ones who initially sought out ways to be revised by the other. Service learning is a step in the right direction and, perhaps, plants a seed in students that can be further realized later.

The study of literature can reveal many instances where one is revised by his or her experience with the other, though, as we have stated earlier, there are few instances where the individual initially seeks his or her own revision. On this note, we have found two more potential examples of being revised by the other, one in J. M. Coetzee's (2000) book, *Disgrace*, and the other in Mark E. Huglen and Basil B. Clark's (2005) book, *Poetic Healing: A Vietnam Veteran's Journey from a Communication Perspective*.

In *Disgrace*, the character David Lurie is seemingly closed to being revised by the other, but eventually changes *because* of a tragic experience. Yet at the close of the novel he is a character who actively seeks his own revision. When David visits his daughter Lucy on her compound deep in the country of South Africa, local intruders rape her and lock him in the bathroom before setting him on fire. From the beginning David did not understand his daughter, but this act of violence made him open up and start to realize the magnitude of his inability to understand her. Lucy states that she will not be forced off of her compound because of this experience. Instead she strives to understand the culture that she is now living in to better understand why this happened to them; she also seeks a different kind of justice than she is used to for this atrocity through the culture in which she is now living.

Margaret Urban Walker writes in her "Moral Repair and its Limits" that after the atrocities that occurred during apartheid Africa, a system was set up in which people voiced their grievances, with no legal action being done, only to have the truth be accepted. This is the system that David was forced to accept because of his daughter's wishes. He wanted justice but had to accept the verbalization of the boy who raped her in front of the local South Africans as enough. Out of this experience with the other, David realized that he had to account for whatever sins he himself had caused, thus by the end of the novel he was a changed man. He chose to stay living there and continue to be revised by that culture instead of going back to his home.

Although Coetzee's David is not a perfect example for our position of actively seeking self revision (because David was initially reluctant to be changed by the other), he does actively seek his own betterment through the other by the end of the novel. It is important to note that the character Lucy does actively seek her own revision by the culture of South Africa throughout the entire book. By the end of the novel, Lucy marries into the culture, which finally materializes and symbolizes her ongoing willingness to seek change.

By enacting the position "being actively revised by the other," we mean actively cultivating something for growth, understanding, and responsible action. Another potential example comes from the book *Poetic Healing: A Vietnam Veteran's Journey from a Communication Perspective*. In this example, the "other" is not a person but nature. A Vietnam veteran—Basil Clark and coauthor of the book—had nearly lost most everything, including his sanity, before sitting down in his garden. He began to look at the plants and started to think about the cycles of life and death in the form of seeds germinating, sprouting, and growing into healthy plants before decaying and dieing. By turning from an internal focus upon his own struggles to an external focus upon the plants, he was able to discover parallels to his own life. He discovered that he needed to start anew, "plant" new seeds in his own life for growth and development.

The weaker part of this example is that the veteran came close to utter destruction before opening up to what the lessons of nature in a garden could teach him, but the stronger part of this example is that the veteran opened himself to something external—an "other" in the form of nature—and learned from that external to heal himself. A garden needs good soil, seeds, water, and sunlight for nourishment, as well as other positive conditions to grow into maturity: The veteran began to realize that he too needed good materials for his body, mind, and soul to heal. Our position of actively seeking self revision peaks through in the veteran's poem "Something in a Garden" in *Poetic Healing*:

> Something in a garden
> Shows that miracles occur,
> Giving daily lessons on
> How to persevere,

> On death, on rebirth, and on not enough care.
> Droughts make roots go deeper.
> Dry too long can kill,
> Water transforms into growth,
> Too much destroys still.
> Yes, miracles are still around,
> In the garden they are caught,
> With balance and cycles
> Ever being taught.

Similarly, human beings need to enter conversations to receive knowledge, wisdom, and understanding not only to act responsibly in the world but also to improve the world. It is this non-confrontational, non-argumentative, yet non-passive and active position we are offering: Actively seeking self revision—being actively revised by an "other."

Conclusion

Being actively revised by the other is a position that moves beyond traditional humanism; beyond multiculturalism; beyond Rorty's call for healthy nationalism; beyond McPhail's call for actively non-argumentative rhetoric and philosophy of coherence; and beyond Burke's fourth rung. By enacting the position "being actively revised by the other," traditional humanists would incorporate multiculturalisms' focus on diversity and difference rather than unity and unification, and multiculturalism would incorporate traditional humanisms' focus on unity.

By enacting the position "being actively revised by the other," multiculturalism would also incorporate Rorty's concern that too much focus on difference incapacitates productive action, and the radical wing of multiculturalism would heed Rorty's call for more community-building and a healthy nationalism. Of course, Rorty would continue to heed the radicals' warnings that too much nationalism can lead to fascism. By incorporating the thesis of this essay, the entire gamut of positions discussed will nudge their way to being actively revised by the other.

Several scholars have already started.[1] Mark Edmundson (2005), in "Humanities Past, Present, and Future," feels "the future will demand more than understanding . . . The future will also demand that we refashion ourselves in the face of change and that we contribute something, too, to the refashioning of a decent society" (p. 46). This sense of refashioning ourselves and being refashioned by others fits with our position of being actively revised by the other.

Paulo Freire's (1970/2000) *Pedagogy of the Oppressed* can also fit with being actively revised by the other.[2] Freire wants to replace "banking" education with "problem-posing" education, where the teacher as the expert expounding "truth" can be replaced by a style of open, authentic dialogue in the classroom. A problem-posing style encourages students to listen to disparate voices to find their own beliefs and helps teachers find and accept diverse points of view. Freire recognizes educational systems need to be greatly modified to accept that "men and women . . . [are] in the process of *becoming*—as unfinished, uncompleted beings in and with an uncompleted reality" (Freire, 1970/2000, p. 84). Students and teachers' beliefs may be changed because of the influence of the other.

Being actively revised by the other cannot be an exclusive position, but must be a part of other positions. As the dogs were wiped out by the intruders in *Disgrace*, or as plants can be wiped out by outside forces in a garden, people's voices can be wiped out during conversations by domineering methods. However, the awareness of our position and the gradual institutionalization of this position as a part of college and university liberal and multicultural education curriculums will set a course for making the world a better place.

Notes

1. Another possible solution to achieving active revision might be the application of more service learning experiences in liberal arts programs. Edward Zlotkowski (2001) states that most people assume that service learning opportunities fit best with humanities departments, yet his studies show that "humanistic disciplines like philosophy, history, and literary studies have contributed relatively little to the movement's growth and increasing sophistication" (p. 89). Zlotkowski argues that more service learning experiences will aid liberal education to "diverge widely from more genteel notions of knowledge for its own sake, [since] such notions . . . diverge from the moral and civic goals that characterize the mission statements of most American liberal arts colleges" (p. 90). Service learning enables students to directly interact with the members of diverse communities in ways that solely academic assignments can not.

2. Barbara Urciuoli's (1999) declares that multiculturalists tend to operate in humanities departments or specific cultural programs. She has noticed a trend where administration promoted "the value of student diversity with the process of learning, the education of citizens and the development of leaders. *We, our*, and *us* were used several times, invoking a general sense of 'College Community' (a frequent phrase), but it was unclear whether the students who were diverse were part of *us* or a resource *for us* as part of the educational process" (p. 290). Urciuoli states her belief that multiculturalism has become yet another commodifiable skill to promote a liberal education.

References

Barry, P. (1995). *Beginning theory.* Manchester, UK: Manchester University Press.

Burke, K. (1955). Linguistic approach to problems of education. In N. B. Henry (Ed.), *Modern philosophies and education, The fifty-fourth yearbook of the National Society for the Study of Education, Part 1 of 2* (pp. 259–303). Chicago: National Society for the Study of Education.

Burchell, D. (2004). Will the real humanism please stand up? *Continuum: Journal of Media & Cultural Studies, 18*(2), 247–259.

Coetzee, J. M. (2000). *Disgrace.* New York: Penguin.

Edmundson, M. (2005). Humanities past, present—and future. *New Literary History, 36,* 43–6.

Freire, P. (2000). *Pedagogy of the Oppressed.* (M. B. Ramos, Trans.). New York: Continuum International Publishing. (Original work published 1970)

Huglen, M. E., & Clark, B. B. (2005) *Poetic healing: A Vietnam veteran's journey from a communication perspective, revised and expanded edition.* West Layfayette, IN: Parlor Press.

Kuh, G. D., & Umbach, P. D. (2005). Experiencing Diversity. *Liberal Education,* 14–20.

Martinez Aleman, A. M., & Salkever, K. (2003). Mission, multiculturalism, and the liberal arts college: A qualitative investigation. *The Journal of Higher Education, 74* (5), 563–596.

McNally, M. D. (2004). Indigenous pedagogy in the classroom: A service learning model for discussion. *The American Indian Quarterly, 28*(3), 604–617.

McPhail, M. L. (1996). *Zen in the art of rhetoric: An inquiry into coherence.* Albany, NY: State University of New York Press.

Norris, E. (2006). Age matters in a feminist classroom." *NWSA Journal, 18*(1), 61–84.

Rorty, R. (1999). *Philosophy and social hope.* New York: Penguin Books.

Urciuoli, B. (1999). Producing multiculturalism in higher education: Who's producing what for whom?" *International Journal for Qualitative Studies in Education, 12*(3), 287–298.

Walker, M. U. (2001). Moral repair and its limits." In *Mapping the Ethical Turn* (pp. 110–129). Ed. T. F. Davis & K. Womack. Charlottesville, NC: University of Virginia Press.

Worrell-Carlisle, P. J. (2005). Service-Learning: A tool for developing cultural awareness. *Nurse Educator, 30*(5), 197–202.

Zlotkowski, E. (2001). Humanistic learning and service-learning at the liberal arts college. *New Directions for Higher Education, 114,* 89–96.

6 Preaching What We Practice: Course Design Based on the Psychology of Form

Richard H. Thames

Forty years ago students called for college to be relevant. Studies should be pertinent to problems of the modern world. What could Plato say about Pleiku? What did Aristotle have to do with Agnew except that both were Greek? Today students call for college to be "revelant." Obviously they have changed the word's spelling. They *seem* to have changed its sense too. Once they complained of studies unrelated to political events; now they complain of studies unrelated to careers. Except for rock songs from the sixties, history's relevance is reserved for resumes. Protagoras never programmed a computer. Gorgias never earned an MBA. My point is not that students then and students now are different, rather that they are much the same. In fact, no matter what the time or place (1928 in England, 1954 in France) students voice the same complaints about their classes. Most demand requirements be restricted to what they believe relevant to their own here-and-now, not some other there-and-then. For most, what is relevant speaks only to immediate concerns. Courses must address the moment and no more.

Modern students might be surprised to learn the Ancient Greek philosopher, Isocrates, had much to say relevant to their complaint, though they no doubt would be surprised by his answer. Isocrates advanced a citizen-orator model for rhetoric (and communication) in particular and education in general, addressing the question of speaking not only well but wisely. Our obligation is to reject student demands for what they consider relevant and persuade them instead of what Isocrates considered relevant to both his day and ours as well as distance tomorrows. Our office is to *educate* them, a duty we too often fail because, in the words of Kenneth Burke, we increasingly view education inappropriately as a (social) science built on the psychology of information as opposed to an art built on the psychology of form. We "scientistically" seek to inform (and often fail at even that), not to persuade, transforming students into leaky containers for data and habits of parochial import only rather than knowledgeable and thoughtful citizens familiar with the larger universe of human discourse.

In this chapter I will proceed by examining how we coach young "orators" in public speaking, then how the scientific assumptions behind such coaching affect how we too often school them as careerists rather than "citizens." I will focus on the fact that few of us practice what we preach, though contrary to what is usually bemoaned in this regard, I will argue that our practice often proves better than our preaching. In route I will look more carefully at Burke's distinction between a scientific psychology of information and an artistic psychology of form, arguing that attention to a psychology of form is critical not just for teaching public speaking well but for teaching well at all. I will conclude with a story concerning what Isocrates called a "rounded education" (*enkyklios paideia*, the phrase from which we get "encyclopedia"), in the acquiring of which teaching based on an artistic psychology of form is essential. Such an education does not acquiesce to student demands for relevance but communicates instead a vision that inspires them to look beyond their immediate distress over politics or jobs or whatever to the blessings of true learning—indeed a lifetime of learning and entrance into what Burke called "the unending conversation."

THE ORATOR: WHAT WE PREACH

Let us start with true confessions. I have never taken public speaking. I have taken homiletics—the art of preaching. In high school and college I avoided public speaking. People considered me a good speaker already, so the course held no challenge. Then in seminary, much to my surprise, I got interested in rhetoric thanks to my homiletics professor, David Buttrick, perhaps the foremost figure in his field at the time. My grades and his recommendation got me a graduate assistantship. Naively assuming I would be assisting someone, I discovered instead that all by myself I was teaching public speaking—a course I had never taken. Luckily my neighbor was teaching it in high school and her sister in college. They volunteered their help, but I am sad to say they did not help that much. I had been preaching for three years under the tutelage of Buttrick. I quickly came to the conclusion that what was taught in public speaking classes had little to do with what I knew from practice worked. I came to the conclusion that public speaking classes prepare students to succeed in one arena and one arena only—public speaking classes.

Exemplars for Pedagogical Analysis

Public speaking courses teach students to write informative speeches that in fact fail to inform. Obviously, informative speeches are meant to inform. But what does it means to inform? What do we really ask audiences to remember when we inform them of something?

Exhibit one: "how-to" speeches like the following from a best-selling textbook, *The Art of Public Speaking* by Stephen Lucas. The purpose of this exemplary speech is "to inform the audience of basic steps in making a stained glass window." What do we really learn from the speech? The audience "feels" informed, but does anyone really learn how to make a stained glass window? Does anyone ever learn how to do anything from how-to speeches? None of us would expect a student to learn "how to write a speech" from a 10-minute talk, but here we have the far more complicated and technically involved process of "how to make a stained-glass window" explained in that amount of time. So the question is, "To what purpose?" The answer, "None, other than the vague purpose of feeling informed." If someone wants to learn how to, he gets a book; he takes a class; he goes to a demonstration. Why listen to a speech that tells him "design the window, cut and paint the glass, assemble the pieces." Does he really learn much more than this? If he does not, then what has he learned?

Exhibit two, again from Lucas: a speech on immigration. To "avoid confusion" the student is advised to turn three of his main points into supporting points instead under a new main heading more clearly related to other headings. Rather than explaining "people immigrate for economic opportunity, political freedom, and religious freedom," the student is advised to say "there are several reasons why people immigrate." But what is more important, remembering what the reasons are or remembering only that there are several? The student is effectively asked to redirect the purpose of his speech. Rather than telling the audience precisely what he wants remembered, he is advised to settle for vaguely informing them.

After such "exemplary" speeches, I ask students what they think. "Very informative," they say. "We learned a lot." But when I ask "what?" they hide. No one is willing to take a test. And no amount of class discussion puts the speech—like Humpty-Dumpty—back together again. An audience may "feel" informed; but if being informed does not mean remembering anything in particular, then what does it mean? Public speaking courses routinely encourage students to inform people but not about anything in particular.

(Pseudo-) Deductive Pattern Recognition and Development

Public speaking courses teach students methods of organization better suited to laboratories than auditoriums. Instructors insist on the deductive pattern of "general then particular," a pattern better suited to describing the systems and increasingly detailed sub-systems students find dissecting cadavers than informing or persuading living audiences.

Exhibit two once more. The student is advised to reorganize his four points under two main headings with supporting points. The first ("over the years, millions have immigrated to America") does not fit with the other three ("the reasons people immigrate"). He should expand the first by adding supporting points—actually more numbers—and consolidate the others under a general heading with three supporting points. My advice would be different: Handle the first point in the introduction—it is not as important as the other three and is assumed in them anyway; then make the others the main points of the speech—they state what should be remembered. But speech professors love conventional outlines with points and sub-points whose hierarchic relationships can be clearly seen—on paper (i.e., the typed outlines students hand to professors prior to speaking). No matter that audiences are unlikely to hear or remember the hierarchy of points and sub-points so carefully arranged. In fact speech professors insist that entire speeches exemplify the general-particular pattern even when the pattern makes no sense.

Requiring all speeches to conform to the general-particular pattern results in points that are really general titles of outline items recast as sentences with supporting sub-points that are themselves but sub-titles recast and presented in no specific order with a final few particulars of support. "Many Reasons for Immigrating to America" becomes "There are many reasons..." followed by "Economic, Political, and Religious" which become "Some immigrated for economic opportunity," etc. If an audience were taking notes, its members would be left with lists (reasons, causes, results, exceptions, steps and stages with no sense of process or development), as they too often are in classes—isolated bits of data to be memorized, penultimately remembered on multiple choice tests, and ultimately forgotten, as if anything specific were ever really known. The general-particular requirement results in ideas reduced to grocery lists to be memorized rather than understood and then forgotten when we leave the store.

The general-particular template requires all speeches to state a central thesis when obviously not all speeches have one. What for instance is the thesis of a problem-cause-solution speech? In public speaking nothing more than a summary of points to follow. "There are four basic steps in making stained glass windows." "The Great Wall of China was built in three stages." "The Eiffel Tower is divided into three parts." "There are four steps involved in getting tattooed." Such sentences are vague summaries, not thesis statements. The thesis statement of my dissertation was, "Underlying the system of Kenneth Burke is an ahistorical, mystical ontology that leads to the depreciation of historical, political acts." Now that is a sentence that says something, something that can be unpacked for 200 plus pages. Why have thesis statements that are no more than summaries? To have a "general" statement at the beginning of the speech, so that the deductive pattern of general-particular can be maintained—even if it is a sham. English teachers flunk students whose outlines contained main points that do no more than summarize sub-points to follow. Speech teachers give grades of "A" because speeches are to be organized in very specific ways—ways that conform to the deductive (or more accurately, pseudo-deductive) prejudices of speech professors.

Inductive Pattern Recognition and Development

The inductive pattern typical of narrative is more dramatic and persuasive than the pseudo-deductive pattern that speech teachers prefer. Through narrative, audiences come to share in an experience created by the speech, an experience out of which insights inductively emerge with dramatic and persuasive impact.

In our immigration speech, from the three reasons why people immigrate, the student could infer something about the American character. What is inferred may vary with the relative importance of each reason; different arrangements imply different degrees of importance and therefore different insights. Whatever order, the insight persuasively emerges out of the experience of the speech. This insight—or thesis—is that toward which the speech moves dramatically. But speech teachers want everything up front: "State the thesis first"—and spoil the drama, spoil the audience's experience of the speech and the persuasive illusion of arriving at the insight with the speaker. There is dramatically no good reason for putting the thesis up front.

Persuasively doing so proves stupid particularly if the conclusion to which you wish to bring your audience is one about which they initially may be hostile. An audience is not totally rational, concurring on a thesis stated up front because it is convinced by the evidence and argument that follow. Sometimes an audience must be seduced. Sometimes the whole point is to start where your audience is and move it somewhere else.

Many Bible stories deal with redefinition: the anointing of David, Jesus's parables, the road to Emmaus. In the third story the disciples are hurrying out of Jerusalem early Easter morn in deep despair. Jesus's crucifixion has dealt a mortal blow to their political hopes for the Messiah. They meet a stranger who persuades them by interpreting scripture that their hopes were misplaced, not tragically dashed by Jesus's death. His suffering and death are central to what it means to be the Messiah who is not a powerful political figure but a suffering servant. When they realize what the Messiah is to be, they realize the stranger they have talked with is the risen Christ.

A speech or sermon about the road to Emmaus could not be given by the standards of public speaking. How can one talk about redefinition without first establishing the definition the audience must see as problematic and therefore seek to change? The story, the speech, the sermon is about the experience of change, the process of redefinition. To be persuaded the audience must be carried through the experience. The audience cannot start with the insight that the process generates; it must arrive there.

If the point of the speech is to convert, to change the audience's mind, to bring it to a new insight or perspective, the inductive approach typical of narrative is more persuasive and dramatically satisfying than the pseudo-deductive approach preferred by speech teachers. Speeches, in short, must be built on a psychology of form exemplified in the sermon rather than the psychology of information exemplified in the speech on immigration.[1]

Orality as Key

The best model for persuasive and informative speech as well is not the scientistic approach of speech teachers but the narrative approach of preachers—indeed of oral cultures. A narrative model built on the psychology of form for both persuasive and informative speeches is superior to the scientistic model built on the psychology of information that speech teachers prefer.

People do not spontaneously generate conventional outlines. They are arguably more an artifact of writing than of speech. People do spontaneously generate stories. Students should be taught not to outline speeches but to plot them instead. Each step in the plot should advance the story or argument. Each step should actually tell us something—not that "people immigrate for several reasons," rather specifically what the reasons are. Drama (as Burke tells us) provides the best model for our purposes—especially French drama. In French (unlike English) drama, the entrance or exit of a character(s) represents the introduction or the advancement of a motive. Scenes in drama would correspond to ideas in speeches. Each idea calls for a structural element in the speech corresponding to a scene—a paragraph, if you will, that aims at articulating or arguing each point.

The structure of messages is of enormous importance in oral cultures because structures package messages in a way that helps recall. Such structures provide vessels for memory. Using this approach a student could tell the story of immigration in America, moving through the reasons over the centuries and finally inferring something about the American character. A student could generate a story about the effects of alcoholism, following a student through the day as his life is adversely affected physically, academically, and socially, moving to a crisis point where he could evaluate his drinking problem but instead decides he needs a drink. What students can do is astonishing when they are challenged. Students produce dramatic, persuasive speeches when given a narrative model to which they are spontaneously drawn anyway.

I believe the immigration speech the student first suggested was superior to the speech Lucas recommended, potentially conforming more to a narrative model as opposed to the scientistic model most speech texts prefer (though on his own the student would probably have produced a list of reasons with no specific order or sense of development, conforming more to the psychology of information model learned from other classes rather than the psychology of form model advocated by Burke)

At the risk of telling "how to" and being hoisted on my own petard, let me sketch a plotted speech on "The Road to Emmaeus" which meets the requirements of dramatic form as defined by Burke—the creation and satisfaction of an appetite; in this case a definition problematized and therefore requiring redefinition:

1. Introduction—description of a Te Deum window picturing Christ enthroned in glory.

2. The disciples see Jesus as their Messiah, their King, the embodiment of all their political hopes for God's people. (Palm Sunday and the early part of Holy Week.) Logic: association with intro.

3. Jesus's crucifixion destroys their hopes. (Good Friday with a ellipsis cutting from Jesus being beaten to his being nailed to the cross.) Logic: dialectic, temporal.

4. Jesus's death leaves the disciples in despair (Holy Saturday and Early Easter on the road to Emmaus.) Logic: causal, temporal.

5. We have known the same despair as the disciples; in our own lives we have traveled the same road to Emmaus. Logic: association.

6. Something happens to the disciples that transforms their despair into joy that braves all hardships. (Post Easter—the acts of the apostles.) Logic: dialectic, temporal (flash-forward).

7. What happened on the road to Emmaus? The disciples meet a stranger who through the interpreting of scripture and the breaking of bread at an evening's meal is revealed to them as Jesus. (The story

of the road to Emmaus—with the underlying structure of a worship service, specifically the Mass.) Logic: temporal (flash-back).

8. Jesus tells them that the Messiah, the Christ, must suffer our pride and hatred to persuade us of God's unending love and forgiveness. Logic: causal.

9. Because, rather than in spite of his suffering, Jesus is the Messiah, the Christ, God's anointed King. (The ascent up Golgotha not as funereal but celebratory—picking up the ellipsis from earlier; the vision of Jesus's being lifted on the cross as his enthronement. A point made more in the Gospel of John than Luke from which the Emmaus story is taken.) Logic: redefinition.

10. Conclusion—Will the congregation continue on a life-long, meaningless road of despair or take back to the world the joyous message that God suffers our pride and hatred to persuade us of his love?

Rhetoric as Key

In speech classes we seldom ask the difficult question "What is a speech for?" Often the answer is only for the exercise of organizing and orally delivering a speech, not for asking an audience to remember something, not for asking it to think or act in a particular way. Public speaking classes prepare us to succeed in the arena of public speaking classes only. What is taught has little to do with what I know from practice works. How many instructors known as good teachers or lecturers follow the pseudo-deductive model? (No speaker with whom I ever shared the dais for convention panels did.) My bet is that, like me, they spontaneously generate narratives or dramatic structures. Of course good lecturers are strangely enough not always appreciated in our discipline or even the academy. The suspicion is they use rhetoric. That is, of course, exactly what they do. That is why they are successful.

The Citizen: What We (Should and Sometimes Do) Practice

If we really practiced what we preach, we would confront failure. But we do not really practice what we preach, because in one sense we have little or no practice beyond speech classes. There is no real-world test, no consequence for failure, nothing at risk. We frequently deal with captive audiences in required classes. Ministers, on the other hand, do have a practice upon which their livelihoods depend. If they are not persuading audiences, they have no audiences and therefore no jobs—to say nothing of the larger goals of saving souls.

But in another sense we do have a practice—organizing and teaching our courses. What we often do makes far more sense than what we say to our students. In our best practices, we organize and teach material quite differently from our own recommendations or those of public speaking textbook authors. Still there are considerable problems. Our challenge is to persuade students to adopt a more charitable attitude toward education, to recognize it as an holistic endeavor offering both immediate and long-term benefits that equip them not just for living but for living well.

Equipment for Living: Socialization vs. True Education

When we acquiesce to student demands for a relevant education—an instant gratification education—too often the outcome is a lesser education that, in both its narrow utilitarian form of training for careers and its broader form of addressing pressing social concerns, is really *socialization*. Such an education's usefulness and significance lies in teaching each generation what must be learned for a particular society to perpetuate itself. High school lessons in civics or history are no doubt suffered through by future lawyers and landscapers alike. Even those supposedly useless lessons are taught for the very useful purpose of inculcating proper attitudes in future citizens. Assuming intellectual demands on a dentist are greater than those on a mechanic, the former attends a university, the latter a technical school. Both in a sense seek vocational degrees. Pre-med students complain as loudly as plumbing apprentices of irrelevant assignments. Dante helps no more to diagnose disease than Petrarch to thread pipe. Students' collar colors may differ, but their utilitarian attitudes do not. There are many kinds of learning associated with the multitude of roles to be played in the myriad institutions that make up a society. A major function of educational institutions is teaching what must be learned to play the roles of social workers, brokers, merchants, judges, nurses, engineers, janitors, and educators. But what is learned has more to do with socialization than true education.

Socialization's utility is restricted to developing automatic responses for recurring social situations in a certain here-and-now. But automatic response is of value only if situations remain unchanged—which of course they never do. Training prepares us for careers. Later interests and opportunities however may lead us not where we suppose but elsewhere. I majored originally in physics and chemistry, finally in psychology, and in route international studies, English, and philosophy. But I received so fundamentally rounded an education that I was able to go from college to seminary (for theology, Biblical studies, and homiletics) and finally graduate school in rhetoric, after which I returned to my beginning by way of an interest in geology and the rhetoric of science. I have hated economics, loved economics, hated it again, and loved it once more. Students think of training only for the job they want which often they do not get, never thinking of their second or third one or even new careers. Our lives are full of changes for which mere training will not suffice.

Socialization supposes no change. Socialization prepares students to function only in today's world, not tomorrow's perhaps vastly different one. Futurologists may frighten adults, but their futures are really no surprise, only the present extended. Students who have been merely socialized are unprepared not for gradual but for sudden or unanticipated change or change so radical as a shift in the commonplace structure of reality like that from the medieval to the modern or the modern to a postmodern worldview. There is no solace in noting such shifts occur infrequently for we may be in the midst of one now. Communication changes, reorganizing knowledge as it advances from hearing and speaking to reading and writing to broadcasting and receiving and now to the internet. A change in consciousness is wrought by a television broadcast from the moon on Christmas Eve or a photograph of Earth against the backdrop of infinite space. The search for a new cultural cornerstone commences as the foundations built on faith in science erode. Whenever or wherever such change occurs, some portion of a culture should be equipped to understand. But socialization equips citizens only to maintain what *is*, not anticipate or cope with what *will be*.

True education, on the other hand, does prepare students to handle change by teaching them *critical thought*. Socialization teaches *habits*, because recurring situations require no thought. The more unique the situation, the more thought is required. True education introduces students to critical thought by teaching them the current here-and-now is but one of many that human beings have chosen, thereby challenging their assumptions about what is or what should be. To be truly educated students should take history, anthropology, sociology, and psychology not to become psychologists, sociologists, anthropologists, or historians but to learn more of what it means to be human and how many different ways human beings have chosen to exercise their humanity. They should read all those things they think irrelevant because they have little to do with the times: Dante and Petrarch ideally in Italian, Homer and Herodotus in classical Greek. They should learn dead languages they will never speak and modern ones they may seldom use, because another language is another world.

True education is really travel to distant times as well as places. True education transports students beyond the town square where conversation covers parochial concerns. Students find they have left the local park bench behind and stepped instead into the universe of human discourse. Stimulated by that conversation, they learn how to question, and they learn how to think.

True education, however, can threaten socialization. Socialization begets security and the comfort of an open hearth. True education may breed alienation and the madness of an open heath. Knowing the modern world is but one of many, the truly educated could question its choice. If too many were to question it too closely, this world (any world) could crumble. The corner market could not stand if men fought round the cracker barrel. True education may provide insurance against sudden or radical change but not without some risk of chaos.

The risk is minimal, however, for true education is seldom sought by more than a few. A bother for some, an adventure for others, true education like travel may not be for everyone—seeing the sights, yes; encountering the culture, not so fast. Intelligence obviously would be required (and might be found in many), the right temperament even more so (and found perhaps in but a few). True education can be as disturbing as culture shock in modern Calcutta or cause the same distress as the Montezumas in Mexico. Finding it chilling rather than bracing, would the multitude ever seek true education? Would its learning ever go from Abelard to Zeno, or would true education give way instead to greater degrees of training and/or socialization to protect sanity and society?

The Psychology of Information vs. the Psychology of Form

Many courses today, especially survey or intro courses in communication, follow a social-science model, that is, they are built on a scientistic psychology of information. They lack drama and often prove boring for students who have no intrinsic interest in the material and especially boring for teachers who do have an intrinsic interest but find themselves presenting the same material year after year. As Burke predicts, material organized in such a fashion cannot bear the burden of repetition. Most mysteries, for instance, appeal to a psychology of information, sustaining interest by means of surprise and suspense; once we know "who done it," we are done, there being nothing left to surprise, nothing new to be known. Given the appeal of information as such, once we have what we desire, we return only to remember what we have forgotten. Our interest is sustained only by new information. So the teacher is constantly compelled to "update" the course, which is fine if it involves a real science and/or really contains new information; more often it contains only new vocabulary—new words for old information.

More humanistically/philosophically oriented courses are typically built on an artistic psychology of form." They are historically or narratively based and evince evolution or formal development. Material organized in such a fashion bears the burden of repetition and proves far more interesting initially because the course has a dramatic arch—that is, the intrinsic appeal of the information is enhanced by the extrinsic appeal of form. Both students who take the course but once and teachers who teach it many times encounter the material, not as "one damn thing after another," this and that piece of information to be compiled into a list and memorized for multiple choice exams, but as moments to be experienced and contemplated in the context of a larger story, often an historical development. Such courses are best taught by faculty committed to presenting the material with a simplicity which (to paraphrase T. S. Eliot) costs not less that everything, the supposedly superficial instead suggesting depths of organically, rationally consistent explanation. Such courses are not so much updated as improved by the unfolding of further implications or the discovering of greater consistencies. Such courses live; such courses grow. They do more than simply convey information; they engage the whole person. Such courses are memorable. Such courses persuade.

Humanistic Course Design

In the first part of this essay, I outlined a plotted speech (a sermon) to illustrate my argument concerning public speaking, so let me now outline an unconventional course in "Persuasion" to illustrate my argument concerning course design. The course was taught by Trevor Melia at the University of Pittsburgh for 25 years and proved wildly popular with average enrollments of five hundred before being required by his department and limited to a hundred. From its inception the course was unique—there was no textbook. Ultimately Melia published one as unique and popular as the course—*Lucifer State: A Novel Approach to Rhetoric*, used in conjunction with various novels as well as films and documentaries exemplifying arguments.[2]

Characterizing the course in the book's introduction Melia wrote, if the student is to grasp the full scope of the discipline, the teacher must convey the idea of rhetoric as a worldview with an ancient and honorable tradition. To do so he must not only uncover rhetoric's roots but also, like Burke in his *Rhetoric*, rediscover rhetorical elements obscured when rhetoric as a term fell into disuse and other specialized disciplines came to the fore. From its beginning rhetoric has been deeply concerned with the world of human affairs, today presumed to be the domain of social science. As a humanistic enterprise, however, rhetoric rejects methods of analysis befitting social science in favor of linguistic methods traditionally associated with literature—witness the novel.

After *Lucifer State* was published, Melia reorganized the course. He had always depicted the first rhetoricians of ancient Greece as sceptical of knowing the truth and therefore disposed to viewing communication as a process not of finding and teaching the truth but of persuading people to accept opinions or beliefs; accordingly, he had argued that a course in persuasion would concern itself with basic questions such as *how are we persuaded to adopt certain beliefs, how are we persuaded to maintain them*, and *how are we persuaded to change them*. He now argued answers would vary with perspectives—that is, points of view associated with a set of assumptions, or stances situated in particular times and places (the stance of perspectivism as opposed to the vertigo of relativism in which the humanities were increasingly involved). He reorganized the course around four basic points of view—psychological, physiological, sociological, and rational—each featuring a different aspect of human being, perhaps to the detriment of others. The variant I teach at Duquesne (a Catholic university) introduces a fifth, the religious, and with it perhaps a shift from Melia's purposefully pluralistic tone to a more integrative one.

The variant I teach is organized as a semester long drama divided into five acts (given five perspectives) and two breaks (for exams)—the psychological and physiological (the semester's first 40%), the sociological (the second 40%), and the rational and religious (the remaining 20%), with each perspective exemplifying rational consistency and ultimately touching on religious questions as each perspective is worked out thoroughly (also the case in Burke's own analyses). A prologue and epilogue address the nature of rhetoric and belief. Each class or lecture is organized as a complete scene in the larger drama.

The course is organized within an Augustinian framework which is ultimately agnostic rather than advocative (i.e., the course is in rhetoric not theology) but treats religious appeals—as Burke himself does—as rhetorically significant (and appropriate to the study of such phenomena as Islamic jihadism). Psychological, sociological, and rational appeals (with reductionistic physiological appeals presented as a contrast but also a caution concerning the always embodied nature of all communication) can evolve into quasi- or pseudo-religious appeals (consistent with the pseudo-communions or false mysticisms Burke criticizes in his *Rhetoric*).[3] The course leads up to and away from the third act in which advertising's materialistic appeal is critiqued as pseudo-religious—that is, the illusion is created of inductively arriving at a principle that henceforth can be deductively unfolded. Students are directed to reflect back upon the appeals of mass movements and cults as potentially pseudo-religious too (following Eric Hoffer's *True Believer* and Arthur Koestler's famous essay on communism as "The God that Failed"). Thereafter as the course unfolds the student is urged to reflect on the potentially quasi- and pseudo-religious appeals in propaganda, hierarchical persuasion, and expertise; discussions of cognitive dissonance and hypnosis within the rational perspective lead to religious quandary. Finally Martin Luther King's rhetoric is interpreted religiously (as a call to redemptive suffering) rather than politically (as inspiring a mass movement) as the course returns to where it began—a study of rhetoric and belief.

Though not religiously advocative, the course is still designed to be persuasive concerning its treatment of rhetoric and belief and is therefore built on a psychology of form rather than information. In teaching as but the scientific presentation of data, persuasion is eschewed except for occasional condescension to rhetorical "enhancements" such as Power Point. In teaching as persuasion, Burke's advice applies—the rhetorical power of presentation is amplified by dramatic form.

True education is facilitated by harnessing form to our teaching. Dramatic form will enhance the teaching of any material—one of my favorite college classes was biology because the teacher was superb; one of my favorite textbooks was statistics because it conveyed the formal beauty of mathematics. Dramatic form will enhance the teaching of any material at any level taught to any purpose—socialization as well as true education. The employment of form, however, is not only more appropriate for but necessary to a truly rounded education such as Isocrates envisioned, such as Burke through his own efforts achieved.

Given the organization of modern curricula, students too often experience college as one class after another, a cafeteria line from which they pick a little sociology, a bit more psych, and so on. There is little sense of intellectual development within majors and less within the university at large. If dramatic form enables students to experience, contemplate, and remember course material not as one thing after another but as moments within the context of a larger story, then making them aware of the larger story of learning will revive love for their own learning as they experience it within that context and thereby give it greater relevance. And so, I offer the following to close.

Equipment for Living Well: The Unending Conversation

The origins of true education can be traced to ancient Greece and the teachings of the Sophists. Like the truly educated of today, the Sophists were travelers. Their journeys through the ancient Mediterranean initially may have shocked them but ultimately must have made them more aware of cultures as constructions. Phoenicians and Greeks, Persians and Egyptians built their worlds on differing foundations. Each was as sure as the others that its walls were one with the fundamental structures of the universe, when all the stones were really set on shifting sand. The Sophists came to believe that the human world is constructed in accordance with human needs or concerns peculiar to a particular time and place; that it is subject to change when those needs or concerns are frustrated or when new ones arise. Each world is the result of choices that have consequences for which we bear responsibility. Each world is the product of coercion or ideally of persuasion—that is, agreement or consensus arrived at by means of democratic debate and decision, compromise based on common concerns.

Some Sophists ignored the risks inherent in their teaching. Gleefully turning critical thought to intellectual arrogance, they urged a careless rejection of merely human institutions, refusing to acknowledge the alternative as anarchy. Others recognized the risks. Gravely shouldering responsibility for what they taught, they developed a careful respect for such unstable but still admirable constructions, insisting on the ethical character of all human endeavor. Among the latter was Isocrates who first articulated the citizen-orator model informing the education of leaders in the classical world. The Greek tradition of a "rounded education" (*enkyklios paideia*, from which we get *encyclopedia*) became the Roman tradition of education in the "humanities" (*studia humanitatis*)—exactly what Burke had in mind when he conceived of an approach to education featuring linguistic action between students and teachers about the feats and foibles of human relations with other humans, texts, art, science, religion, nature, and so on.[4]

What began with Isocrates and continued with Cicero was revived in the Renaissance and eventually adopted as the heart of education. Today universities may consist of several professional schools but at their core is always a series of requirements taught in a College of Liberal Arts and Sciences insisting that a true education cannot confine itself to utilitarian talk of a here-and-now that could soon become another there-and-then, but must engage itself in a conversation that has lasted more than two thousand years. From that conversation emerges not just a greater appreciation for the life we have been given but a greater awareness of our particular time and circumstance, a greater willingness to respond when time and circumstance demand, and a greater capacity to act with wisdom culled from the ages when the call comes. From that unending conversation comes a rounded education that is always and everywhere relevant.

Notes

* This chapter was originally two-and-a-half essays (half of the third having been misplaced). The author would like to thank the editor not just for the suggestion that they be combined but also for actually producing a draft that persuaded him to do so. The author considers this arrangement well within the Burkeian tradition in that one of Burke's most important essays ("Mysticism as a Solution to the Poet's Dilemma") was reconstructed from notes by Stanley Romaine Hopper after Burke lost the original.

1. Only later in the semester of my public speaking class are students introduced to *inductive* and *deductive* reasoning, then *dialectic* (e.g., thesis, antithesis, synthesis) as the basis for dramatic development (contradiction or conflict calling for resolution). An actual story may be the origin of the speech (e.g., the "Road to Emmaus") or the story may be constructed for a speech whose points have already been determined (e.g., the effects of alcoholism). Students are first introduced to *problem-cause-solution* speeches; starting with such speeches, they are told speeches can also be organized using any one (or combination) of the following: *cause*, then *time* and *space*, then *degree* (often conceived of temporally as the first/last item or spacially as the top/bottom item on a list), then *category* (the above list being categories of logical connection) and after that *association* (by which the above list of categories is organized given any list is difficult to remember unless some organization or development exists among the categorized items, organization and memory being closely associated canons of rhetoric).

2. Trevor Melia, Nova Ryder, Jean Jones. *Lucifer State: A Novel Approach to Rhetoric*, 3rd ed. Pearson Custom Publishing. Melia originally published the book in 1981 and a second edition (containing exegetical essays) in 1983 with Kendall/Hunt Publishing. After his retirement demand for the book diminished and it eventually went out of print. Jean Jones (Edinboro University of Pennsylvania) edited the third edition in 2005 with new supplementary materials. While the book was with Kendall/Hunt, an edition of my lecture notes was published in 1999 as a companion to the novel—*Persuasion's Domain: An Introduction to Rhetoric and Human Affairs*. The lecture notes, now extensively revised, are still published by the Department of Communication and Rhetorical Studies at Duquesne University and can be obtained for a small reproduction fee from the department.

3. See in this regard, the introduction to the Meridan Books 1962 combined edition of the *Grammar* and *Rhetoric:* "May other analysts join me in the task of tracking down the ways in which the realm of sheerly worldly powers becomes endowed with the attributes of 'secular divinity'" (523).

4. The *Motivorum* trilogy (later a tetralogy) was to cover the classical *trivium* of logic (the *Grammar*), rhetoric (the *Rhetoric*), and literature (the *Symbolic*), to which was added an ethics (tentatively *On Human Relations*). The three books were to be Burke's equivalent to Aristotle's *Logic, Poetics,* and *Rhetoric.*

7 Motives and Metaphors of Education

James F. Klumpp and Erica J. Lamm

Education is arguably the most complex of human institutions. Although it is probable that other animal species pass useful behaviors from one generation to the next in patterns of habit and imitation, no species but humans perform the complexity of choice, value, and commitment to intergenerational education. As Kenneth Burke might have said, education is, if nothing else, *talk about*, and only humans talk about their *talk about* that is education. Hugh Dalziel Duncan (1968), a sociologist and disciple of Burke, designated education, one of eleven institutions of society (pp. 16–17). Duncan carefully described how human action within the context of these institutions acquired character in the communication with which each institution conducted its activities and through which participants gave meaning to the activities. Duncan pointed us toward Burke's work to understand human action in these institutions, and in this essay we accept his challenge to apply Burke's ideas on metaphor.

To Burke and Duncan, what humans do with words is no less than organize the institutions that mark their lives and weave the institutions thus created into the fabric of living. We can read that performance, that is, we can analyze the structure to understand the choices, values, and commitments culturally inscribed. That is the task of this essay: reading education through metaphors with which its performance is shaped. The metaphors lay open some of the moments of contingency when education becomes this rather than that. The payoff of such a reading should be a greater understanding of the variety of education and of the consequences of the choices we make that choose from that variety.

THE RHETORICAL POWER OF METAPHOR

Metaphor was a central concept for Kenneth Burke, the first figure he treated in his seminal essay "Four Master Tropes" (Burke, 1945/1969, pp. 503–505).

In that essay Burke tied metaphor to the taking of perspective (cf. Burke, 1935/1984b, pp. 89–96). Taking a perspective on our world, Burke argued, involves an organizing of perceptions, and perceptions are organized through the power of the language we use to engage that world.

Metaphor is not only central for Burke, it is one of the most common concepts in our language. Insert the word in Academic Search Premier data base and one gets 6349 hits; insert it in the Google search engine and one gets 22.4 million "hits." Burke's initial definition recalled the most common understanding of the term: "seeing something *in terms of* something else" (Burke, 1945/1969, p. 503). Metaphor in this common sense is a figure of speech, noted by Aristotle in his *Rhetorica* as a device that when appropriately chosen adds clarity and distinction (1405a).[1] I. A. Richards provided the analytic engine to understand this sense of metaphor: metaphors manifest a tenor—a quality or meaning—and a vehicle—the transfer of meaning from the familiar to the novel (1965, pp. 94–101). Grammatical theory often differentiates pure metaphors from similes. The latter overtly carry the tenor—the coming of spring was like an anticipated birth—the former do so by force of their logic—he was a breath of fresh air. Either way, the logic of metaphor is a logic of similarity. A rhetor asserts the similarity of two things to communicate the quality of the novel based on a quality of the familiar.

Even in this simple notion of metaphor, there are two energies in the concept as a linguistic device. The first is the sense in which a metaphor explodes beyond its constrained presentation. The vehicle carries both denotative and connotative meaning. Denotatively those hearing a metaphor ask: "How far does the speaker intend the similarity to extend?" Thus, metaphors move beyond the control of the speaker, unless s/he elaborates the limits of the comparison. Connotatively, meaning spills out of the metaphor far beyond the speaker's knowledge as the experiences of both the reference and the novel come rushing forth.

The second energy is the sense in which a metaphor triggers the imaginative powers of its audience. Metaphors are enthymematic, attaining their power in the participation of the experience of the listener. That the tenor of the metaphor is active is necessary to the metaphor serving properly as a vehicle. Thus, metaphors are fully rhetorical. Success in their persuasive use requires that the speaker analyze his/her audience and anticipate the power of construction triggered by the metaphor.

In the last half of the twentieth century the movement known as the linguistic turn took metaphor far beyond its connection with style to emphasize its resources to shape understanding and action. This movement, which dominated in theory and philosophy during the era, centered on the powers of language to frame and structure human thought and action. In many disciplines the ideas of Richard Rorty, Suzanne Langer, the late Ludwig Wittgenstein, and the deconstructionists reshaped the direction of inquiry. George Lakoff and Mark Johnson's (1980) *Metaphors We Live By* offered the fullest treatment of metaphor in the linguistic turn. Lakoff and Johnson argued that quite literally a person's orientation to life was framed by the metaphors that s/he had available for talking about everyday experience. Among the most intriguing metaphors were those that drew diverse experiences together into a coherency structured by the metaphor. Describing the economic disadvantage of a class of people as a disease invokes a plethora of expectations including the danger posed by the condition to the continued welfare of individuals suffering from the disease, the need for diagnosis of the cause of the ailment, the possibility of treatment with the well mastered application of previous knowledge, and the dire possibilities if the ailment is ignored. Metaphor, Lakoff and Johnson argued, guides our attitudes and our actions in relationship to our everyday experience of simple or complex problems. Kenneth Burke was a cornerstone of the linguistic turn. Burke worked through many of the movement's key ideas decades before the movement attained its full influence. Central to Burke's thought was the idea that human action was unique in the universe because it was shaped in language. His attack on the behaviorists, who viewed human behavior through the screen of the animal nature of the species, was the precursor to the central argument of the linguistic turn: that human action was profoundly shaped by the constitutive power of language acts.

Burke's influence drew upon three accomplishments. The first of these was his filling out the behavioral dimension. As Burke's work matured he developed the link between perception and action The choice of language framed understanding of events in our lives, providing the complex of cues with which we negotiated meaning and then coordinated response. He argued, for example, that decisions do not follow thorough understanding of all aspects of a situation; rather, as we encounter the situation, we begin to work to define it and as that process proceeds the possibilities for response diminish to the point at which defining the situation is the most powerful part of the process of deciding response (Burke, 1935/1984b, pp. 29–36). In this defining of the situation, the resources of language are brought to the service of motivated human behavior. Burke first called these clusters of vocabulary *orientations*, and later *motives* (Burke, 1935/1984b, pp. 19–36). Thus, Burke's notion of motivation, like that of the symbolic interactionists, featured the ways in which the performance of language interpenetrates human action. In the face of events, people discuss the meaning and, as an ambiguous agreement on the meaning emerges, people respond in ways consistent with the meaning.

In the opening pages of *Attitudes Toward History* Burke described the choices of patterns of vocabulary as the primary choices that govern responses to the events encountered in everyday life (1937/1984a, pp. 3–4). These choices form *attitudes*, that is, the posturing of expectations that guide the complex of action. Drawing ways of interpreting from the language of their community, interactants reenter the complex social response, thus leading Burke to refer to the interpretive resources of language as "equipment for living" (Burke, 1941, p. 293). The cues to complex behavior emerge from such communicative encounter with experience.

Burke provided another essential insight into human action in his "Definition of Man." One of the six characteristics that he described as the essence of humankind was "rotten with perfection" (Burke, 1966, pp. 18–19). The notion of perfection is the notion that once action adopts a vocabulary those responding act to round out that vocabulary, marking their expectations in its terms and responding to its development with the vocabulary chosen. Indeed, so strong is the momentum of this dedication to a way of knowing and acting that the society will act to the point at which their actions become dysfunctional and lead to results that the vocabulary did not anticipate. At that stage a crisis is generated that leads to again questioning interpretation and seeking new ways of understanding with different vocabularies.

Thus Burke located the roots of human action in the intricate dance of language in which people work with others to interpret the situations in which they find themselves. Choices in those moments, formulated in the familiar patois of everyday encounters structure the complexes of action that define human activity.

Burke's second great contribution to the linguistic turn was an analytic scheme that allowed interpreters to describe the motivational shape of a text. The five terms of the *pentad*—act, agent, agency, purpose, and scene (1945/1969, p. xv)—point to emphases that project understandings. Built into the use of the pentad are ways of seeing motivation. In accounts of action, certain elements will be emphasized to explain why action is appropriate or necessary. Perhaps events will be seen as driven by the character of the individuals who perform in the situation. Or perhaps those individuals merely respond to the exigencies of the situations in which they find themselves, thus action is shaped by the scene of the action. Sometimes coordinated human action is driven by a union of purpose. The other analytic device provided by the pentad are the *ratios*—the possibility that each term of the pentad shapes the others, agent-act or scene-agent, for example—which may be invoked to describe the influences that give coherence to an account.

Burke's theory, however, was not simply a theory to describe text; it was primarily a theory to understand the influence of linguistic performance on social structure. Thus, Burke elaborated his notion of *identification*, the degree to which the joint participation in human action is coordinated through language. People identify with motives as the conversation about meaning proceeds. In the rich texture of a motive, people recognize the roles authorized or even required of them. They accept these roles and play them out with the performance of their linguistic attachments.

The complexity of social structure is most clear in *hierarchy*. Hierarchy is, to be sure, an ordering of people, elevating some to status over others. But, Burke argued, the key to hierarchy in social structure lies in its roots in language (Klumpp, 1999). Language differentiates and values. The resources of this quality of language are transformed into similar differentiation and valuing in social structure. By understanding the structures of motives, the observer understands the structure and the stability of hierarchy. As people talk, they invoke appropriateness, attitude, and didactic commands in the language of a motive. A motive explains to us why it is right that students should listen to their teachers, for example. The power of appropriateness implies acceptance of one's position in a hierarchy. Thus, a social justification is enacted as a dimension of the communication through which people coordinate action. To Burke, in sum, a motive is not simply a way of seeing or a way of acting, but also a way of projecting judgment on action that reinforces the power of particular ways of acting to dominate a culture.

Burke's final contribution to the linguistic turn was his emphasis on the synthetic quality of motivation. Grounded in the notion of the human pursuit of perfection, Burke's view of the power of symbolic motivation explained how it becomes the force that shapes action. Burke argued that humans see the situations of their lives as reinforcing the appropriateness of familiar ways of seeing. These ways of seeing also entail attitudes toward the elements of the situation. They foretell the actions that are appropriate in response, thus providing momentum to action.

But there is also a language of guidance, a ritual of language, through which a motive's values, attitudes, and actions are shaped. Burke multiplied the concepts that explain this power to constrain action. For example, he recalled Thorstein Veblen's idea of trained incapacity: people will persist in acting in ways they are trained even after those ways no longer produce the results once promised (Burke, 1935/1984b, pp. 7–9). Burke described how each human choice represents a balance between permanence and change: the effort to see or do things in familiar ways, and the need to innovate to meet new situations. Linguistic motives negotiate this dialectic relationship. The energy of seeking to perfect a vocabulary drives action until an alternative is posed. That alternative comes from a process Burke called "perspective by incongruity," that is, a different metaphor restructures perspective, and with it action (Burke, 1935/1984b, pp. 89–92). Thus, novelty emerges from the fertile possibilities of the tracing of a new metaphor.

In the end, the synthetic power that sets Burke's method apart from the radical analytic method of behaviorism was the energy of motive—or metaphor—to organize action. Sociality emerged from the need to find the right perceptual framework to organize human action. The continuity of culture emerged from the ritualistic performance of a motive over time accompanied by the judgments of appropriateness pronounced in the ritual. The giving of reasons—the rationality of action—emerged from the interactional reinforcement of social action performed through language. Thus, these basic orientational forms, metaphor or motive, came to lie at the center of how the linguistic turn understood human action.

Guided by Burke's perspective, we seek to compare and contrast the metaphoric base of different views of the institution of education. We want to explore the map of appropriateness and necessity that shapes and justifies educational practice. We want to trace the different rhetorical powers invoked by those immersed in the institution. We seek to give shape to the forces which drive educational choice and implement choices throughout an educational system.

PLATO AND THE VALUES AT THE CORE OF WESTERN EDUCATION

If Plato is the father of Western philosophy, he is no less the architect of education's elevated place in Western values. Plato's republic was a decidedly undemocratic state, but it was a state that valued education and elevated the educated—the philosopher king the greatest among them—to rule daily life.

Plato constructed this viewpoint on education around the pillars of an extended antithesis now called platonic dualism and an extended metaphor in the allegory of the cave. Within these two pillars, metaphors of human experience declared the hierarchy. To Plato, human drama takes place against an unchanging backdrop. The term that best characterizes that backdrop is "Truth." In Plato, truth is not for the human to make but for him/her to discover. Human action can proceed with or without awareness of the truth. With awareness, it shapes into harmony and happiness; without, it leads to discord and a failed society (Plato, *Republic*, 518). The human searcher must not only find the truth, s/he must also perceive the needs of the state. Governing for Plato is not a matter of simply following patterns of proper behavior; rather there is a mosaic of behavior through which humans are guided by their intelligence and abilities. The state is shaped through human knowledge and action (*Republic*, 519).

The master metaphor for this relationship of action and backdrop is becoming and being. Becoming is an ephemeral world in which material life is lived. Day-to-day life is linked to sensation rather than reason, so is always becoming and perishing. Being endures. Becoming is the realm of human opinion, being the realm of knowledge.

So the question becomes how to relate becoming to being across the dualism of their difference. Plato accomplished this with the metaphor of sight. In the allegory of the cave, the world of everyday human experience is lived in the cave. Humans are tied by their foibles, and from their constrained perspective their eyes witness only shadows of the real. They have no perception of the real because they cannot see it. So, they naively assume that what they see is real. It is those who are privileged to leave the cave whose sight witnesses the real and the true. With that sight comes knowledge of being (Plato, *Republic*, 514–16).

At this point, Plato has established a human hierarchy: those tied into the shadow world of the cave and those privileged to see the real and true. The geology of Plato's cave metaphor depicts this hierarchy as up/down. The privileged go up out of the cave to learn the real and the true. Plato has now introduced the two great hierarchical metaphors of Western thought: up/down and light/dark. The education of the philosopher takes the soul up from the darkness of the cave, toward the light of being. In the light of the upper regions the soul comes to know truth. Thus, education is a revealing attained through the open eyes and clear sight lines of reason, of philosophy. The responsibility of those that do see is to descend again into the world of becoming to bring knowledge to everyday activity (*Republic*, 519).

The allegory has established the dualism of the enlightened and those confined in the cave. Plato's *Republic* established the responsibility of the former to lead the latter. Thus, for Plato the education of the enlightened becomes pragmatic in the return to the cave. The result is an instrumental knowledge that bridges the world of being and becoming. Socrates sat out with Glaucon's help to divide the everyday world into various subject matters. Knowing the truth of those subject matters enables the knower and confers the responsibility to lead.

Much of contemporary education grounds its values in Plato. There is the motivation to seek knowledge that lies beyond everyday experience in the realm of the invariant. Similarly there is the idea that knowledge once obtained confers responsibility to return to day-to-day life. Education acquires a nobility both from its connection with the world of being and from the responsibility to return to the world of becoming to guide those who have not been permitted the gift of sight.

In the *Republic*, Plato endorsed universal education, but the idea seems inimical to his view of the philosopher king. It is in the *Laws*, his last writing, often interpreted as a more realistic version of the *Republic*, where a rationale for universal education emerged. This account began with a description of the education of the tradesman or the ship captain. The metaphor of this education is growth, the life cycle (*Laws*, 765–766). Education is an ongoing development of passion and ardent desire in the human. The preparation for any trade begins in childhood with play at the trade. Plato gave a child's tutor responsibility for instilling not only a mastering of the chosen life-trade, but also a love of the calling (*Laws*, 643).

Alas, Plato offered, this is not true education. Rather he would restrict true education to training in virtue or citizenship. This is education in how to rightly rule and how to obey *(Laws*, 643–644). Thus, Plato prescribed universal education in a smoothly functioning polis, in which all develop appreciation for the virtues that promote good living. In return, Plato argued, the citizens of the state must attend always to the education of youth *(Laws*, 644).

In these two works at the dawn of Western culture, Plato's richly metaphorical portrayal provided many of the key orientations of Western education. He described an education elevated from the practical day-to-day crafts of the economy. Education addresses the soul, elevates the educated above the uneducated, and bestows a responsibility to return the special endowments of education to the governance of the state. Education enlightens life. Education is a striving for the better. The path of education is marked by the life cycle, beginning in youth and proceeding to full responsibility. Reason is privileged over sentiment. We will see other metaphors challenge the characteristic objective of education, but the values Plato placed on education will endure.

Locke and Freire: From *Tabula Rasa* to the Banking System

The *tabula rasa* (empty tablet) view of the mind dates from Aristotle (*De Anima*, 429a). John Locke, an empiricist, took this view as the basis for his philosophy of education. Locke "suppose[d] the mind to be, as we say, white paper, void of all characters, without any ideas . . ." (1690/1975, p. 104). Thus, all knowledge comes from experience. These experiences "impress" the mind, which has certain characteristics that enable it to "receive" the information. Therefore, the mind possesses no innate truths but has natural tendencies and the structure and capacity for understanding (Cooney, Cross & Trunk, 1993, p. 49).

Locke's view was the starting point for his entire philosophy of education. Teachers are responsible for writing their knowledge onto the blank slate of their students. This view influenced how he believed people learned new knowledge and what he thought the educational system should look like. Locke's metaphors structure many educational encounters, even today.

The blank slate has spawned related metaphors of expression. The container metaphor—teachers pouring information into the brain of their students—has been prominent in U.S. higher education. The latest variation is the banking metaphor—teachers deposit information into the student's knowledge bank. The metaphors are different, however, in the implications their authors draw from them. For Locke, the student's empty mind was ready for knowledge, and this was, in a way, empowering. It meant that students had the capacity to learn, and this was a positive thing. As the metaphor has evolved, however, the teacher has become an active participant who formulates and organizes the material that is presented to the student with more or less effectiveness. The quality of education rests on the teacher's choices of material and presentational strategy. The student is passive or is capable only of accepting or obstructing the reception of the material.

Focusing on the passive student of later forms, Paulo Freire (2004) called this metaphor oppressive. Freire argued that in the student's passive role "the scope of action allowed to the students extends only so far as receiving, filling, and storing the deposits" (2004, p. 72). The banking metaphor provides no vision of creativity and critical thinking for students. Freire argues that the banking system of education is a mirror of the oppression of society as a whole. "The more students work at storing the deposits entrusted to them, the less they develop the critical consciousness which would result from their intervention in the world as transformers of that world. The more completely they accept the passive role imposed on them, the more they tend simply to adapt to the world as it is and to the fragmented view of reality deposited in them" (Freire, 2004, p. 73).

The container or banking metaphor guides ways of thinking about the content of education as well. Teachers must have a certain volume of knowledge before they can provide an education to the young. The extent of education is judged by the amount of content: more written on the slate, more poured into the container, more deposited in the bank. To be more educated is to know more.

Locke uses another metaphor in his discussion of the mind of a child: water. "I imagine the minds of children, as easily turned, this or that way, as water itself" (1693/1989, pp. 83–84). In this metaphor, the mind of a child can be shaped by gentle pressure from an adult. The passiveness of the child is again emphasized. The metaphor, however, leads to expectations that teaching is easy. Blank slates are easily written upon, water is easily directed, and, of course, containers are easily filled.

Locke took the metaphor a step further and explained that the pressure we use on children at a young age shapes their lives for years to come. "The little, or almost insensible, impressions on our tender infancies, have very important and lasting consequences: and there it is, as in the fountains of some rivers, where a gentle application of the hand turns the flexible waters into channels, that make them take quite contrary courses; and by this little direction, given them at first, in the source, they receive different tendencies, and arrive at last at very remote and different places" (1693/1989, p. 83). Locke's elaboration of the metaphor, in fact, intensified the complexity of responsibility of the teacher. What children learn when they are young shapes them into the kind of adults they become. Parents and educators are the people responsible for this shaping. Students, the channels of the metaphor, lay passively waiting for the immense responsibility to be played out in their maturing.

The education system formed by this quantitative metaphor of teacher as active source and students as passive receivers has been questioned by recent educational research. In fact, evidence is that students actively process the knowledge brought to them. Far from being passive receivers, they augment or diminish the material they receive through the connections that they make of the material to their own experiences. The "banking model" is now a controversial viewpoint (see Siegler, 1989; Siegler & Alibali, 2004), but remains among the most widely used perspectives on the role of teachers and students.

The Student as Consumer and the Business Model of Education

The metaphors of education we have treated to this point structure the action within the institution in a way that privileges the power and status of the teacher. His/her responsibility lies with the traditions that one generation passes to another through knowledge. Students remain the passive receivers, shaped by their education. Today a second powerful metaphor responds to this depiction of education and competes for prominence: the student as consumer.

"The metaphor of student as customer is based on the view that students are customers who must be served and whose needs must be met if the relationship with the educational institution is to be successful and continue" (Hoffman & Kretovics, 1994, pp. 104–105). This metaphor empowers the student as a demander of education and depicts the teacher as a supplier.

Education is a product, purchased by the student or his/her parents with tuition, or by the state through appropriations. Different colleges and universities provide products of differing character and differing quality. The student selects the product s/he wishes to purchase.

An economic structure has grown in the private sector to service the educational consumers. *US News and World Report* is the most noted of several publishing structures that rate colleges and universities and generate manuals and advice materials to guide consumer choice. A quick review of the forms to aid the choice reveals the changes in frame promoted by the consumer metaphor. The range of information that wise consumers gather before choosing a product extends far beyond traditional academic concerns: location of campus, social life, food in the dorms, student attitudes.

Colleges and universities seeking to attract students shape the public images to these needs. For example, the University of Maryland (1996, 2005b) promotes visits to campus for potential students/consumers. The university offers suggestions for an activity visit:

> Wonder what the University of Maryland is really like? Visit! Attend Maryland Upclose, or join a tour group. For full immersion, go for the truly live: by hanging out with a real Maryland student, attending classes, eating in the dining hall and kicking back, as college students are known to do now and then. When you are here, don't forget to: Walk the mall. Buy your first Terp t-shirt at the bookstore. Taste our homemade ice cream at the Dairy. Check out that huge climbing wall at the Campus Recreation Center. (2005b)

To be sure, students are urged to sample classes, but the range of activities that the campus presents to the student-consumer for his/her choice is much wider. The result has been the building of increasing campus "support" bureaucracies and the diverting of student funds into the non-teaching elements of the university. "The student experience" becomes the focus of planning and strategic thinking for those in charge of university budgets.

To many educators, the consumer metaphor damages the learning process through the motives it creates in the classroom. Instead of attending class to learn, students now attend class to "get their money's worth." Natasha Sajé (2005) invoked yet another metaphor spawned by the consumer metaphor when she lamented, "It's like working for a tip, except the payoff isn't cash under the plate; it's having one's contract renewed. Administrators worry that the 'customers' will shop elsewhere if they are not pleased" (p. 50).

The move in higher education to thinking about students as consumers or customers has been accompanied by the move to the management of the university as a business. Nowhere is this move as evident as in the growing popularity of Total Quality Management (TQM) in higher education. The University of Maryland is typical. In 1996 the university created the "Campus Assessment Working Group" (CAWG) "to lead the University in creating a culture of evidence that will make it much easier to make decisions based on data." As a child of the TQM movement, CAWG did not collect just any data, some data is better than other. CAWG declared, "CAWG's primary focus is on students, but the group hopes to build on success in this area to also help understand the needs of other key constituents, such as faculty and staff.... CAWG has committed to creating profiles of student attitudes, perceptions, and concerns that will be available to a wide campus constituency" (1996). CAWG helped the university respond to student needs.

The connection between Deming's quality management theories and education was drawn by Dobyns and Crawford-Mason (1994) in their book, *Thinking about Quality: Progress, Wisdom, and the Deming Philosophy*. In their description of the quality management program at Westinghouse High School in New York, Dobyns and Crawford-Mason focus on education as a business, a factory, or a place of production. Dobyns and Crawford-Mason begin the chapter on education with the maxim: "Inspection doesn't produce quality; testing doesn't produce education" (p. 171). Quality management, however, produces better potential-employees. When community businesses were asked to comment on the preparation of Westinghouse graduates, they told the school to add a public speaking course. The school complied, as an example of the "classic business-supplier relationship, where each helps the other succeed" (p. 180). Students are the products being supplied to businesses, and business naturally want only the highest quality products.

Obviously the consumer/business metaphor dictates particular emphases in education. Many of these emphases raise important issues about the metaphor. For example, who are the true customers of education? While students are key stakeholders in the educational process, the community, future employers, and the parents who are paying the tuition are all potential stakeholders. Dobyns and Crawford-Mason (1994) see multiple stakeholders in their case study: "Westinghouse is run for the customers-students, parents, and staff on the inside; colleges and business on the outside" (p. 180).

This metaphor has been met with mixed reviews in the academy. Some view the application of Deming's total quality methods to higher education as a helpful tool for improving how American higher education functions. Many have turned this metaphor on its head and argued that the damage it does to education is far worse than any potential benefits of applying marketing concepts to learning. Either way, the metaphor motivates students, teachers, administrators, and American society to think about education as a business satisfying the demands of stakeholders, and to design education to meet these demands.

"No Child Left Behind"

"No Child Left Behind" is the title of George W. Bush's educational initiative. The phrase is, of course, itself a metaphor. Evoking images of a forlorn child gazing through tears at a school bus receding into the distance, the metaphor carries powerful political weight. The Bush initiative passed Congress with widespread support from members of both political parties. Governmental programs are important because they are the predominant funding mechanism for America's public schools. A campaign such as "No Child" is of value if it delivers the support for a quality educational system. At the same time, however, legislation affecting the educational system can have a powerful effect on the actions and motivations that drive the school system. It is, therefore, wise to see the metaphors beyond their political force and ask what they imply for education.

If we examine the speeches and other discourse generated from the "No Child" campaign, we will note that the discourse has called regularly upon two related metaphors. Although the discourse seldom provided what we might call a philosophy of education—an examination of the assumptions and principles of educating the young—the dominant metaphor framed education as the teaching of skills. The skills metaphor was, we shall note, tied to the strongest metaphor of the discourse, the educational system as an industrial factory. The featuring of this metaphor placed the emphasis on the management of the educational system.

The skill metaphor was not new with the Bush administration. Indeed, we encountered the metaphor in Plato's description of education for the crafts. But Plato declared this training to be something other than true education. Nevertheless, since the dawn of the industrial era the notion of providing skills for workers through the public educational system has been a hallmark of Western democracies. The creation of the land grant university in the 1860s, the idea of universal education that drove the development of state commitments to public education, and the development of professional schools in the late 1800s, all reflected this notion of education.

The vocabulary of the skills metaphor has been pervasive in the Bush administration's vision of education. The White House's (2004) promotional brochure, *Education: The Promise of America*, fixed the goal of Bush's program as "ensur[ing] that all children are proficient in reading and math." This proficiency was "needed to succeed in college and a globally competitive workforce." A key section of the report was entitled, "Skills for the 21st Century: Better Training for Better Jobs."

The vocabulary was drawn from a metaphor that saw the purposes of education framed within the needs of the national economy and the economic rewards that the economy endows upon the trained. Children succeed in this metaphor when they acquire the skills that provide them gainful employment and provide fully contributing workers to the national economy. The deficiencies of the current educational system are located within such definitions of fulfillment. Reading, as an example, is considered a skill that students must acquire to succeed in life. Failure to read is a "personal tragedy and social injustice" (Bush). Any notion of the enrichment of literature as an end—or as a means—of teaching reading is absent in this discourse. Reading is instrumental to training and thus the central educational skill.

Teaching in this metaphor is itself a skill. The "No Child" act promised to "give teachers the skills and knowledge they need in the classroom." To do so the act would "promote scientifically-based reading instruction programs" (White House, 2004, p. 6). Teachers' skills would be developed through a number of programs and the plan recognized that they required resources to skillfully perform their tasks. "No Child" would "reward effective teachers who are successful in raising student achievement and producing real results for all children" (White House, 2004, p. 7).

As policy, the "No Child Left Behind" Act focused most directly on the management of schools, and the dominant vocabulary from which the metaphor for management drew was the industrial firm. This metaphor shares much with the business metaphor spawned by the student-as-consumer movement, but the emphases of the Bush vocabulary are different. Here the key stakeholder is not the consumer/student but the national economy. The metrics that drive the metaphor focus not upon consumer wants but upon the production of students useful to the national economy. While the President often commented that "Education is a local responsibility" (Bush), he assumed federal control over the efficiency and productivity of the system. "Accountability" was the key word employed repeatedly, drawn from the vocabulary of business. "I am an activist for accountability," Bush declared. The role of the federal government was akin to the accounting department of large corporations, assessing the productivity of the component parts of the system and advising management on weaknesses and changes mandated by the measured assessments of the accountant.

There are several aspects of the metaphor of the industrial firm that we want to examine. The first is the production model for education. Students were described as "educated graduates" "produced" by the educational system (White House, 2004, p. 13). As inputs, some are "ready to learn," and improving them in this regard is "one of the best investments America can make" (White House, 2004, p. 18). Teachers are the workers of the system, some "well-trained" in the "required skills," others needing training in the proper methods of instruction. In the narrative, it is on the abilities of these teachers to mold the students that the success of education depends. The variable quality of the system to produce quality students rests on the skills of those teachers. The best methods that these teachers should adopt are "scientifically-based" and "proven to work" (White House, 2004, p. 6). The value of education rests on the contributions of their products—the students—to meeting the needs of the 21st century economy. Thus, value is externally defined by its place in the context of the economy.

Value is further defined by its ability to be measured and scientifically validated. Industrial factory production operates on the principle of interchangeability: that the components of the production system are defined by precise dimensions to permit substitutability. Thus, the language of measurement becomes a central characteristic of the metaphor. The primary linguistic strategy of the "No Child" legislation is its mandating of a metric for measurement of education. The accountability that Bush declares to be his central concern is achieved through extensive testing and the comparisons that become possible with measurement. This accounting system makes possible judgments like: "Fourth- and eighth-grade students made substantial increases in reading and math in the state of New Mexico" (White House, 2004, p. 9).

Finally, the industrial factory metaphor frames education as a linear process in which advancement over a defined sequence is privileged. Progress is measured not by maturing but by the ebb and flow of test scores. Students "fall behind in reading" when they do not score with other students on reading tests. Schools are judged failures and candidates for reorganization when their students do not achieve the scores of other schools. Students are expected to increase their scores as the years pass in their education. We began this treatment of the metaphors of "No Child Left Behind" by noting the political power of a metaphor that carried the image of a child watching through a veil of tears as a bus recedes into the distance. But ultimately, the metaphor of the child left behind is an ambiguous metaphor, and the measurement of production suggests another meaning for this metaphor: a child left behind by other students who have advanced to a higher test score. If the political power of this metaphor helped to win the bill's passage, the operation of the system it established trades on this other meaning of the metaphor. This is the linearity of the industrial metaphor. The progress of children through the educational system is marked by their improvement on tests. A child left behind fails to score as fellow students have scored. Thus, the phrase ties together the vision of education that drives the initiative.

Criticisms of "No Child Left Behind" have focused on its assumption of the uniformity of student experience. This uniformity is inherent in the language that drives the program. It is this uniformity that allows Bush to champion the program as a method of achieving equality when he touted the program in a speech before the convention of the National Urban League. The principles of accountability and of a system designed to employ sound scientific principles to advance the acquisition of skills assumes a uniformity of interchangeable parts. The more unique individual students become, the more the industrially designed factory system begins to become a complicated challenge to accountability.

The "No Child Left Behind" initiative promised increased resources to education. Its focus upon success and the ideal of each child treated the same provided the impetus for educational reform. As a language of education it drove the management of education more than it drove the philosophy of education. In a speech to the National Urban League, Bush introduced his secretary of education by observing, "when it came to picking the Secretary of Education, I didn't—wasn't interested in picking a theorist or a philosopher, I was interested in picking a doer." The vision of "doing" at the heart of Bush's initiative was one that was controlled by the management style of the modern industrial model. Despite Bush's eschewing a concern with educational philosophy, his vision of the management of education created pressures for an education of a certain type driven by the metaphors of skills and training. Education in this model was also compelled to define steps along its linear path in a metric that would demonstrate to management its achievement. Measuring the quality of education through scientific testing values quantifiable outcomes over learning as exploration or creativity or critical thinking. Thus, education developed in a direction required by the central language of "No Child Left Behind."

Burke suggested that "in a complex world there are many kinds of action. Action requires programs—programs require vocabulary" (1937/1984a, p. 4). The metaphors we choose shape the actions carried out in their names. The vocabulary of "skill," "accountability," "effectiveness," "measuring progress," "achievement gaps among students," "producing educated graduates" texture a system with a particular character. That system carries certain attitudes toward education, students, and teachers. That system describes, and prescribes, privileged action within the schools.

"Student as Nigger": The Burning Prose of Jerry Farber

We have been looking at powerful metaphors, some close to what we call "dead" or unconscious, that mold the great institution that is American education. We turn now to a metaphor used in a different way, as a strong rhetorical device to stir indignation and disrupt the dominant system.

During the height of the social unrest of the 1960s, Jerry Farber (1969), then a faculty member at California State University at Los Angeles, wrote an essay he entitled "Student as Nigger." The essay was first published in the *Los Angeles Free Press*, the largest circulation underground newspaper in Los Angeles at the time. It was soon picked up by the Liberation News Service, disseminated, and published in other underground papers in major American cities. Farber later put the essay and other writings in a small book of the same name published in 1969.

Farber's essay and his chosen metaphor were polemic. The essay was an example of what Burke called *rejection*. Rejection, Burke noted, is a partial frame. It does not provide the rich texture, the roundness, to achieve the power to mold human action that we have seen in other metaphors. Rejection, Burke wrote, "takes its color from an attitude towards some reigning symbol of authority, stressing a *shift in allegiance* to symbols of authority" (1937/1984a, p. 21; emphasis in original). This was the force of Farber's essay, to participate in the movement of the counter-culture to undermine the power of dominant institutions of society, in Farber's case, the dominant university system. Farber's metaphor was not dead, but very much alive and contributed its power to the essay.

Then as now, Farber's title stunned. The title's use of what we today merely refer to as the "N" word to fully emphasize its repugnance was the essence of the essay's strategy. The metaphor was slavery, the title laid bare its intensity. As a rejective frame, slavery provided perspective on the university system through the incongruity that was created by the weaving of the slavery metaphor into a descriptive account of higher education. Farber offered no orienting metaphor to restructure higher education; nothing rounded out a vision of education as it should be. The power of the essay was the power to destroy the hegemony of other metaphors of education.

Farber's strategy interwove two descriptive characterizations: the slave plantation of the nineteenth century and the contemporary university. The valuing in the essay arose in his audience's repugnance toward the former. The condemnation carried from the memory of the former to the reality of the latter. Farber constructed the contemporary world with vague narratives of events. The people in those narratives were unnamed and thus faceless, identified only by their roles: students or professors, girls or teachers. Action was driven by the social expectations of the university. "A student at Cal State is expected to know his place. He calls a faculty member 'Sir' or 'Doctor' or 'Professor'—and he smiles and shuffles some as he stands outside the professor's office waiting for permission to enter." (Farber, 1969, ¶ 3) The automatons of these narratives act out their part with little consciousness or whisper of choice.

The slave plantation was enthymematically evoked from cultural memory rather than explicitly constituted in a narrative. Knowing one's place, smiling and shuffling outside a professor's office recalled the memory of slaves bowing and shuffling in the presence of the white plantation owner. Slaves required permission to enter the big house. Students follow orders or they are punished with low grades. "They're like those old gray-headed house niggers you can still find in the South who don't see what all the fuss is about because Mr. Charlie 'treats us real good.'" Farber (1969) even identified himself as "Simon Legree on the poetry plantation." The vestiges of slavery were also invoked. "Students have separate and unequal dining facilities." Faculty "cling" to their "white supremacy." The treatment of sex in the university featured "castration" and fear of oversexualized students. Farber offered no narratives to fix the system of slavery and discrimination, but they rang with familiarity nonetheless. Sometimes the plantation was invoked with simile and sometimes with allusion, but always to insure that the condemnation was sharp.

In fact, the only resistance to this playing out of the relationships of the plantation came in the admirable quality of the slaves/students to resist in attitude what they played out in behavior. "They've got that slave mentality: obliging and ingratiating on the surface but hostile and resistant underneath." In the face of Farber's Simon Legree, "even the Toms are angry down deep somewhere." "The saddest cases among both black slaves and student slaves are the ones who have so thoroughly interjected their masters' values that their anger is all turned inward." Descriptions followed of students suffering psychological breakdowns from low grades or terror from being questioned in class.

Farber drew the circle of responsibility for this failing beyond the teacher or student, pointing to the educational system in totality. He explicitly argued that the professorate is not to blame. "So students are niggers. It's time to find out why, and to do this we have to take a long look at Mr. Charlie." The Governor and Legislature reduce them to laying "flat on their stomachs with their pants down, mumbling catch phrases like 'professional dignity' and 'meaningful dialogue.'" They are basically spineless or "short on balls" in the face of the system in which they are caught.

Farber's was the voice of resistance. He was offensive, and thus declared his resistance. He declared that slavery was not dead and that the system that had never freed the slaves cannot provide an education of the young in anything but a slave culture. The slave metaphor provided a perspective by incongruity. Burke described a vision of a stage on which action was being played out in two scenes forestage and back. On the backstage dinosaurs fought and killed in an orgy of blood and gore. On the forestage contemporary society played out. As the action proceeded, the two scenes were linked only by the backplay serving as a sort of symbolic commentary on the actions of the foreplay. Ultimately, the division breaks and the dinosaurs and their violence move forward to consume the forestage (Burke, 1935/1984b, pp. li-lii). Farber's technique did the same. The metaphor of slavery colored the actions in the contemporary university and rejected the manner and style of modern education as destructive of human dignity.

It is well to return to the limitations of Farber's perspective captured in Burke's characterization of frames of rejection. Farber provided no vision of education. His was a treatment of social relationships within the institution of education. They were undemocratic, a problem for the New Left with which Farber identified, but beyond that they diminish the humanness of universities. But the work of his metaphor did not reframe education in a better or even a different norm. It was a metaphor that aided his mission by forcing his viewpoint into our consciousness in a way that we did not soon forget.

Teaching as Revolution: A New Metaphor for Education

In the metaphors of education we have examined thus far hierarchies of status or power have formed in the classroom. Either teachers dominated, passing their knowledge to those who lacked knowledge, or students dominated as consumers shaping education with their demands. bell hooks focused upon this ratio of power as the key lesson of education, and urged an alternative metaphor. Hooks identified education as the practice of freedom, and learning as revolution. She looked back on her own education and found that: "My all-black grade schools became the location where I experienced learning as revolution" (hooks, 1994, p. 2). She sought to spread that experience to all of education.

Burke suggested that social hierarchy is based in language (Klumpp, 1999). Hooks echoed Burke and Farber, underscored the social power of language to perpetuate social hierarchy. "I know that it is not the English language that hurts me, but what the oppressors do with it, how they shape it to become a territory that limits and defines, how they make it a weapon that can shame, humiliate, colonize" (hooks, 1994, p. 168). In her metaphor of education as the practice of freedom, hooks reclaimed language to reshape and remake it into a tool for revolution. "Shifting how we think about language and how we use it necessarily alters how we know what we know" (p. 174). By shifting the fundamental structure of education from hierarchy to equality, even revolution, we alter how we behave and how education functions.

Although the commitment to equality alters the philosophy of education, hooks identified an altered educational practice as key. "Education as the practice of freedom is not just about liberatory knowledge, it's about a liberatory practice in the classroom" (hooks, 1994, p. 147). To make her point, she contrasted education as liberation with the banking metaphor. "This [learning from students] is one of the primary differences between education as a practice of freedom and the conservative banking system which encourages professors to believe deep down in the core of their being that they have nothing to learn from their students" (p. 152). Hooks proceeded to describe a classroom in which all are learning through the interaction of those engaged in the educational process. "To begin, the professor must genuinely *value* everyone's presence. There must be an ongoing recognition that everyone influences the classroom dynamic, that everyone contributes" (hooks, 1994, p. 8). When everyone's language is valued, hooks suggested, education can actually *become* liberatory.

This idea of education as freedom is not a metaphor that is common in the classroom; indeed, hooks suggested that most professors are not comfortable in classrooms where hierarchies are leveled and all thoughts valued. "Given that our educational institutions are so deeply invested in a banking system, teachers are more rewarded when we do not teach against the grain. The choice to work against the grain, to challenge the status quo, often has negative consequences. And that is part of what makes that choice one that is not politically neutral" (hooks, 1994, p. 203).

An attitude of equality in the classroom is accompanied in hooks' framework by an ethic of sharing. Teaching is much more than "depositing" information into a student's mind; it requires a belief "that the teacher's work is not merely to share information but to share in the intellectual and spiritual growth of students" (hooks, 1994, p. 13). Hooks believes this growth is essential to quality education: "To teach in a manner that respects and cares for the souls of our students is essential if we are to provide the necessary conditions where learning can deeply and immediately begin" (p. 13). It is this manner of teaching, what hooks terms an "engaged pedagogy," that is called for in her metaphor of teaching as freedom.

It is not, however, only teachers who need to alter their paradigm. hooks acknowledged that one of the problems with instituting this revolutionary metaphor lay in student expectations. Students, through the metaphors they have lived all their lives, have been conditioned to see teachers as leaders and themselves as followers. The key to enacting this new metaphor is, as hooks' friend philosopher Ron Scapp asserted, to reframe the responsibility of learning such that it rests on the students' shoulders: "To acknowledge student responsibility for the learning process is to place it where it's least legitimate in their own eyes. When we try to change the classroom so that there is a sense of mutual responsibility for learning, students get scared that you are now not the captain working with them, but that you are after all just another crew member—and not a reliable one at that" (hooks, 1994, p. 144).

Among the contributions of hooks' metaphor is to emphasize that even the definition of education as the passing of a culture from generation to generation is a construction of the metaphors of education. Hooks proposed not to perpetuate the inequality and oppression of the culture that she inherited. Rather, she saw the power of education to remedy the defects of one generation as another was taught. "Liberation" is a powerful motivational term in the American lexicon. hooks exploited this power. "Revolution" has its own place in the American myth. hooks borrowed the term not simply for its motivational power but also for its power to indicate the drama of the new. Her educational system reoriented, reversed past character, and achieved its purposes through the power of language to alter human behavior.

Conclusion

We have explored a range of metaphors drawn from literature that structures American education. The linguistic acts we have studied are in some cases a philosophical pondering of the nature of education. Plato, Locke, and the proponents of the consumer metaphor come to mind as examples of this linguistic power. Even as their philosophical contemplation described education, the valuing inherent in language use acted out the attitudes and values presented as a prescribed educational system. Other linguistic acts we have studied are more consciously persuasive. George W. Bush and his administration sought political power through their influence on the educational system. This is not to say that they had any less concern for students than Jerry Farber or bell hooks. These three metaphoric campaigns worked by lamenting the shortcomings of the educational system they described. Farber chose a metaphor that stung, that shocked even. His metaphor destroyed the passive day-to-day performance of old metaphors of education. Bush and hooks chose metaphors that served the dual purposes of drawing adherents to their perspective and structuring reforms. They offered a new way of seeing and performing education which they envisioned replacing the metaphors that structure the current system of education.

Burke emphasized the power of metaphors to gather the resources of language into human institutions. His insights were illustrated in these metaphors of education. The metaphors structured social cooperation as they envisioned the relationships within which learning occurs. They set a purpose for education with which teachers and students could join in a dedication to teaching and learning. They provided a range of attitudes toward these modes of education from an accepting of a natural relationship to a stark rejection of a system marked for change. All analyze the day-to-day performance of education in terms that illuminate its qualities and its characteristic behaviors.

What we are left with as our examination concludes is the image of contingency and the responsibility of choice in education. As a human institution, education is shaped through our applying the powers of linguistic performance to the practical need to coordinate human knowledge. An awareness of the possibilities of this linguistic performance empowers us all to consider the responsibilities that go with the immense power of education.

NOTE

1. References to the works of Aristotle and Plato refer to applicable lines of text, not page numbers, as is the common practice when working with such classical texts. In this way, readers may go back to the text in any version and obtain the material used in this chapter.

REFERENCES

Aristotle. (1954). *De Anima*.(J. A. Smith, Trans.). In R. McKeon (Ed.), *The basic works of Aristotle* (pp. 535-605), New York: Modern Library.

Aristotle. (1954). *Rhetorica* (W. Rhys Roberts,Trans.) In R. McKeon (Ed.), *The basic works of Aristotle* (pp. 1325-1453), New York: Modern Library. Burke, K. (1941). *The philosophy of literary form*. Baton Rouge, LA: Louisiana State University Press.

Burke, K. (1966). *Language as symbolic action: Essays on life, literature, and method*. Berkeley, CA: University of California Press.

Burke, K. (1969). *A grammar of motives*. Berkeley, CA: University of California Press. (Original work published 1945)

Burke, K. (1984a). *Attitudes toward history* (3rd ed.). Berkeley, CA: University of California Press. (Original work published 1937)

Burke, K. (1984b). *Permanence and change* (3rd ed.). Berkeley, CA: University of California Press. (Original work published 1935)

Bush, G. W. (2001, August 1). *President discusses education at the National Urban League Conference*. Washington, DC: The White House. Retrieved September 1, 2005, from http://www.whitehouse.gov/news/releases/2001/08/20010801-1.html

Cooney, W., Cross, C., & Trunk, B. (1993). *From Plato to Piaget: The greatest educational theorists from across the centuries and around the world*. Lanham, MD: University Press of America.
Dobyns, L., & Crawford-Mason, C. (1994). *Thinking about quality: Progress, wisdom, and the Deming philosophy*. New York: Times Books.
Duncan, H. D. (1968). *Symbols in society*. London: Oxford University Press.
Farber, J. (1969). *The student as nigger*. Los Angeles: Contact Books. Retrieved September 1, 2005, from http://roark.ry4an.org/readings/short/student/
Freire, P. (2004). *Pedagogy of the oppressed*. (M. B. Ramos Trans.). New York: Continuum.
Hoffman, K. D., & Kretovics, M. A. (1994). Students as partial employees: A metaphor for the student-institution interaction. *Innovative Higher Education, 29*, 103–120.
hooks, b. (1994). *Teaching to transgress: Education as the practice of freedom*. New York: Routledge.
Klumpp, J. F. (1999). Burkeian social hierarchy and the ironic investment of Martin Luther King. In B. L. Brock (Ed.), *Kenneth Burke and the twenty-first century* (pp. 207–241). Albany, NY: State University of New York Press.
Lakoff, G., & Johnson, M. (1980). *Metaphors we live by*. Chicago: University of Chicago Press.
Locke, J. (1975). *An essay concerning human understanding*. (P. H. Nidditch, Ed.). London: Oxford University Press. (Original work published 1690)
Locke, J. (1989). *Some thoughts concerning education*. (J. W. Yolton & J. S. Yolton, Eds.). Oxford: Clarendon Press. (Original work published 1693)
Plato. (1980). *Laws*. (A. E. Taylor, Trans.). In E. Hamilton & H. Cairns (Eds.), The collected dialogues of Plato, including the letters (pp. 1225-1513). Princeton, NJ: Princeton University Press.
Plato. (1980). *The republic*. (P. Shorey, Trans.). In E. Hamilton & H. Cairns (Eds.), The collected dialogues of Plato, including the letters (pp. 575-844). Princeton, NJ: Princeton University Press.
Richards, I. A. (1965). *The philosophy of rhetoric*. New York: Oxford University Press.
Sajé, N. (2005). Teaching for tips. *Liberal Education, 91*, 48–51.
Siegler, R. S. (1989). Mechanisms of cognitive development. *Annual Review of Psychology, 40*, 353–379.
Siegler, R. S., & Alibali, M. W. (2004). *An introduction to children's thinking*. Upper Saddle River, NJ: Prentice Hall.
University of Maryland (1996). *CAWG at work: Creating a culture of evidence*. Retrieved September 1, 2005, from http://www.oirp.umd.edu/CAWG/Articles/cawg.html
University of Maryland (2005). *The choice is yours*. Retrieved September 1, 2005, from http://www.uga.umd.edu/admissions/visit/default.asp
White House, The. (2004, September 26). *Education: The promise of America*. Washington, DC: Author. Retrieved September 1, 2005, from http://www.whitehouse.gov/news/releases/2004/09/20040926.html

8 A Burkeian Approach to Education in a Time of Ecological Crisis

Robert Wess

> *The only cure for digging in the dirt is an idea. The cure for any idea is more ideas. The cure for all ideas is digging in the dirt.*
>
> —Kenneth Burke

Kenneth Burke's (1955) major statement on education, "Linguistic Approach to Problems of Education" (herein referred to as LAPE), is arguably the least studied of his major essays. Attention to it is long overdue. Other statements bearing on education appear in various places in his work; some of these are cited below. But LAPE is the central text for any consideration of the pedagogical implications of Burke's thought.

Studying this essay for this purpose, however, initially poses two main difficulties. The first is that it needs updating. As we will see, there are good Burkeian reasons to think that this 1955 text needs revising to be made relevant to our situation in 2009 (and beyond). Significant help in moving in this direction can be found in LAPE itself, in its "Epilogue" (to which we will turn later), where Burke imagines a possible future that in some respects resembles our situation today. The second difficulty is suggested by the essay's opening sentences, which are pitched at a level more philosophical than pedagogical: "Beginning absolutely, we might define man as the typically language-using, or symbol-using, animal. And on the basis of such a definition, we could argue for a 'linguistic approach to the problems of education'" (Burke, 1955, p. 259). It is true that Burke immediately adds, "Or we could settle for much less, merely pointing to the obviously great importance of the linguistic factor as regards both education in particular and human relations in general" (Burke, 1955, p. 259). This pointing to a mere descriptive truism is ambiguous at best and question-begging at worst. One can agree that language is central but exactly how should language be defined? Burke's own answer to that question in the section that follows, "Language in Educational Theory," quickly leads back to the generalization of the opening sentences. A more appropriate title for this section might be "An Approach to Education Focusing on Language." For in this section there is no survey of educational theories current in the 1950s with special attention to the place of language in each. Instead, there is extended attention to Burke's philosophic definition, especially its two sides: (1) "language-using, or symbol-using," and (2) "animal." Because the focus of LAPE is going to be on the first side, Burke takes time to caution us not to overlook the second. In the process, he uses the term "ecological," so that we will have occasion to return to this passage in exploring a Burkeian approach to education in our time of ecological crisis.

To address this second difficulty, one needs to begin not in the context of debates about pedagogical techniques but in a broader context that helps to illuminate how philosophizing about humankind bears on educational practice. Help in this regard may be found in the history of the humanities that R. S. Crane (1967) offers in *The Idea of the Humanities*.[1] Crane is particularly magisterial in his attention to linkages between philosophical premises and pedagogical practices, linkages suggesting that humanistic education is tied inextricably to generalized conceptions of what human beings are. A few highpoints from his history are sufficient to provide a context in which to see that Burke both continues the tradition Crane traces insofar as his philosophy informs his pedagogy and transforms it insofar as his philosophical premise leads to a radically different vision of the aim of education.

Crane contends that the history of humanistic education is properly traced back beyond the Renaissance to Roman antiquity, when the word "humanity" (*humanitas*) referred, Crane explains, to the arts "by which those who earnestly desire and seek after them are most highly humanized, in the sense of being endowed with the virtues and knowledge that separate man most sharply from the lower animals" (1967, p. 156; see also pp. 23–24). Because of the centrality of rhetoric and oratory in Roman culture, speech was the attribute that was typically pinpointed to distinguish humans from animals. Crane quotes Quintilian identifying speech, even more than reason, as the "gift from heaven . . . [by] which mankind excels all other living things" (1967, p. 25). Turning to the Renaissance, Crane finds continuities with the Roman tradition combined with innovations stemming from the Christian reconception of humanity, whereby humanistic education mutated to focus preeminently on "nourish[ing] our love toward God" (1967, p. 33).

With the rise of modern science, and the attendant quarrel between the ancients and the moderns, a new consensus formed around the idea of a "necessary law of human development": while human nature may be permanent in one sense, this nature equips humans to progress by learning from experience (Crane, 1967, pp. 78–79). New philosophies (Locke's, Berkeley's, Hume's, Kant's) focus on how humans come to know: "[H]uman history becomes a kind of collective enterprise of inquiry in which a single fixed subject matter—the nature of things—is gradually approximated, after inevitably imperfect beginnings, through stages the order of which cannot be reversed" (Crane, 1967, p. 88). This paradigm of progress, however, ultimately worked against the humanities as progress came to be associated mainly with the sciences, such that by the nineteenth century the humanities became something that needed defending. The assumptions about human beings informing these defenses are easy to see (Crane, 1967, p. 144, 147, 150):

1. the "permanent" side of humanity, cultivated preeminently in the humanities, is as important as the "progressive" (Whewell)

2. "[m]en are men before they are lawyers, or physicians, or merchants, or manufacturers . . . What professional men should carry away from a University is not professional knowledge, but that which should direct the use of their professional knowledge, and bring the light of general culture to illuminate the technicalities of a special pursuit" (Mill)

3. humans need "the cultivation of a state of mind in which partial principles of knowledge, taste, and conduct are harmonized and related in a balanced whole" (Arnold)

Such defenses of the humanities continued into the twentieth century in ways familiar to us all. In this process, there is a truncation in the scope of the humanities that often goes unnoticed. For the opposed sides in these polemics—"permanent" humanity and "progressive" science—both derive equally from attributes that distinguish the human from the nonhuman. As far as we know, nonhuman animals produce neither Shakespeares nor Einsteins. But these defenses, by opposing the "Shakespeare" side to the "Einstein" side, end up identifying the humanities with only a part of the human being, even as humanists claim to speak for the "permanent" or "whole" human being. Perhaps it is time to pose the issue of whether these two sides can work together rather than against one another. We will return to issue in concluding.

In emphasizing that language is the attribute that most distinguishes humans from nonhumans, Burke perhaps reminds one of the Romans more than any of his other predecessors in the long tradition of philosophizing about humanistic education. It is true that Burke focuses on written language more than spoken (a la Quintilian), but that difference is secondary to the similarity in their spotlighting of language.[2]

What is perhaps most notable, however, is less Burke's similarity to the Romans or any other predecessor than his difference in one respect from everyone in long tradition that Crane traces. For the distinction between humans and nonhumans used over and over in this tradition typically works to elevate humans over animals, whereas for Burke it works to lower humans as much as, if not more than, it elevates them.[3] When this distinction is used to elevate humans, the aim of humanistic education is typically to perfect idealized human capacities. Contrastingly, for Burke the linguistic prowess that distinguishes humans from nonhumans not only gives humans great powers of various kinds but also induces humans to stoop to actions unimaginable among nonhuman animals. For example, Burke (1935/1984b) proposes in *Permanence and Change* that all living things, even fish, are "critics" insofar as they survive by learning to make discriminations in their environment (e.g., food vs. bait), but humans, by virtue of the linguistic powers of abstraction and generalization, greatly expand such discriminations in ways that are negative as well as positive: "No slight critical ability is required for one to hate as [their] deepest enemy a people thousands of miles away" (pp. 5, 6)—something unimaginable among nonhuman animals. For Burke, consequently, the central problem for education to address arises from language-using in particular and symbol-using in general. In Burke's words,

> *the proper study of mankind is man's tendency to misjudge reality as inspirited by the troublous genius of symbolism*. But if we were trained, for generation after generation, from our first emergence out of infancy, and in ways ranging from the simplest to the most complex, depending upon our stage of development, to collaborate in spying upon ourselves with pious yet sportive fearfulness, and thus helping to free one another *of the false ambitions that symbolism so readily encourages*, we might yet contrive to keep from wholly ruining *this handsome planet and its plenitude*. (Burke, 1958, p. 63; italics added)

For Burke, then, no matter how much language may elevate humans, language is also a threat to nothing less than the planet itself. Burke (1966) even uses the phrase "rotten with perfection" to designate the human drive for perfection in order to accentuate the danger that this drive may prove destructive (pp. 16–20).

Burke's philosophical conception of humans as symbol-using animals thus leads to an approach to education that parallels in some respects John Dewey's influential pragmatic approach. Dewey's *Democracy and Education* (1916/1980) begins on the level of a fundamental distinction that frames Dewey's educational theory: "The most notable distinction between living and inanimate beings is that the former maintain themselves by renewal. . . . Life is a self-renewing process through action upon the environment" (p. 4).

Because death interferes with this process in each individual living being, each species must reproduce itself, and in some species of which the human species is the paradigmatic example, such reproduction requires education (p. 5). Dewey's framework provides the proper context for Burke's educational theory, despite their differences on other matters. Dewey, for example, optimistically envisions an educational process in which human reproduction is a process of progressive change (1916/1980, pp. 85, 87), whereas Burke is more cautious. In one of his Dewey reviews, Burke suggests that Dewey may over-valorize intelligence insofar as he thinks that because "intelligence is good, it will naturally choose good values" (1973, p. 386). Burke, by contrast, stresses that to be intelligent one has to be concerned with ways intelligence can become dangerous and destructive ("rotten with perfection"). Despite such differences, Burke shares Dewey's conviction that education is best considered from the standpoint of the processes of life and the human need for education to continue human life. At the foundational level, Burke's pedagogy aims to keep humans from endangering themselves and the planet on which they depend for their existence.

Ecology in Burke's Perspective of Education

LAPE exemplifies Burke's theory of the concrete, situated nature of discourse. Burke (1941/1973) begins *The Philosophy of Literary Form* with the claim that discourses are "answers to questions posed by the situation in which they arose" (p. 1). For Burke even an attempt to write to escape one's situation is presumably still, however obliquely, a response to one's situation. He advises, for example, that "whenever you find a doctrine of 'nonpolitical' esthetics affirmed with fervor, look for its politics" (Burke, 1950/1969b, p. 28). Hence, it would not be a surprise if his general views on education needed to be applied somewhat differently, with different emphases, in different situations. Burke says as much, as we will see, in LAPE's "Epilogue."

In the case of LAPE, the Cold War was the situation to which Burke was responding.[4] Appearing in 1955, the essay was written against the backdrop of the earliest days of the nuclear arms race, which created new fears in response to dangers of unprecedented magnitude. Burke reminds us of the magnitude of these fears in LAPE's closing sentence, which refers to "the new weapons that threaten not only our chances of living well but even our chances of living at all" (Burke, 1955, p. 301). This nuclear threat was the most immediate threat to "this handsome planet and its plenitude," great enough in its magnitude to overshadow the emerging ecological crisis that concerned Burke as early as 1937, long before the Cold War. What Burke saw on the historical horizon in the 1930s made its way to the popular media in 1970, appearing in a *Fortune* magazine article, "Our New Awareness of the Great Web":

we may assume that most predictions put forward in 1937, like those of other years, would now be worth recalling only as examples of fallibility. But at least one prediction published in that year has since come to seem exceedingly perspicacious. It appeared in a book [*Attitudes toward History*] by Kenneth Burke, a literary critic. "Among the sciences," he wrote, "there is one little fellow named Ecology, and in time we shall pay him more attention [1937/1984a, p. 150]." (Bowen, 1970, p. 198)[5]

Since the 1970s, this "new awareness" has, of course, only increased. Burke's own concern with ecology is evident in repeated references to it in his works and his concern becomes particularly prominent in later works.[6] While in 1955 the near-term threat of the "new weapons" overshadowed the long-term threat to the ecological health of the planet, it is not hard to imagine that if Burke were writing LAPE over fifty years later, in 2009, today's ecological crisis would overshadow the nuclear threat.

Furthermore, as noted earlier, ecology is not altogether absent from LAPE. Attention to the "animal" dimension of Burke's definition of humankind directs attention to the human body and its dependence on the ecology of the earth that makes life possible. Burke stresses, "Man *as an animal* is subject to the realm of extraverbal, or nonsymbolic, a realm of material necessity that is best charted in terms of *motion*" (Burke, 1955, p. 260). This material realm, Burke adds, combines competition among organisms for resources with mutuality in "the relationships prevailing among various organisms, or 'substances,' in their 'ecological balance'" (Burke, 1955, p. 262). However much language-using transcends the materiality of living, it thus nonetheless resides in a body rooted in the materiality of life. Burke captures this interplay in his cycle from "dirt" to "idea" to "dirt" quoted in the epigraph above (Burke, 2003, pp. 353–354). Ideally, the interplay should be positive, with the material conditions of life allowing language to flourish, and with language working to sustain these conditions. Language, however, can become counter-productive, fostering conditions that become a threat to the ecological processes that make it possible.

Education, Language and Ecological Crisis

Like Burke, C. A. Bowers theorizes education from the standpoint of its underlying philosophical assumptions. Writing on education and ecology since the 1970s, C. A. Bowers has published nearly twenty books to establish himself as a leader among educational theorists who concern themselves with the ecological crisis. We will make use two of his books from the 1990s: (1)

Educating for an Ecologically Sustainable Culture: Rethinking Moral Education, Creativity, Intelligence, and Other Modern Orthodoxies; and (2) *The Culture of Denial: Why the Environmental Movement Needs a Strategy for Reforming Universities and Public Schools.* Parts of LAPE do some of the things that Bowers thinks education needs to do, and other parts suggest how Burke may help to solve the biggest problem of all, precisely the one for which Bowers, ironically, seems unable to offer a plausible solution.

For Bowers (1997), educational practices endanger the ecological health of the planet when they are based, as is typically the case in the United States, on the philosophical assumptions informing modernity, with its valorizing of "the individual as the basic social unit," its tendency to view "[c]hange . . . as inherently progressive," its suspicion that "[t]raditions, except for family holidays, patterns, and events, are . . . inhibiting progress," its conception of "development . . . in economic and technological terms," and its unquestioning "reliance on science" (pp. 7–9; see also pp. 40–50, 105–126; 1995, pp. 154–158, 161–162).[7] These are the values that brought us the modern world, and it is the modern world that has engendered the ecological crisis. Bowers credits postmodernity with challenging some dimensions of modernity, but leaving others in place (1997, pp. 70–75). We are in, Bowers suggests, "a classic double bind situation where the promotion of our highest values and prestigious forms of knowledge serves to increase the prospects of ecological collapse" (1997, p. 3). Even environmentalists, Bowers likes to point out, sometimes preach environmentalism on one hand while subscribing to some of these values on the other (1995, pp. 168–169; 1997, pp. 27–29, 145, 222).

Bowers is adept at showing how educational practices cultivate among students the values of modernity even when the philosophical orientation informing modernity is not the explicit subject matter of a given course. For example, "[w]ithin a wide number of subfields of education, creativity is still understood as free, natural, and expressive of the individuals' inner powers of origination" (1995, p. 45). Pedagogies based on this assumption (e.g., write from your own personal experience) instill modernity's valorization of individualism, its discrediting of tradition, and its equation of the new with the valuable. Bowers even regularly subjects parts of Dewey to criticism. Bowers approves of Dewey's dismantling of modernity's isolated individual mind a la Descartes and the tradition of epistemological philosophy that he inaugurated (1995, pp. 13, 187; 1997, pp. 146–147), but Bowers faults Dewey's confidence in the scientific method and his tendency to equate change to progress (1995, pp. 137–138; 1997, pp. 86–87, 120, 147). Bowers's view of Dewey is thus similar to Burke's.

What is needed, Bowers contends, is a change at the foundational level to put in place a philosophical orientation that displaces modernity in favor of "wisdom derived from experience-based understanding of how humans are nested in cultural communities, and how these cultural communities are nested in ecosystems that are subject to unpredictable changes" (1997, p. 139; see also 217). One might add (though Bowers does not) that Dewey's foundational focus on species reproduction is compatible with this orientation, so that one could retain this part of Dewey's thought even if one wanted to dispense with the others that Bowers foregrounds in criticizing Dewey. In any case, one might visually contrast modernity to Bowers's alternative. On the side of modernity, one sees a linear line of constant change, with individuals looking forward rather than back and working unceasingly to extend the line, with every extension conceived as progressive. On the side of Bowers's ecological alternative, one sees stability based on concentric circles in harmony with one another: the ecosystem is the largest, cultures are circles within the encompassing eco-circle, and individuals are small circles within cultures.

Much in LAPE answers Bowers's call for study of "how individuals learn their cultural patterns without being aware of the deeper layers of symbolic construction . . . [which explain] how the individual is unconsciously nested in a cultural ecology shaped by the past" (1997, pp. 154–155, 171). For Burke's pedagogy aims to cultivate an awareness of the symbolic "equations" informing one's attitudes and actions. What does the "hero" equal? The villain? Etc. The significance of such equations becomes clear when one considers, for example, "the difference between the equation 'reason equals respect for authority' and the equation 'reason equals distrust of authority'" (1955, p. 270). Such differences prompt different actions. Burke summarizes,

> Having thus, without heckling, systematically let the text say its full say, even beyond what its author may have thought he was saying, we have the basic admonition as regards man, with relation to his specialty, "symbolic action." We see "exhortations" of terrifying importance being prepared for, even when a writer has no such intentions in mind. For, if certain elements equal "good" and certain elements equal "bad" . . . then in contemplating the "dynamics" of such "equations" (their implied hortatory value), do we not contemplate the very essence of human foibles? (Burke, 1955, p. 271)

The core premise, then, is that humans typically respond not to objective realities but to symbolic realities constructed through such equations. In this sense, language speaks us more than we speak it, sometimes even inducing us to "hate as [our] deepest enemy a people thousands of miles away" if we lack the education Burke would promote. Burke's pedagogy aims to make students see language as the cause of "man's tendency to misjudge reality." It is a pedagogy that, Burke concedes, would be irksome to instructors who see themselves using language in the classroom to talk about not language but "objective reality" (Burke, 1955, p. 277). Writing in the 1950s, Burke was thus anticipating the social constructionism that became commonplace in the closing decades of the twentieth century, according to which our relation to reality is mediated by constructs built up through linguistic and cultural processes. We will return to this anticipation later, when we consider LAPE's "Epilogue."

Correcting Problem Ecological Orientations

The deep problem that Bowers never addresses adequately is to envision how we might move from where we are today to his philosophical model of circles nested inside one another and thus start down the long road to the acceptance it would need to enjoy to displace modernity's linear line of progressive change. What Bowers does instead is (1) to spell out how one can find this model in so-called "primal" or "primitive" cultures (1995, pp. 165–168; 1997, pp. 4–5, 6, 206–209), and (2) to argue that we need to return to this model, without offering any scenario outlining how such a return could occur. While he concedes, albeit rarely, that not all these cultures worked to benefit their ecological milieu (1997, p. 10), he nonetheless contends that we must make ourselves over in the image of these cultures lock, stock, and barrel, without evaluating either the plausibility of such a transformation or even considering whether it would be desirable in every respect.

For example, because in these cultures "elders" typically enjoyed great authority, Bowers praises one educational reform for including an "oral history" exercise that fosters the respect for elders needed for them to recover the position of authority they once enjoyed (1995, pp. 187–188). But Bowers leaves unanswered a host of questions that come to mind. He even contradicts himself insofar as elsewhere he recognizes elders today are generally "false elders" because they promote modernity (1995, p. 172). If elders are indeed part of the solution, what is needed is a way to get from today's "false elders" to the "true elders" of tomorrow. Even more important, Bowers needs to ask if elders are indeed an important key to the solution we need. One can imagine cultural situations in which elders, simply by virtue of their years of experience, would possess the knowledge one would want people in authority to have, but it is not clear if such situations will ever return. Part of the difficulty here seems to be that Bowers sees science as inextricably tied to modernity so that science in particular needs to be displaced along with modernity in general. When he envisions elders carrying forward "accumulated knowledge," he seems to envision elders taking the place of science. But one needs to consider that while science has played a part in bringing about the ecological crisis, it is also playing an essential part in helping us (1) to understand the crisis (it is science that explains global warming to us) and (2) to look for ways to address it (e.g., science is involved in the search for alternative forms of energy). Science per se may not be the problem so much as the extent to which science has become a very expensive enterprise and has often received the funding it needs by proposing to conduct research that advanced economic developments that proved ecologically retrograde. Science that serves an ecological master might prove to be quite different from the science that served the god of economic development.

Rather than following Bowers in his effort to return to fully fleshed out cultural forms of the past such as the role of elders and others that he discusses (communal ceremonies, mythopoetic narratives, etc. [1997, pp. 4–5]), one could concentrate instead on developing a strategy to establish philosophical foundations for Bowers's ecological model of nested circles. Establishing such a model is a necessary first step, and by concentrating on this step, one may ultimately do more by virtue of initially aiming for less. LAPE offers a useful guide for the development of such a strategy.

In the case of the philosophies informing modernity and Bowers's ecological alternative, we are using the notion of philosophy not in the narrow sense of a specific philosophical doctrine, with its technical precisions, but in the broad sense in which a philosophy is a way of life that may pervade a culture. At the level of a "way of life," Burke suggests in LAPE, any "attempt [at] charting the good life" needs to use the strategy of "both-and" rather than "either-or." In Burke's words, "where two opposed principles are being considered . . . what we want is something that avoids the typical vices of either and combines the typical virtues of both. . . . [W]e can readily propose that any troublesome *either-or* be transformed into a *both-and*" (293). Before we apply this both-and principle to today's ecological crisis, it will help (1) to see how it works in LAPE and (2) to turn to LAPE's "Epilogue," where similarities between the future Burke imagines in 1955 and our reality in 2009 bring us to the point at which we can use Burke's both-and principle to envision a first step toward establishing an ecological model of nested circle that seeks harmony and stability to displace modernity's model of linear progress that has brought us to the edge of ecological catastrophe.

The Both-And of Ecology

In the Cold War situation of 1955, as we saw earlier, Burke put heavy stress on the admonitory in urging the development of pedagogical strategies to sensitize students to the "equations," coming from their culture, that were informing their ambitions. The admonition of admonitions was to learn not to mistake a symbolic reality, constructed of such "equations," for objective reality. This emphasis on the admonitory, Burke recognizes, runs counter to the tendency to put education "wholly under the sign of the promissory," whereby students see, consistent with modernity's stress on individualism, education as a way to get a good job and get ahead in the world. Even in the humanities, Burke suggests, "courses are expected to help students 'get ahead' as individuals. Humanistic education thus becomes the attempt to teach and to acquire the kind of 'insignia' that are thought to be proof of cultural election" (Burke, 1955, p. 271). Under Burke's tutelage, the "realities" prompting such ambitions would be "deconstructed" (*avant la lettre*), exposed as social constructs rather than the realities they purport to be. In the process, Burke hopes, such "realities" would lose their appeal, their power as incentives to action. In this fashion, Burke's pedagogy would transform students by freeing them "of the false ambitions that symbolism so readily encourages." This stress on the admonitory is part of Burke's response to the Cold War, because Burke sees education's rewarding of individualistic ambition as intensifying the competitions that "mak[e] for the kind of war now always threatening" (1955, p. 272).

But admonition is negative, and for Burke it is essential that this negative not exclude the positive: both-and rather than either-or: "But our zeal for the negative or admonitory in education should not seem to prevail over its counterpart, the lore of 'positive' appreciation" (1955, p. 290). Attention to "equations" is negative in exposing the linguistic constructedness of what was thought to be reality, but the very same attention becomes positive insofar as one aesthetically appreciates the linguistic resources by which one was persuaded to mistake a linguistic construction for reality itself. One gives up one's previous "persuasion" (negative) but one has a new appreciation for the formal devices that produce persuasion (positive). Furthermore, great art often centers on precisely this human "tendency to misjudge reality." As Burke suggests,

> Have we proposed a distrust of ambition? Then see, on the other hand, what great tragic assertions have been made of this distrust, as with the grotesqueries of *Macbeth*, or the stateliness of murder in *Julius Caesar*. Do we discern how the motives of sheer ownership figure in relations between husband and wife? Then note how these are made almost exultant in *Othello*. (1955, p. 291)

In other words, the pleasures of appreciation that await the student benefiting from LAPE's pedagogy in particular encompass the pleasures to be found in much Burkeian criticism in general.

The aesthetic, then, completes the transformation Burke's pedagogy is designed to produce. Students come to it with their energies excited by the putative realities of their individualistic "get ahead" American culture. These energies are dissipated insofar as these realities are deconstructed, but in this process of deconstruction, these energies are redirected to the aesthetic. The aesthetic becomes in effect a kind of new reality. While language separates us from reality in one sense, it is a reality in its own right. It is a reality, moreover, about which one can speak with certainty: "'Truth' is absolute, in the sense that one can categorically make assertions about certain basic resources and embarrassments of symbols. It is nearly absolute, as regards certain 'factual' statements that can be made about the terms of a given work" (Burke, 1955, p. 276).

Furthermore, aesthetic appreciation helps one not only to get outside one's own orientation but also to appreciate the orientations of others and thus ascend the dialectical ladder that Burke puts forward as an "educational ladder" to measure progress by one's capacity to transcend the local to the cosmopolitan (1955, p. 283). The full implications of Burke's both-and pedagogy appear when Burke turns to religion, which is the framework within which he considers the antagonists in the Cold War: the capitalism of the U.S. and the dialectical materialism of the U.S.S.R. Burke emphasizes that his approach is "not doctrinal, but formal. That is, it does not ask: 'Is such a doctrine literally *true* or *false?*' Rather, it asks, 'what are the relationships prevailing among the key terms of this doctrine?'" (Burke, 1955, p. 298). "The same considerations apply," Burke adds, "to purely 'secular religions,' notably such political philosophies as capitalism or dialectical materialism" (Burke, 1955, p. 299). As he continues,

> It is the thesis of this essay that, since all divergent doctrines must necessarily confront one another as doctrinal "idioms," a framework for the lot could be provided only by the perfecting of some terminology for the study of idioms in general. A terminology as so conceived must necessarily adopt some point of view in which all could share. And a formalistic view is such a one, at least in principle. (1955, p. 299)

Burke concedes that his "secularly formal (or, if you will, '*aesthetic*') approach to the literal particularities of dogma must be insufficient, as judged by the tests of advocates who would proclaim one doctrine and no other as the whole and only truth" (1955, p. 298; italics added). "Admittedly," Burke goes on, "such an approach is not enough to resolve specific issues that lead to blunt, head-on collisions. One cannot ask an educational program to do the impossible. But one can ask that it provide a positive equivalent for the area of commonalty which even opponents must share, if they are to join the same battle" (1955, p. 299). Similarly, Burke (1945/1969a) suggests that *A*

Grammar of Motives works "toward the purification of war" by drawing attention to a level of linguistic resources that "even wholly rival doctrines of motives must share in common" (p. 442). In this fashion, Burke uses his both-and strategy to fashion an educational pedagogy designed to cultivate a "way of life" that pursues peace.

Toward a Positive Aesthetic of Ecology

As noted earlier, LAPE's "Epilogue" points beyond 1955 toward the future. It begins, "But suppose that all did turn out as we would have it, so far as educational programs went? What next? What might be the results?" (1955, p. 300). Burke imagines two possibilities: "absolute piety" or "absolute drought" (Burke, 1955, p. 301).

Why "drought"? Humans might become sensitized enough to the "fogs of language," Burke suggests, "to so distrust the motives of secular ambition, as clamorously established by all who help make secular aims 'glamorous,' that the entire pageantry of empire would seem as unreal as a stage set" (Burke, 1955, pp. 300–301). As Burke (1950/1969b) spells out in detail in *A Rhetoric of Motives* (pp. 201–203), humans need something positive to live by, "a real and ultimate universal ground" (p. 203). What LAPE's "Epilogue" envisions is a world where, by virtue of the "fear of symbol-using," all the realities that motivated "secular ambition" (the positives) have been exposed as mere "stage set[s]" that entice the unwary. In a world where everyone is "wised up" by Burke's pedagogy, what would be left to motivate action?

The main argument in LAPE assumed that however uncertain we may be about language-using animals insofar as it is an open question as to whether they will use their linguistic prowess to destroy the conditions that make their life possible, we can be certain when it comes to the statements we make about how language works to produce its persuasive effects. In this fashion, language seems to become what *A Rhetoric of Motives* says humans always need: "a real and ultimate universal ground." LAPE divorces universal forms of language from content to put forward the best ground available on which to build the consensus needed to avert nuclear catastrophe, and in the process, these forms become a new reality that stimulates the pleasures of aesthetic appreciation. The "Epilogue," by contrast, complicates this picture, forcing a reevaluation. For it suggests that in the long run, language cannot serve as the "real and ultimate universal ground" that humans need. A world seen by everyone as a mere "stage set" would be a world in which the linguistic constructedness informing its "reality" would be apparent to all. But such a world, the "Epilogue" suggests, would be less an aesthetic utopia than a demoralizing disappearance of incentives for action. From the futuristic standpoint of the "Epilogue," one can see retrospectively that in the context of 1955, the positivity of the aesthetic was enhanced insofar as linguistic constructedness was not widely embraced. In such a context, it is a positive that one can fight for, as Burke does in LAPE. But in the future that the "Epilogue" imagines, it is widely accepted that it is the only positive left in town, and in this context it is not enough. It is a reality capable of exciting the energies of aesthetic appreciation in students benefiting from Burke's pedagogy in 1955, but it is not a reality that can serve as the "real and ultimate ground" humans need for the long run.

It would appear, moreover, that this possibility Burke envisioned in 1955 has to at least some extent been realized in the world in which we live in 2009. After a generation spent teaching the likes of Derrida and Foucault in particular, and social constructionist theory in general, the academy has sensitized students to the "fogs of language" that mediate our relations to reality. In my field of literary studies, constructionist pedagogy has centered particularly on the trio of gender, race, and class. A generation of students has been taught that social hierarchies in these areas are not rooted in biological realities, as was once thought to be the case, but are in fact linguistic constructs forged in history. The lessons Burke offered in 1955 have been taught over and over, though perhaps less often in the Burkeian comic spirit of aesthetic appreciation than in a melodramatic spirit of debunking that was sometimes polarizing. Furthermore, limits to the "fogs of language" that the "Epilogue" records have also been evident in the sense that however insightful constructionism has been into the ways of culture, the reign of constructionism has also often left us with the sense that it cannot be all that there is.

It is this sense that helps how to explain how "absolute piety" can arise alongside "absolute drought" as an alternative to it. Emphasis on the "fogs of language" heightens a sense that there must be something beyond these "fogs": "In seeing beyond the limitations of language, many might attain a piety now available to but a few" (Burke, 1955, p. 300). However much the human world is a "stage set," this "stage set" does not exhaust the reality of planet earth and its place, however humble, in the universe. The ecological crisis reminds us of this on a daily basis, and the revival of religion in our time may be due at least in part to a reaction against the notion that there is no way out of these "fogs."

In this fashion, Burke takes in his "Epilogue" the remarkable step of seeing beyond the essay he has just completed, and he deserves to be credited with a remarkable degree of prescience. Moreover, by envisioning the educational discourse he just completed so changing the situation that a new discourse would be needed for this new situation, Burke dramatically demonstrates his commitment to the principle, discussed earlier, that discourses are always responses to situations (1941/1973, p. 1).

If we use Burke's "absolute drought" and "absolute piety" to define the opposed extremes in our situation today, how can we devise a both-and ecological discourse of nested circles that would strategically appeal to both these extremes and thus move us toward a reorientation from modernity toward a new philosophical foundation for an ecological pedagogy to meet the ecological crisis of our time?

Conclusion

Fleshing out the "both-and" needed in 2009 might best be conceived as a bargaining process that allows each side, "absolute drought" and "absolute piety," a chance to keep something at the cost of giving up something else. Some on each side will no doubt prefer the oppositional "either-or" to giving up anything, but a "both-and" would offer a third alternative to those on either side who are not altogether comfortable with the polar opposition. Proposing a solution in purely religious terms would be a mistake because it would only reinforce the foundational premise of the religious absolutists, but offering religious absolutists an absolutism of a different kind may entice at least some of them to forego their "either-or" for a place in a "both-and" structure that includes people with and without faith instead of dividing them into opposing camps. Similarly, one cannot stay strictly within the premises of the social constructionism, because that would again simply be reaffirming one side of the "either-or." The constructionists need to concede that there is a reality beyond constructs and that the relation of constructs to this reality needs attention.

A passage in Burke that could serve as a focal point for such bargaining is Burke's image of the human condition at the end of *Permanence and Change:*

> We in cities rightly grow shrewd at appraising man-made institutions—but beyond these tiny concentration points of rhetoric and traffic, there lies the eternally unsolvable Enigma.... [F]or always the Eternal Enigma is there, right on the edge of our metropolitan bickerings, stretching outward to interstellar infinity and inward to the depths of the mind. And in this staggering disproportion between man and noman, there is no place for purely human boasts of grandeur, or for forgetting that [humans] build their cultures by huddling together, nervously loquacious, at the edge of an abyss. (1935/1984b, p. 272)

Combining the "fogs of language" ("nervously loquacious") with the "ultimate reality" ("abyss") beyond them, this passage visualizes three concentric circles nested inside one another: ultimate reality (encompassing circle), cultures (circles inside this reality), and individuals (huddling inside their cultures). Furthermore, just as Burke suggests that no matter what we see ourselves doing, we are in fact building cultures at the edge of an abyss, David Orr's maxim that "all education is environmental education" (1992, p. 90) suggests that no matter what we see ourselves doing pedagogically, we are training students to act on the earth in particular ways that will have impacts on the environment, be they good or bad. Recognizing that all education has environmental effects, however, tends automatically to sensitize one to the sense in which our cultures are nested inside the encompassing ecological circle that we may substitute for Burke's "abyss" (a substitution justified by Burke's considerable attention, as noted earlier, to ecology in other writings).

Examining first the constructionist side of the "both-and," one example may suggest what Burke's concentric circles can offer constructionists and what constructionists must give up to accept the offer. Consider the issue of gender. In literary studies, this issue, like the issues of race and class, is often framed as an opposition between "essentializing" and "historicizing." Essentializing is identified with grounding patriarchy in biology, thereby making it an absolute independent of culture; whereas historicizing is identified with exposing patriarchy as a mere construct relative to the historical circumstances in which it was forged and sustained (e.g., see Jehlen). From a feminist standpoint, constructionism is thus liberating. Gender constructs become real insofar as they are actually lived, but such realities have their roots in processes of cultural construction, not in the encompassing ecological circle. Consequently, unlike biological absolutes, one construct relative to one cultural situation can displace another relative to an earlier situation.

The limitation of this historicizing/essentializing opposition is that it prompts constructionists to attack affirmation of an essentialism of any kind as an affirmation of essentialisms of all kinds (cf. "Being driven into a corner," in the "Dictionary of Pivotal Terms" in Burke's [1937/1984a] *Attitudes Toward History*). It is this line of attack that constructionism must give up. It can keep its theory for constructed realities that really do have their origins in cultural processes of language-using; LAPE's pedagogy will continue to have a place in the new Burkeian pedagogy for 2009 and beyond insofar as the "fogs of language" will necessarily be a part of cultural life. What constructionism must give up is the view that constructionism is all there is. It must concede that there is an essentialism of the earth, that is, realities independent of language and culture in the encompassing ecology of the earth. However free culture is to go its own way in some areas, when it comes to the absolute realities that sustain life, culture must adapt or self-destruct. Furthermore, however much constructs have their origins in human language, they can impact the earth beyond language, as when consumerism stimulated by constructs results in degradation of the earth and the long-term endangerment of humankind as well as many other species.

Turning to the other side of the needed "both-and," what is the bargain to be offered to "absolutist piety"? What can it keep? What must it give up? Returning to Burke's image of concentric circles, we need to focus on the encompassing ecological circle. This circle is absolute insofar as it is independent of the relativism of constructs, which have their origins in culture.[8] It is a geocentric absolute of the earth rather than a cosmocentric absolute of the heavens above (for more on this geocentric/cosmocentric distinction, see Wess [2003]). Cultures are built "nervously" because the ecological circle is limited to the circle of the earth. Even being a sinner condemned to hell brings the comfort of participating in God's cosmic drama, which is good news compared to the dismal news that one is limited to a few years of life on a speck in the cosmos. However common the "god-talk" in the "loquaciousness," there is no foundation for "boasts of grandeur." Religious absolutists, then, can have an absolute, but it must be an absolute of the earth. A Burkeian pedagogy for 2009 and beyond, then, while continuing LAPE's pedagogical strategy for countering the ambitions, both domestic and international, fostered by America's "get ahead" culture, would also seek to counter the cosmocentric ambitions of those who seek to see themselves as the instruments of God's will.

The strategy informing this bargain seeks to drive a wedge between two groups of religious absolutists. One group would agree with James Watt, Reagan's first secretary of the Interior, who did not worry about the ecological crisis because he thought that "after the last tree is felled Christ will come back," a fact Bill Moyers (2004) recounts in a speech he gave upon receiving the Global Environment Citizen Award from the Center for Health and the Global Environment at Harvard Medical School. Some forms of religion, Moyers thus reminds us, may even welcome ecological disaster. The other group of absolutists thinks about the earth differently. In the Pacific Northwest, for example, a group of Catholic bishops recently issued a "Pastoral Letter" on the Columbia River designed to "bring the mission of care for God's creation more fully to the heart of religious life" (Ashton, 2000). Religion can find an absolutism in the "both-and" envisioned here if it is willing to submit to a geocentric test rather than to dismiss life on earth in the name of a higher, more perfect cosmocentric test. In other words, even if these absolutists want to hold onto transcendence upwards, they must concede that the necessary first step is transcendence downwards to the earth (for a Burkeian theorizing of such transcendence downwards, see Wess [2003]). As Burke argues, "It would be much better for us, in the long run, if we 'identified ourselves' rather with the natural things that we are progressively *destroying*—our trees, our rivers, our land, even our air, all of which we are a lowly ecological part of" (Burke, 1970, p. 414). Speaking geocentrically here, Burke suggests how in identifying with nature, geocentrists and cosmocentrists can find common ground. It is possible for people with and without faith to come together in recognizing the need for attention to ecological reality.

This "both-and" is rooted deeply in Burke who simultaneously taught us much about the constructive powers of verbal action, while rooting language in the motion of our bodies and the process of life on earth. The Burkeian pedagogy needed for today and years to come attends more fully to both the language-using and animal sides of the human animal than did Burke's 1955 pedagogy, which de-emphasized the animal side for reasons peculiar to his situation in 1955. By attending to both these sides, one can draw on Burke for help in creating a space for the constructionists and religious absolutists willing to enter it to dialogue together to forge the earth-centered orientation we need. In the process, they can displace the philosophical orientation informing modernity with a new philosophical foundation linking ecology, culture, and the individual in mutually supporting concentric circles.

Such a foundation may, in addition, help to overcome the opposition between the sciences and the humanities that has been with us too long. For a Burkeian pedagogy for today's ecological crisis calls attention to the need for humanists to heed science in its inquiry into the question of what it means to be a human being. In addressing this question, humanists must take into account what it means to be an inhabitant of the earth, and it is science that gives us the best answers to the questions of what humans have been doing as inhabitants of the earth and of what they need to do differently. Burke never denies that science can produce knowledge about the realm beyond language; he only insists that science cannot operate independently of the action of language-using:

> Men can so arrange it that nature gives clear, though impartial and impersonal, answers to their questions. The dialectical motives behind such methods usually escape our detection, though we get a glimpse of them when Galileo speaks of experimental testing as an "ordeal." Stated broadly the dialectical (agonistic) approach to knowledge is through the *act* of assertion, whereby one "suffers" the kind of knowledge that is the reciprocal of his act (Burke, 1945/1969a, p. 38).

The crucial human component is in the determination of the questions to put to nature. Science produces knowledge but this knowledge results from the questions humans ask in pursuit of their purposes. The Burkeian pedagogy for today's ecological crisis returns us to Burke's 1937 prediction that one day humans would need to put questions to nature best answered by the science of ecology. Science may be viewed as humankind's way of "digging in the dirt," but there is a big difference between digging to adapt to the ways of the dirt (ecology) and digging to shape dirt into the mud castles dreamed up by voracious human ambitions.

Burke's 1955 pedagogy aimed to stave off conflict by attending to the ways language instills false ambitions and thereby fosters unnecessary competition and conflict. A Burkeian pedagogy for today needs to continue this effort, but it must also broaden its scope to the horizon of the earth. Ambitions are false not only when they foster unnecessary competition and conflict but also when they foster activities that worsen the health of the ecology of the earth. While this new pedagogy would thus continue to expose the "fogs of language," there is no danger that such exposure will leave us in the end with a mere "stage set." For this pedagogy combines such exposure with attention to the "ultimate reality" of the ecology of the earth.

In the long run, the fate of the earth may be tied inextricably to whether we can learn that the truth of what it means to be a human being starts with the truth that we are inhabitants of the earth and must act accordingly. A Burkeian humanistic education can get us started in the right direction at long last.

Notes

* I would like to thank Josh Beach for his careful reading of an earlier version of this essay. His suggestions strengthened it, but whatever shortcomings remain are, of course, my responsibility.

1. Crane (1967) expresses particular indebtedness to Richard McKeon, a colleague at the University of Chicago, for his views on the humanities (p. 3). McKeon was also a friend of Burke's from the time of the student days they shared at Columbia University. Crane's history is based on a series of lectures he gave in 1943 at the University of Chicago, where Burke taught in the summer of 1938.

2. In LAPE, Burke is explicit about his reasons for focusing on written rather than spoken language (1955, pp. 265–66). He also explains that "symbol-using" is technically more correct because it encompasses all the arts that together distinguish humankind among all animal species. Nonetheless, "[v]erbal symbol-using (like its variant mathematics) enjoys a special place among the lot because the individual word has a kind of conceptual clarity not found in individual notes, colors, lines, motions, and the like" (p. 266).

3. Burke's reevaluation of the traditional human/animal distinction anticipates current reevaluations among contemporary theorists. A good place to start an investigation of these is Cary Wolfe's *Animal Rites: American Culture, the Discourse of Species, and Posthumanist Theory*, Chicago: University of Chicago Press, 2003.

4. See Jessica Enoch (2004) for an insightful and convincing study of the Cold War background for LAPE.

5. See Marika Seigel (2004) for an invaluable historical contextualization of Burke's 1937 prediction. Seigel also makes a convincing case that ideas about ecology helped Burke to formulate his well-known "comic attitude."

6. Perhaps the most notable examples of Burke's concern with ecology in his later works are his "Helhaven" essays, "Toward Helhaven: Three Stages of a Vision" and "Why Satire, with a Plan for Writing One." Both are included in *On Human Nature: A Gathering While Everything Flows, 1967–1984*, edited by William H. Rueckert and Angelo Bonadonna, Berkeley: University of California Press, 2003. This satire is built around "Helhaven," where technology is ironically used to reproduce on the moon simulacra of the conditions on earth that existed prior to their destruction at the hands of human technological prowess.

7. For a study of Burke that focuses in particular on Burke's critique of modernity, which is similar to Bowers,' see Paul Jay, *Contingency Blues: The Search for Foundations in American Criticism*, Madison: University of Wisconsin Press, 1997. Jay gives Burke a central place in nineteenth and twentieth century critiques of modernity in American culture.

8. Similarly, Samuel Southwell (1987) interprets Burke's incorporation of the "abyss" in the image from *Permanence and Change* as evidence that Burke never limits himself solely to the "life-world" of the "loquaciousness" but always also reaches beyond it, "into the abyss, grappling for a foundation" (p. 66).

References

Ashton, L. (2000, November 11). Pulpits turn green as ecology joins theology. *Corvallis Gazette-Times*, A10.

Bowen, W. (1970, February). Our new awareness of the great web. *Fortune*, pp. 198–99.

Bowers, C. A. (1995). *Educating for an ecologically sustainable culture: Rethinking moral education, creativity, intelligence, and other modern orthodoxies*. Albany, NY: State University of New York Press.

Bowers, C. A. (1997). *The culture of denial: Why the environmental movement needs a strategy for reforming universities and public schools*. Albany, NY: State University of New York Press.

Burke, K. (1955). Linguistic approach to problems of education. In N. B. Henry (Ed.), *Modern philosophies and education, The fifty-fourth yearbook of the National Society for the Study of Education, Part 1 of 2* (pp. 259–303). Chicago: National Society for the Study of Education.

Burke, K. (1958). Poetic motive. *Hudson Review*, 11, pp. 54–63.

Burke, K. (1966). *Language as symbolic action: Essays on life, literature, and method*. Berkeley: University of California Press.

Burke, K. (1969a). *A grammar of motives.* Berkeley, CA: University of California Press. (Original work published 1945)

Burke, K. (1969b). *A rhetoric of motives.* Berkeley, CA: University of California Press. (Original work published 1950)

Burke, K. (1970). Poetics and communication. In H. E. Kiefer & M. K. Munitz (Eds.), *Perspectives in education, religion, and the* arts (pp. 401–418). New York: SUNY Press.

Burke, K. (1973). *The philosophy of literary form: Studies in symbolic action* (3rd ed.). Berkeley, CA: University of California Press. (Original work published 1941)

Burke, K. (1984a). *Attitudes toward history* (3rd ed.). Berkeley, CA: University of California Press. (Original work published 1937)

Burke, K. (1984b). *Permanence and change: An anatomy of purpose* (3rd ed.). Berkeley, CA: University of California Press. (Original work published 1935)

Burke, K. (2003). Counter-gridlock: An interview with Kenneth Burke, 1980–81. In W. H. Rueckert & A. Bonadonna (Eds.), *On human nature: A gathering while everything flows, 1967–1984* (pp. 336–389). Berkeley, CA: University of California Press.

Crane, R. S. (1967). *The idea of the humanities and other essays critical and historical* (Vol. 1.). Chicago: University of Chicago Press.

Dewey, J. (1980). *Democracy and education.* In *John Dewey: The middle works, 1899–1924, volume 9: 1916.* Ed. Jo Ann Boydson et al. Carbondale, IL: Southern Illinois University Press. (Original work published 1916)

Enoch, J. (2004). Becoming symbol-wise: Kenneth Burke's pedagogy of critical reflection. *College Composition and Communication, 56*(2), 272–296.

Jehlen, M. (1995). Gender. In F. Lentricchia & T. McLaughlin (Eds.), *Critical terms for literary study* (2nd ed., pp. 263–273). Chicago: University of Chicago Press.

Moyers, B. (2004). *Battlefield Earth.* Retrieved December 8, 2004, from http://www.alternet.org/envirohealth/20666/

Orr, D. W. (1992). *Ecological literacy: Education and the transition to a postmodern world.* Albany, NT: State University of New York Press.

Seigel, M. A. (2004). "One little fellow named Ecology": Ecological rhetoric in Kenneth Burke's *Attitudes toward history. Rhetoric Review, 23,* 388–404.

Southwell, S. B. (1987). *Kenneth Burke and Martin Heidegger, with a note against deconstruction.* Gainesville, FL: University of Florida Press.

Wess, R. (2003). Geocentric ecocriticism. *ISLE, 10*(2), 1–19.

9 "By and Through Language, Beyond Language": Envisioning a Burkeian Curriculum

Bryan Crable

In a 1959 letter to Wesley Hartley, of the American Council on Education, Kenneth Burke reflected upon his own (limited) experience with formal education, and upon the lessons that he drew from it. Though he assured Hartley that his experience had not soured him on higher education—even recommending that "[e]very student should at least experiment with college"—it had, he felt, left him with a rather pessimistic view of educational *policy:* "In matters of education, I find myself more and more forced to the not very startling conclusion that one man's[1] meat is another man's poison. Thus, I doubt whether there can ever be such a thing as a single educational policy which would be beneficial to all."[2] Given this statement, we might easily infer Burke's attitude toward the current debate over both current educational practice and educational reform—or proceed with a Burkeian analysis of the discourse generated by this debate (e.g., Staton & Peeples, 2000).

However, a focus on such matters might lead us to overlook Burke's own attempt to recast American educational policy in his essay, "Linguistic Approach to Problems of Education." Quite atypically, Burke planned the essay in close conjunction with Kenneth Benne, from the Adult Education Association, and specifically wrote it for an audience of professional educators and policy-makers.[3] Its systematic application of dramatism to the philosophy of education further marks it as a unique entry among Burke's many books and essays. Perhaps due to these unusual qualities, Burke was quite worried about its reception by his standard audience of critics, social theorists, and philosophers (e.g., Kenneth Burke to Stanley Edgar Hyman, 8 March 1955, KB). In one respect, his fears were justified; though he initially received compliments on the essay from a few colleagues (e.g., Stanley Edgar Hyman to Kenneth Burke, 9 March, 1955, KB; Kenneth Burke to Stanley Edgar Hyman, 10

March 1955, KB), the essay has gone largely unnoticed in the fifty years of rhetorical scholarship following its publication.

Undoubtedly, its relative anonymity can be traced partly to its intended audience (since scholars in literary criticism, communication, and sociology rarely look to education for work on Burke), and partly to its publication in an edited collection; both characteristics conspire against its easy inclusion in the Burkeian canon. The current essay, like others in this volume, thus attempts to reclaim Burke's text for contemporary scholarship, arguing that we can learn a great deal from it about both the nature of symbolic action and the proper education of the "symbol-using animal." In order to establish this argument, I first offer an overview of this little-cited essay, including Burke's explanation of dramatism, its application to the philosophy of education, and the curriculum that would embody a dramatistic revision of current practice.

Following this overview, I revisit the significance of Burke's theoretical preoccupation with the difference between "nonsymbolic motion" and "symbolic action." After examining this central polarity in more depth, I contend that Burke's (1955) educational program in "Linguistic Approach to Problems of Education" does not fully embody the dramatistic critique of scientism. In sum, I argue that Burke's revised curriculum, though quite different from educational practice of his (and our) time, does not go as far as Burke himself does in undermining traditional views of language and reality. I subsequently offer—as a thought experiment—an alternative dramatistic curriculum, one that, beginning with early childhood education, *solely* focuses upon language—as something to be learned and as something to be discounted. I offer this as a contribution to our current conversations on educational reform, a Burke-inspired "tour de force" that asks (a la "What are the Signs of What?"): "what might be discovered if we tried . . . such a view" (1966, pg. 360)?

Tracing the student's move through primary and secondary education, I thus unfold a paradoxical, playful program for linguistic appreciation—*where the only principles studied through ninth grade are those of symbolic action*. This curriculum gradually provides the student with the foundation necessary to study nonsymbolic motion; firmly maintaining that school children are not symbolically sophisticated enough to adequately discount terminologies of motion, this program consequently delays the study of natural science to late secondary and early college education. After detailing this revised dramatistic curriculum, the chapter ends by weighing its weaknesses against the assumptions reinforced by our present educational system. Though no solution can fully immunize beings "rotten with perfection" against themselves, I conclude that this thought experiment provides a new perspective on these matters, insight which may prove useful as we continue to debate and recast American educational practice.

Burke's Premises: Dramatism Explained

One of the most striking features of Burke's article, "Linguistic Approach to Problems of Education," is its scope: The account that Burke provides of the dramatistic perspective ranges across a good number of his central texts, themes, and concepts. Indeed, upon reading the essay, no less an interpreter than Stanley Hyman remarked, "I found the piece a useful summary of the whole works [of Burke], with a handy bibliography" (Stanley Edgar Hyman to Kenneth Burke, 9 March 1955, KB). Burke's encapsulation of the dramatistic position surely was designed to help his audience, likely unfamiliar with his previous work; as a result, any reader needing a holistic introduction to (or refresher on) Burke would be well-served by consulting this essay.

Burke's summary, though, goes far beyond an annotated bibliography, or even a brief tour of his writings. Burke instead opens the essay with an extended reflection upon the central tenet of dramatism: the human being is best understood "as the typically language using, or symbol-using animal" (1955, p. 259). Burke fully unpacks this statement for the reader, with an eye toward establishing a clear contrast between the dramatistic approach to human social life and its antithesis, "scientism," or the "scientistic" approach. First, by defining humans as symbol-users, Burke highlights the fact that humans are actively engaged with the world, and are not merely passive receivers of stimuli; we *use* (and, as Burke emphasizes, are used *by*) symbols. Or, as Burke writes, dramatism begins with the belief that language is symbolic *action*, "a mode of conduct" (1955, p. 259). This is the first key difference between the dramatistic and scientistic approaches; rather than building its perspective around the notion that human beings actively engage the world, scientism is founded upon a separation between human beings and their environment (in the sense that the knower, in order to know, must be separated from that which is to be known). On the scientistic account, humans passively receive stimuli through sense organs, and (cognitively?, neurologically?) work to convert these stimuli into a faithful account of the surrounding environment.

The scientistic account correspondingly presumes that the central function of language is to help human beings accurately represent this environment, and convey those representations to others. In short, scientism treats language as primarily a vehicle for storing and sharing knowledge; or, as Burke frames the issue, scientism conceives of language epistemologically, in terms of the conditions necessary to capture and convey truths about some aspect of the world. Burke argues that this sharply contrasts with the dramatistic approach, which is fundamentally ontological, concerned with language as the primary way through which things *are constituted, or made significant* for human beings. Language, for dramatism, is not a mirror, reflecting what is already there; rather, it is that which enables us to "draw the lines" that separate the things, events, persons, and places of our world from their surroundings—a demarcation that is necessary if we are to identify, define, relate to, or reflect upon what is "already there." On Burke's view, language does not represent a preexisting world, as in scientistic accounts. Rather, language is that activity through which we *fashion* the only world that we can encounter, the symbolically ordered world that forms the backdrop for our everyday acts.[4]

These different conceptions of language indicate a further contrast between dramatism and scientism. By defining humans as symbol-using animals, Burke, as we have already seen, stresses the irreducibility of language; according to Burke, symbolicity is *the* distinctive feature of human existence. As a result, he holds that certain of our motivations and characteristics are solely traceable to the workings of the symbolic realm. Only human beings, for example, can be overcome by the stanzas of a poem, or driven to greater and greater efforts by a cultural idea of "success." However, Burke insists that this realm alone cannot account for human motives—that, instead, "Man *as an animal* is subject to the realm of the extraverbal, or nonsymbolic, a realm of material necessity that is best charted in terms of *motion*" (1955, p. 260). Despite our best efforts, he reminds us, there are certain features of existence that cannot be symbolized away: "Man cannot live by the *word* for bread alone" (1973, p. xvi).

In other words, dramatism presumes that human existence is twofold, that it is characterized by a dialectical mix of symbolic action and nonsymbolic motion.[5] Consequently, for Burke, only an approach that accounts for both aspects of our humanity—without reducing one to the other—can claim to be truly comprehensive or synoptic. Unlike scientism, dramatism fits the bill, since it recognizes both the awesome creative power of our symbolic abilities and their dependence upon the processes of the nonsymbolic realm. Since both realms are ever-present in human existence, only a terminology that sees the primacy of symbol-use (without losing sight of its nonsymbolic foundation) is appropriate for the treatment of human motivation; because scientism makes symbol-use a secondary, and not primary, phenomenon, Burke finds it appropriate for the study of the natural world, but ill-suited to the study of the social world (1955, p. 269–270). Although Burke insists that the two realms cannot be collapsed into one, scientism begins with a terminology only appropriate to the nonsymbolic realm of motion.

To the extent that the scientistic approach confines its observations to this speechless realm, Burke offers no objection; however, all too often, scientism broadens its focus, extending its terminology to cover the realm of human affairs and behavior—in the process, effectively reducing persons to things, verbalizers to mute nature (1955, p. 260–264). As a result, Burke argues for a strict division of labor between these two approaches: scientism should be confined to examinations of the nonsymbolic, dramatism given domain over the realm of symbolic action.

Although Burke's essay next turns to consideration of dramatism's basic terminology, this discussion continues his extended comparison of these two modes of inquiry. In one sense, he notes, dramatism arrives at its central principles quite empirically, as does scientism. However, instead of deriving its key insights from microscopic comparison or laboratory experiment, Burke argues that dramatistic empiricism entails investigation of the great dramas of human literature. From close examination of these canonical texts, Burke writes, dramatism isolates central principles, principles that hold for the study of nonfiction and fiction alike—for our everyday lives, like works of art, are best approached as products of symbolic action, organized around explicit or implicit dramatic structures. Though he admits that there is never a full parallel between everyday symbolic acts and those identified as the great works of literature, he insists that "co-ordinates *developed from the analysis of formal drama* should certainly be applied to fluctuant material of this sort" (1955, p. 265). Moreover, he claims that both forms of drama are illuminated by the effort.

Burke then lists some of these central, interrelated coordinates that dramatism derives from the study of literature, and thereupon applies to human action more generally. These coordinates are terms quite familiar to the Burkeian scholar, and include the pentad (act, agent, scene, purpose, agency), the pentadic ratios, identification, symbolic purification, transcendence, mystery, and the hortatory negative (1955, p. 268–269). In other words, Burke's essay uses the contrast between dramatism and scientism to make the case for the overall coherence of his perspective: despite the seemingly disparate nature of Burke's key concepts, all are commonly derived from the study of the grand works of human literature. Once these central principles are firmly in hand, Burke argues that dramatistic analysis can begin: the close examination of particular works of symbolic action, with an eye toward the "fearsome appreciation" of the power, and the corresponding danger, of our symbolic prowess (1955, p. 270–271).

Dramatistic Pedagogy: Symbolic Action as Education

Having armed his reader with as comprehensive a background as possible in dramatism, Burke shows its relevance to the field of education—outlining the educational program best suited to the needs and characteristics of the symbol-using animal. A dramatistic philosophy of education, Burke tells us, is founded upon one guiding principle: "man's distinctive trait, his way with symbols, is the source of both his typical accomplishments and his typical disabilities" (1955, p. 271). As befitting an approach identifying both the insights and blindnesses that accompany symbol-use, Burke argues that education should attempt to reveal the points at which particular emphases or perspectives became more hindrance than help, in terms of the perpetuation of the "good life" for all human beings.

In order to carry out such a program, Burke suggests that educational institutions become comprehensive repositories for the products of symbolic action; each institution, in other words, should assemble as complete a collection of human discourse as possible, ranging from literature and biography to the pronouncements of religion and politics—and including even the contemporary lore of advertising. Such a collection would provide the raw material for dramatistic educational efforts; rather than memorizing dates or key quotations, students would be tasked with analyzing this material for what it reveals about the dynamic relationship between symbolic insight and blindness (1955, pp. 271–274). Education would thus become a never-ending reflection upon ourselves, focusing upon the most characteristically human of our products, symbolic discourse. Furthermore, in this way education would truly embody the attempt to learn from the past; we are most likely to avoid repeating the past, Burke tells us, if we do not simply memorize a particular item from history, but "[place] it within the unending human dialogue as a whole" (1955, p. 273).

However, Burke acknowledges, in order to ensure that such "smiling hypochondriasis" pervaded all educational efforts, all courses in the curriculum would have to be restructured. Rather than simply inculcating students in a disciplinary vocabulary, classes would revolve around student analysis of particular examples of symbolic action, efforts designed to reveal and critically evaluate the examples' characteristic insights and blindnesses. More specifically, students would apply the rules and steps of three interrelated procedures to these texts; the first is "indexing" (a method familiar to many Burkeian scholars). This process, which he argues can be applied to any example of symbolic discourse, consists primarily in identifying the key "equations" of the work—or, in other words, answering the question "what equals what?" for this particular author, in this particular text (1955, pp. 274–276).

Following a complete "charting" of the text's equations, the student moves beyond this list, and identifies the ways in which this list reflects not only the author's particular cluster of motives, attitudes, and values, but the constellation of motives, attitudes, and values endemic to her society, at that point in its history. In other words, the index created for each work becomes a way to isolate the elements of an individual's symbol-use that are particularly symptomatic of *her society's* ways of seeing and not seeing. Finally, after completing these two procedures, Burke writes that the student is encouraged to widen the scope of her examination, and comment upon what the results suggest about symbolic action across *all* social and historical contexts. Moving systematically across levels—from individual symbolic act, to social texture, to universal condition—Burke argues that students and educators alike gain heightened insight into the awesome power of human symbolic action (1955, pp. 274–278).

In this sense, dramatism would function as the philosophy guiding the entire educational process, though, as noted earlier, it would still maintain an uneasy truce with scientism, insofar as the latter's terms are properly confined to the realm of nonsymbolic motion (e.g., 1955, p. 282). Burke points out that scientism must, at times, defer to dramatism—at least insofar as scientism itself relies upon an interrelated set of terms for the charting of motion—but he acknowledges the vital role played by scientific terminologies in any curriculum, even one built upon a dramatistic foundation. As a result, Burke does not banish science altogether; he instead reorganizes the curriculum in such a way that science takes its proper place within an ordered system, one oriented by the distinction between symbolic action and nonsymbolic motion. In this way, Burke attempts to respect each discipline's relative autonomy, while still holding to his belief that scientistic terminologies should be confined to their proper subject matters.

First, Burke identifies the portion of the curriculum devoted to tracking the workings of nonsymbolic motion; here we see the traditionally "hard" or "natural" sciences, such as "physics, mechanics, chemistry, astronomy, geology, mineralogy, oceanography" (1955, p. 278). Second is biology, which falls somewhere between the realms of action and motion; biology frequently deals with beings that are not limited to the speechless existence of rocks or water, but still do not display the reflexive, narratival abilities of the human being, the typically symbol-using animal. Burke describes this as the study of "sign-affected motion," or, we might say (using terminology from Burke's [1966] *Language as Symbolic Action*) "motion plus" or "action minus."

Burke admits, of course, that the disciplines focused upon the realm of symbolic action are somewhat more complex to classify. Burke begins by grouping together those disciplines treating "*practical* action" (a subdivision of the larger realm of symbolic action). Here are collected the "ethical (the doing of good), political (the wielding and obeying of authority), economic (the construction and operation of utilities and powers)" (1955, p. 280). Thus, we see the study of political science, sociology, ethics, and economics to be separated from, on Burke's scheme, those fields devoted to the study of *symbolic* action (in a more restricted sense)—though Burke further demarcates this latter grouping into "artificial action" and "neurotic action." Under the heading of "*artificial*" would be the disciplines oriented toward the creations of human symbolicity, including language study, history, philosophy, rhetoric, and theology, as well as the aesthetically oriented fields of literature, art, and music. "*Neurotic* action" would cover the interrelated fields of psychology, psychiatry, and therapy (1955, pp. 280–282).

Action-Motion Revisited: Is Burke's Curriculum Dramatistic Enough?

Burke's discussion of curriculum ends with an appeal for the logic of his classification of the various disciplines listed above. He argues that it reflects little more than a slight reorganization, one simply centered in the recognition of the distinction between symbolic action and nonsymbolic motion—hence it should not be seen as a radical redrawing of the traditional disciplinary lines of demarcation (1955, p. 282). Though largely accurate, I believe that this statement conceals a central weakness in Burke's essay. Indeed, I contend that the educational program laid out in Burke's essay actually *undermines* his philosophical position, thus preventing his curricular proposal from fully embodying dramatism's critique of scientism.

As we have already seen, Burke's suggested curriculum strikes a balance between the study of symbolic action and the study of nonsymbolic motion. Burke consistently argues that, when confined to the proper sphere—that of the speechless realm of motion—the various sciences should be given a good deal of autonomy. However, at the same time, Burke states that the overriding concern of education is attention to the power and subtlety of the "socioanagogic": "there is a 'pageantry' in objects, a 'socioanagogic' element imposed upon them, so far as man is concerned, because man necessarily approaches them in accordance with the genius of his nature as a symbol-human species" (1955, p. 263).

In sum, Burke argues that one of the most overlooked, and thus insidious, forms of symbolic blindness occurs when symbol-users mistake their own linguistic categories, values, and/or hierarchies for the workings of the natural world (e.g., 1955, pp. 261–263, 277, 282, 289, 295). It is tempting at times to read Burke's discussion of the socioanagogic as simply a reflection upon how the things of the world can take on a social dimension—as when the color purple became associated with the trappings of royalty. I believe, however, that it would be a mistake to reduce Burke's argument to these terms. The full significance of Burke's argument—especially for his philosophy of education—can be seen only through a more careful examination of Burke's later writings on his two key terms, symbolic action and nonsymbolic motion.

As we have already discussed, Burke sees the relationship between symbolic action and nonsymbolic motion to be central to any thorough account of human existence; he terms their relationship "the basic polarity" of human existence (1978, p. 809). By defining these terms as polar, Burke highlights the inseparability of action and motion; he stresses that human existence is a necessary interrelation of symbolic and nonsymbolic elements. Thus, while we must recognize that symbol-use is fully dependent upon the motions of the body, we must also admit that "man's *generic animality* is experienced by him in terms of his *specific 'symbolicity'*" (1955, p. 261). Moreover, by discussing the action/motion pair as polar, Burke also stresses that the divide between the two is insurmountable, that these two terms cannot be reduced to one; just as the processes of the nonsymbolic are not dependent upon symbolic discourse, the realm of symbolic action introduces motivations not reducible to simple outgrowths of nonsymbolic motion (1978, p. 814).[6]

However, these two widely-recognized features of Burke's account do not exhaust his discussion of the terms' relationship. Indeed, because the polarity is "unbridgeable," Burke writes that action and motion are related in another sense: symbolic action is necessarily *about* symbolic motion. In other words, Burke contends that symbolic action arises as an attempt to comment upon, or account for, the otherwise mute realm of nonsymbolic motion (1978, pp. 814–815; 1970b, pp. 276–277). It is this aspect of the terminological relationship that Burke labels "*duplication*." Burke summarizes this point in his equation of the symbolic realm with the introduction of "STORY" into nature: "The taste of an orange is a sensation. The words, 'the taste of an orange,' tell a story. They are in the realm of symbolic action, a realm that duplicates the realm of nonsymbolic motion but is not reducible to it (though not possible without it)" (2001, p. 204). Symbolic action is, first and foremost, a reflection upon or story about the nonsymbolic, since symbols confer the ability to talk about the features and elements of our world (2003, pp. 198–199). Burke therefore describes symbolic discourse as a primary duplication of the nonsymbolic: *the translation of the nonsymbolic into the terms of symbolic action.*

This fundamental duplication, symbolic action as the doubling of the nonsymbolic, will, Burke says, "necessary manifest itself in endless variations on the theme of DUPLICATION" (1978, p. 821). Burke provides some examples of this: "Sex is not complete without love lyrics, porn and tracts on sexology. The nonsymbolic motions of springtime are completed in the symbolic action of a spring song" (1978, p. 822). However, for present purposes, even more important is one variation on or extension of this primary duplication, which Burke terms *imitation*.

Burke writes that imitation is one form of duplication, one that indicates not merely the doubling of motion in myriad instances of symbolic action, but the subsequent, symbolic *inspiriting* of the nonsymbolic. Imitation suggests that, as symbol-users, we never gaze simply upon the nonsymbolic, but upon its doppelganger—its spiritual (or symbolic) double. Because symbol-use and human existence are of a piece, we necessarily approach the nonsymbolic through the symbolic, with the result that the former realm is always viewed "in light of" the latter. In explaining this point, Burke offers a parallel from Plato's thought: "once we turn from the realm of motion to the realm of symbolicity and try to envision everything in terms of that ideal symbolic universe, then all actual things in nature become in effect but *partial* exemplars of what they are *in essence*" (1978, p. 821).

Here Burke's discussion offers a Platonic parallel—since we do not look directly upon the nonsymbolic, but rather upon its symbolic duplicate, we only see the nonsymbolic as refracted through the categories of the symbolic. Our symbolic conceptions, in other words, haunt our vision of the nonsymbolic; although we are continually driven to separate human constructions from what is "really there," it is only by using symbolic categories (tied to a particular social group) that we can talk about these "natural" or nonsymbolic elements of existence. The "natural," accordingly, can never be more than the symbolic double of the nonsymbolic realm that we seek.

At the same time, our unique power to linguistically "carve up" the world into recognizable things, events, and people often leads us to forget that the world we see around us was not already so carved when we came onto the scene. Moreover, since our linguistic categories—the terms that we rely upon in our "drawing of the lines"—are dependent upon a particular socio-historical order, the world that we thus encounter is one that is aglow with the norms, values, and assumptions of our particular community. This is the phenomenon Burke defines as "*imitation*," which is the sense in which the things and events of the "natural" world are simply imitations of the symbolic categories, values, and hierarchies through which we approach the nonsymbolic. In short, the stories we tell of the nonsymbolic are so persuasive that we rarely attend to them as duplications; by collapsing the difference between our stories and their subject (the nonsymbolic), we simultaneously invest the things and events of "nature" with the attitudes, categories, and orderings of the symbolic. The world we see correspondingly glistens with the meanings that we provide it; the danger, Burke reminds us, is that this process of duplication and imitation is easily forgotten by human symbol-users.

It is for this reason that Burke, in his essay on education, finds the overriding concern of education to be attention to the socioanagogic—or, in other words, to the processes whereby the world we study is simply the imitation of our symbolic duplication of it. Accounts of the "natural" world consequently reveal more about our particular cultural or disciplinary categories than they do about the "nature" we claim to discuss. It is at this point that we must return to Burke's discussion of education, and its attempt to strike a compromise with the vocabularies of scientism. If we revisit this discussion armed with Burke's discussions of duplication and imitation, I argue, we find that only an education in the nature of symbol-use can successfully combat the unthinking substitution of an imitation for its nonsymbolic "original." In other words, I believe that Burke's radical insight lies in the complex relationship between action and motion—and in the processes by which one is insidiously mistaken for the other. Thus I take his suggested curriculum in "Linguistic Approach to Problems of Education" and, using this concept of imitation, push it "to the end of the line"—in the hopes that this thought experiment will, when added to debate over educational reform, suggest additional, and perhaps different, questions about how best to educate the typically symbol-using animal.

When discussing his suggested curriculum, Burke's (1955) essay strikes a surprising compromise, I feel, given the human tendency to slight the importance of symbolic action:

> Perhaps, the world being what it is, this enterprise [dramatism] could be but one course in a curriculum, rather than the guiding principle behind educational policy in general. But if so, at least it would be conceived of as a kind of "central" or "over-all" course, a "synoptic" project for "unifying the curriculum" by asking the students themselves to think of their various courses in terms of a single distinctive human trait (the linguistic) that imposes its genius upon all particular studies. (1955, p. 274)

Burke's compromise, in other words, involves relinquishing dramatism's preeminent role in the programmatic education of young, impressionable symbol-using animals. Symptomatic of this compromise is his organization of the curriculum—which places dramatism and scientism on more or less equivalent terms. However, if we take Burke's writings seriously, such an arrangement threatens to undermine the importance of Burke's alterations to the traditional curriculum. In other words, though a course of study in dramatism (or even a branch of the curriculum, devoted to "artificial" or "neurotic" action) might implore students to use its teachings to illuminate their studies as a whole, these appeals would be offset by the assumptions reinforced in other, scientistic parts of the curriculum. Indeed, Burke himself tells us as much—in his argument that we are *all too ready* to forget the symbolic constitution of our world. This forgetfulness, I would suggest, cannot be combated on the one hand while it is being facilitated on the other. To reorganize the school along dramatistic lines is not enough, unless this reorganization also creates the best possible environment for the appreciation of the power and danger of human symbolicity—including those symbolic activities recognized under the umbrella of "science."

Said another way, the difficult thing is not to get human symbol-users to see the world in light of their vocabularies (scientific or otherwise). Rather, Burke teaches us that *the difficult thing is to get them to see that this is what they do* when they provide an account of the "natural" world. Consequently, I would have us ask: what insight might be gained through forgetting, for the moment, Burke's compromise with science? What might a dramatistic curriculum, taken "to the end of the line" look like?

A Dramatistic Curriculum: A Return to the Trivium in Early Childhood Education

Translated into dramatistic terms, the goal of each discipline in the school curriculum is to teach students a coherent system of categories and concepts that carves up some portion of the world, for some particular purpose. By adopting a discipline's terminology, students are not simply given a new tool to use in studying the world, but a new version of the world to study—and a version which can be refined through further working-out of that terminology's explicit and implicit implications. Consequently, by retaining something approaching the traditional division of the curriculum, Burke does not go as far as he might in envisioning a dramatistic curriculum; the curriculum proposed in his essay would certainly educate students more fully in the insights of dramatism than in current curricular models, but this education would be limited by the conservative or traditional influence of the other disciplines, especially those based in scientistic terminologies. Burke even admits this, when he notes that "the linguistic approach can be irksome to instructors who would persuade themselves and their classes that they are talking about 'objective reality' even at those times when they happen to be but going through sheerly linguistic operations" (1955, p. 277).

With this curriculum, Burke seems to have accepted that, at best, his program of education will achieve an "uneasy compromise" between dramatism and scientism. However, I believe that his arguments regarding human symbolicity are more revolutionary than the curriculum Burke proposes here. What if we, for heuristic purposes, refused Burke's compromise with scientism? Said another way: what might a curriculum look like that followed Burke's insights to their entelechial end? A curriculum, in other words, that offers a thorough training in the dangers of symbolic duplication and imitation—the dangers inherent to *any* vocabulary? Although a model for such a curriculum might be drawn from many sources, I suggest one with a storied heritage: the medieval trivium. Or, more correctly, a Burkeian version of it: Grammar, Rhetoric, and Symbolic.[7] These three subjects would provide the young symbol-using animal with all (or nearly all) she would need to know in order to gain the necessary admiration of and respect for her (and her culture's) symbolic prowess. To help flesh out this pedagogical thought experiment, let me offer a brief sketch of each of these stages of this entelechial curriculum.

First, in this new dramatistic curriculum, grades one through three would focus specifically upon Grammar. Though this would certainly entail the learning of language and grammar in the familiar sense, there would be a difference in emphasis. Students would be asked, in essence, the following question: what does it mean to sum up and entitle a variety of concrete situations under a unifying word? By calling attention to the students' own halting symbolic efforts, children would be taught to attend specifically to the nature of symbolic discourse—and to the transformations specific to the conversion from orality to literacy, from the spoken symbol to the written. Examples drawn from the students' own discourse could be supplemented by stories or books highlighting the magical relationship between human beings and their world—thus instilling a respect for the transformative nature of symbols, and the transformable nature of the world human symbol-users inhabit. Throughout this course of study, students would be prompted to discuss these examples in terms of a central dramatistic principle: symbolic act as constitution.

Here would be the teaching of the symbolic act as a "decreeing of substance" (e.g., Burke, 1969, p. 373). By learning that symbolic discourse both constitutes and reflects past constitutions, students could then be taught the radical responsibility that travels with such abilities—the responsibility for the creation and maintenance of the world as we know (and are able to know) it. This would be followed by the child's first exposure to the blindness that is the obverse of each insight—the constitution rejected in each new decreeing of substance. In these studies of Grammar, by drawing special attention to the plasticity of language and, subsequently, the world—and by tying this discussion to the initial stages of literacy—the young symbol-user is taught to pay attention to the linked processes of duplication and imitation. Such attention, I believe, would help combat the easy forgetfulness of symbol-use, the forgetfulness that turns an inevitable outgrowth of symbolicity into a destructive (and self-destructive) blindness.

The following three grades, four through six, would then turn to the implications of symbol-use for the creation of cooperation among human beings: Rhetoric. Building from their earlier studies of Grammar, students would first be taught the importance of order (or hierarchy) in symbolic discourse. Through exposure to significant social texts, including stories of the founding of nations (stories, even, about the U.S. Constitution), students would begin to learn that the process of symbolic constitution necessarily results in an ordering of nonsymbolic and symbolic resources—which enshrines a certain hierarchy or valuation within the very substance of the constituted world. Further, attention to such significant social texts allows these young symbol-users to appreciate the particular constellation of values, hierarchies, and relationships common to their culture. By making these elements of symbolic discourse explicit, students would again be shown the responsibility inherent in symbol-use; since symbolic constitutions necessarily establish or reinforce certain orders, then their corresponding insights and blindnesses become all the more important to identify and analyze. Here, then, would be a central defense against our all-too-common inattention to the socioanagogic features of contemporary social life.

Moreover, following such introductory explorations of the relationship between symbolicity and order, students would begin to learn the connection between such orderings and their own individual identities. Here would be the ideal point for Burke's suggested tripartite analysis of accumulated examples of symbolic action. On the basis of their intertwined education in Grammar and Rhetoric, students would be able to take the wide-ranging examples of symbolic discourse accumulated in their school (as per Burke's suggestion) and index them—with an eye toward the relationship between the particular author's constitutions and those of her cultural contemporaries. Examination of the works of others thus prepares the students for the more difficult analysis of their own symbolic efforts to display the signs of a particular social order (or set of orders). Since these studies will come at a time of early adolescence, when such stirrings toward individuality are often met with confusion, hostility, or fear, these studies will be able to draw on highly relevant examples from the students' own lives. Indeed, students' related tendencies toward cliques and victimization would not simply be regulated by the school, but would form material for analysis—since such efforts would be ideal illustrations of the difficulty inherent in the proper formation of identity within the bounds provided by one's culture.

These Rhetorical studies of identity—in relation to the dominant and rebellious orders of the day—then provide the foundation for the final phase of this dramatistic curriculum: the Symbolic. Though Burke himself famously vacillated on the nature of the final projected (and uncompleted) volume on motivation, students completing an intensive six-year study of Grammar and Rhetoric would be better prepared to explore the freedom inherent to adulthood in the symbolic realm.[8] Though their studies to this point would have emphasized the power of symbolicity, the responsibility it entails, and its ultimately social (or cooperative) nature, students studying the Symbolic would also be prepared to grapple with the infinite variation of acts possible to the symbol-using animal.

Here, through examination of great works of human symbolicity, students would begin to see the liberties that can be taken with any social order—liberties that tend to be expressed artistically, through the production of symbolic acts that reveal orders not constituted, reverse accepted orders, reduce an order's complexity to one element, or explore the necessarily infinite surplus of nonsymbolic and symbolic material that resists incorporation into a dominant order. Here also would be one central promise of the dramatistic curriculum—the systematic support of students' artistic impulses and inclinations. Rather than dulling their senses to the possibilities open to the symbol-using animal, such a curriculum forces students to appreciate that social orders are never fixed—just as any human constitution is never fixed, but must be continually reenacted in subsequent constitutions to remain alive and relevant for future generations. This insight makes plain the eternal possibilities for artistic play within (and toward) social structures.

In addition, the studies of the Symbolic would examine the idiosyncratic nature of the individual identity formed by years of socialization. Though ever alert to the ways in which the identities thus formed are unable to cope with the anxieties inherent to human existence (and the pathologies that result), the examination of individual identities as distinct constitutions in and of themselves would likely prove medicinal to the young adolescent striving to arrive at a more mature conception of her own identity. Further, by approaching individual identity as a problem of constitution (and identification), students would be encouraged to recognize both their freedom to constitute a self and the responsibility that self must bear as a member of a cooperative social order. Indeed, such a course of study would underscore the message of the entire curriculum: we can never forget that, as human symbol-users, the world we see everyday—not to mention the selves who "see" it—is formed through systematic symbolic duplication of the nonsymbolic.

This education would thus challenge its students to constitute the selves, and the world, best suited to the maintenance of the "good life" for all.

After completion of this rigorous course of study—and after achieving a requisite facility with the central object of study, symbolic action—students' courses would begin to reflect something more akin to Burke's suggested curriculum from "Linguistic Approach to Problems of Education." In other words, beginning in tenth grade, students would take their knowledge of symbolic action to the study and application of the various terminologies so central to present-day education—including the sciences of motion. Though this would obviously delay students' exposure to the orientation and terminology of such hallowed human projects as science and philosophy, it is at this point that Burke's suggested curriculum makes sense, because it is at this point that students would be properly equipped to discount them as terminologies, like any other.

Having learned about the intricacies of symbolicity for nearly a decade, students would not easily be fooled by terminologies that would seem (to the dramatistically untutored) to simply reveal a "nature" separate from human beings. The graduates of the dramatistic trivium would rather be in a position to recognize scientific vocabularies for what they are: quite helpful (for purposes of prediction and control) duplications of the nonsymbolic, but no more a revelation of an absolute reality than the terminologies of mysticism or poetry. Further, they would be in a position to recognize when symbolic duplications become imitations, when their insights threaten to become dangerous forms of blindness. These students would, in sum, be trained not in what is easy (the unthinking taking of symbolic for nonsymbolic), but what is hard (the recognition of this temptation as endemic to our symbolicity). Contrary to Burke's compromise with scientism in "Linguistic Approach to Problems of Education," this curricular thought experiment suggests that these are the only students that should be learning science, for they are the only ones equipped to analyze it properly as symbolic action.

Conclusion: Is This More Than a Thought Experiment?

I would be disingenuous if I did not admit that the previous section will likely strike most readers as fanciful. I also acknowledge the discomfort that such a position would necessarily produce in other disciplines; I myself felt a certain hesitation in showing this essay to (or even discussing this argument with) my scientistically-oriented colleagues. Further, it does not seem obvious that those in history, theology, or economics would immediately embrace such a proposal, since it similarly relegates their specialized studies to later in the curriculum. As Burke writes of his own experimental reversal of the belief that "words are the signs of things" (his claim that "things are the signs of words"), "There is so much that is substantially correct in this commonsense view . . . we tinker with it at our peril" (1966, p. 363). In terms of the present argument, not only is there "so much that is substantially correct" with our current curricular arrangements, but there is a great deal of danger in taking my thought experiment too far (or too seriously); in a time when science education is under attack from literalist readings of the Bible (e.g., Antolin & Herbers, 2001), I would not want my entelechial curriculum to be mistaken for an extension of such political/theological efforts.

Moreover, a logistical objection might be raised to this educational program, one familiar to readers of Plato. In his *Republic*, which similarly outlines a radical curriculum for the proper education of young symbol-users, a key question arises: who will educate their educators? If, as Burke suggests, contemporary culture reflects a deep-rooted bias toward scientism, technologism, and (ultimately) self-destruction, where will be found the army of educators espousing the virtues of dramatism? As in William James's famous "turtle" anecdote (it is turtles all the way down), a quick response of "college" obviously pushes the question back but does not answer it. Thus, even if we were to spontaneously adopt such a curriculum as a society, we would seem singularly ill-equipped to organize and implement it.

Although I recognize the validity of these objections, I would suggest that there is also much that is valuable in this hypothetical curriculum; the central insight of dramatism lies in its analysis of the workings of symbolic action, and especially in Burke's emphasis upon the temptation to subtly transform our symbolic duplications into imitations. When discussing his own experimental assertion, Burke writes that "even if we didn't dare assert that it should flatly replace the traditional view, we still might hope that it could supply a needed modification of that view, like adding an adjective to a noun" (1966, p. 363). Indeed, though there is increasing recognition of the relationship between language and the teaching of math and science (e.g., Sensenbaugh, 1992; Omer, 2002; Bruna, Vann, & Escudero, 2007), this awareness could be deepened through an incorporation of a more rigorous, dramatistic understanding of symbolic constitution. Moreover, Burkeian studies of Rhetoric could offer a radically new perspective on the origin—and *persistence*—of gender bias in science, and in science education specifically (e.g., Tindall & Hamil, 2004). Similarly, Burke would applaud attempts to organize early childhood education around operations of sorting and classifying (e.g., Platz, 2004), as well as attempts to move away from transmission or "conduit" models of education (e.g., Gozzi, 1998)—thus redefining "literacy" in terms of relational, contextual performances (e.g., May & Wright, 2007; Smyth, 2007; Whitehead, 2007). At the same time, Burke's discussions of our human symbolic existence suggest that our educational problems—and the solutions—are even more fundamental than recognized within this literature; even these progressive attempts do not fully grasp the vital role played by symbolicity in the constitution, and ordering, of our world. In this way, we might profitably take the hypothetical curriculum proposed here, and use it to strengthen the theoretical foundations of our current (and less problematic) programs of reform.

Indeed, I would argue that, whether discussing educational programs or social interaction, we ignore Burke's insights on action and motion at our peril. We live in a moment when the constitutions "life," "death," "parent," and "marriage" are not recognized as such—and where the debates over these issues provide case studies of the symbolic imitation of the nonsymbolic. This calls for the study of Grammar. We live in a time when, over three hundred years after Francois Bernier's division of human beings into five separate "races" (e.g.,Bernasconi & Lott, 2000), something as "natural" as prehistoric human remains, found on the North American continent, are inspirited (at least for some white supremacists) with the category "Caucasoid" (e.g., Hitt, 2005). This calls for the study of Rhetoric. Finally, we live in a time when individuality is measured by the uniqueness of one's cellular ring tone—but a child's disruptive activity in an over-structured environment results in diagnosis and medication. This calls for the study of the Symbolic.

Mining the dramatistic curriculum outlined above, drawing out the central insights of Burkeian dramatism, I believe that we can significantly contribute to the debates over educational policy and reform—and, in this way, raise a generation more qualified to intelligently confront these (and other) challenges endemic to human symbolicity and sociality. Educational policies which do not begin with Burkeian, dramatistic premises largely remain blind to the workings of symbolic action—and, in future generations, will result in little more than continued fascination with our imitations of the nonsymbolic realm. These are the stakes, I argue; this is why Burke's essay on education is as relevant today as it was when written fifty years ago.

Burke ends his essay by touching upon some of the central implications of his philosophy of education. He argues, in Deweyan fashion, that the dramatistic approach to education is the one best designed to reconcile the individual and her community, as well as the various world communities in their shifting forms of alliance and enmity. This is because, as Burke contends, a dramatistic philosophy of education, with its focus on the nature of symbolicity, institutionalizes an attitude of tolerance and understanding—a vital attitude when the alternative is rejection, victimage, and violence. I thus see Burke's essay as leaving us with a critical question, or perhaps a challenge: by recognize the necessary intertwining of symbolic and nonsymbolic, can we construct a curriculum better suited to the education—and, given the scope of modern technology, long-term *survival*—of the characteristically symbol-using animal?

NOTES

1. Although contemporary scholarship recognizes that the masculine is not a universal, I have not changed the wording of quotes. My own usage, though, reflects my commitment to the use of inclusive language in scholarship.

2. This quote is taken from an unpublished letter from Burke to Wesley Hartley, 12 January, 1959, from the author's private collection. A carbon can be found in the Kenneth Burke Papers, housed in the Rare Books and Manuscripts Collection, Pattee Library, Pennsylvania State University, State College, PA. All subsequent letters from this collection will be parenthetically indicated by "KB."

3. Burke discusses the context of the planning of the essay in an August 20, 1953 letter to Hugh Dalziel Duncan. This letter is part of the Hugh Dalziel Duncan Papers, housed in Special Collections, Morris Library, Southern Illinois University, Carbondale, Illinois.

4. In this section of the essay, Burke argues another related point (and makes it clear that they are separate, though connected, points): dramatism is a literal account of human symbol-use, not simply a metaphor, as in "All the world's a stage." For more on this specific point, and on the difference between ontological/epistemological and literal/metaphorical approaches, see Crable (2000), "Defending Dramatism as Ontological and Literal."

5. Burke would not have us forget, however, that the two realms interpenetrate. For example, the drive for "success" can have quite physiological effects; our definition of what counts as "food" is dependent upon socialization. Or, as he puts it more generally, "the two realms must be *interwoven* in so far as man's *generic animality* is experienced by him in terms of his *specific 'symbolicity'*" (1955, p. 261).

6. For more discussion of this aspect of the action/motion polarity, see Crable (2003), "Symbolizing Motion."

7. Here I am referring to Burke's projected three-volume work on human motivation, *On Human Relations*, which resulted in only two published works during Burke's lifetime, *A Grammar of Motives* and *A Rhetoric of Motives*. The third and final volume of this trilogy was to be *A Symbolic of Motives*, but was unfinished. For Burke's earliest discussion of his planned trilogy (which changed a great deal over time), see his *Grammar* (e.g., xv–xviii). My use of the terms Grammar, Rhetoric, and Symbolic refer to their respective subject areas consistent with Burke's view.

8. With William Rueckert as the editor and Burke as the author, Burke's unfinished book was finally published in 2006 by Parlor Press under the title, *Essays Toward a Symbolic of Motives: 1950-1955*.

References

Antolin, M. F., & Herbers, J. M. (2001). Perspective: Evolution's struggle for existence in America's public schools. *Evolution, 55*(12), 2379–2388.

Bernasconi, R., & Lott, T. L. (Eds.) (2000). *The idea of race.* Indianapolis, IN: Hackett.

Bruna, K. R., Vann, R., & Escudero, M. P. (2007). What's language got to do with it?: A case study of academic language instruction in a high school 'English Learner Science' class. *Journal of English for Academic Purposes, 6*, 36–54.

Burke, K. (1955). Linguistic approach to problems of education. In N. B. Henry (Ed.), *Modern philosophies and education: The fifty-fourth yearbook of the National Society for the Study of Education, Part 1 of 2* (pp. 259–303). Chicago: National Society for the Study of Education.

Burke, K. (1966). *Language as symbolic action: Essays on life, literature, and method.* Berkeley, CA: University of California Press.

Burke, K. (1969). *A grammar of motives.* Berkeley, CA: University of California Press. (Original work published 1945)

Burke, K. (1970a). Poetics and communication. In H. E. Kiefer & M. K. Munitz (Eds.), *Perspectives in education, religion, and the arts* (pp. 401–418). New York: SUNY Press.

Burke, K. (1970b). *The rhetoric of religion: Studies in logology.* Berkeley, CA: University of California Press. (Original work published 1961)

Burke, K. (1973). *The philosophy of literary form: Studies in symbolic action* (3rd ed.). Berkeley, CA: University of California Press. (Original work published 1941)

Burke, K. (1978). (Nonsymbolic) motion/(symbolic) action. *Critical Inquiry, 4*(4), 809–838.

Burke, K. (2001). Sensation, memory, imitation/and story. In G. Henderson & D. C. Williams (Eds.), *Unending conversations: New writings by and about Kenneth Burke* (pp. 202–205). Carbondale, IL: Southern Illinois University Press.

Burke, K (2003). Theology and logology. In W. H. Reuckert & A. Bonadonna (Eds.), *On human nature: A gathering while everything flows, 1967–1984* (pp. 172–209). Berkeley, CA: University of California Press.

Burke, K. (2006). *Essays toward a symbolic of motives: 1950-1955.* (W. Rueckert, Ed.). West Lafayette, IN: Parlor Press.

Crable, B. (2000). Defending dramatism as ontological and literal. *Communication Quarterly, 48*, 323–342.

Crable, B. (2003). Symbolizing motion: Burke's rhetoric and dialectic of the body. *Rhetoric Review, 22*(2), 121–137.

Gozzi, Jr., R. (1998, Spring). The conduit metaphor in the rhetoric of education reform: A critique of hidden assumptions. *The New Jersey Journal of Communication, 6*(1), 81–89.

Hitt, J. (2005, July). Mighty white of you: Racial preferences color America's oldest skulls and bones. *Harper's*, 39–55.

May, S., & Wright, N. (2007). Secondary literacy across the curriculum: Challenges and possibilities. *Language and Education, 21*(5), 370–376.

Omer, L. S. (2002, Winter). Successful scientific instruction involves more than just discovering concepts through inquiry-based activities. *Education, 123*(2), 318–321.

Platz, D. L. (2004, Fall). Challenging young children through simple sorting and classifying: A developmental approach. *Education, 125*(1), 88–96.

Sensenbaugh, R. (1992). *Reading and writing across the high school science and math curriculum*. Bloomington, IN: EDINFO Press.

Smyth, J. (2007). Pedagogy, school culture and teacher learning: Towards more durable and resistant approaches to secondary school literacy. *Language and Education, 21*(5), 406–419.

Staton, A. Q., & Peeples, J. A. (2000, October). Educational reform discourse: President George Bush on "America 2000." *Communication Education, 49*(4), 303–319.

Tindall, T., & Hamil, B. (2004, Winter). Gender disparity in science education: The causes, consequences, and solutions. *Education, 125*(2), 282–295.

Whitehead, D. (2007). Literacy assessment practices: Moving from standardized to ecologically valid assessments in secondary schools. *Language and Education, 21*(5), 434–452.

10 Educational Trajectories for Open and Democratic Societies: Kenneth Burke's "Linguistic Approach"

David Cratis Williams

In an important but long neglected essay[1] entitled, "Linguistic Approach to Problems of Education" (1954), American rhetorical theorist and critic Kenneth Burke proposed to approach education in a deductive manner; that is, starting with an ontological premise: "Beginning absolutely, we might define man as the typically language-using, or symbol-using, animal. And on the basis of such a definition, we could argue for a 'linguistic approach to the problems of education'" (p. 259). On the next page, Burke reiterates this basic premise, but adds an admonitory twist: "Man literally is a symbol-using animal. He really does approach the world symbol-wise (and symbol-foolish)" (p. 260). Burke proceeds to argue that education ought to stress this generative dimension of who we are: our symbolicity. If individually each of us is a "symbol-using, symbol-making, and symbol-misusing animal" (Burke, 1966, p. 6), and if collectively we engage each other in what Burke has called "a great *drama* of *human* relations" (1954, p. 263; emphasis in original), then our educational processes should start from those premises as well, and in so doing we should dwell upon the ways that we use symbols and that they use us. Dwelling upon the ways that we use symbols and the ways that symbols use us will lead us toward what Jessica Enoch (2004) calls "critical reflexivity," or what Burke talks about in teleological terms as "maximum consciousness" (1984, p. 171).

For Burke, the attainment of maximum consciousness is possible only within a "comic" orientation toward the world, or through what Burke calls "the comic frame":

> The comic frame is charitable, but at the same time it is not gullible. It keeps us alive to the ways in which people "cash in on" their moral assets, and even use moralistic euphemisms to conceal purely materialistic purposes—but it can recognize as much without feeling its disclosure to be the last word on human motivation. Dealing with man in society, it requires maximum awareness of the complex forensic material accumulated in sophisticated social structures. By astutely gauging situation and personal resources, it promotes the realistic sense of one's limitations. . . . (1984, p. 107)

The comic frame is, according to Burke, the ideal perspective for criticism: "whatever poetry may be, criticism had best be comic" (1984, p. 107). Comic criticism is critically reflexive; it makes "a man the student of himself" (Burke, 1984, p. 171). Indeed, conceived of as "a man" being a "student of himself" (coming to "know thyself"), the comic frame is already itself framed as both a critically reflexive pedagogy and a methodology for self-consciousness, and as such "maximum consciousness" is a more meaningful educational objective than factual knowledge:

> The comic frame, as a *method of study* (man as eternal journeyman) is a better personal possession, in this respect, than the somewhat empty accumulation of facts such as people greedily cultivate when attempting to qualify in "Ask Me Another" questionnaires, where they are invited to admire themselves for knowing the middle name of Robert Louis Stevenson's favorite nephew (if he had one). Mastery of this sort (where, if "Knowledge is power," people get "power" vicariously by gaining possession of its "insignia," accumulated facts) may somewhat patch up a wounded psyche; but a more adventuresome equipment is required, if one is to have a private possession marked by mature social efficiency. . . . In sum, the comic frame should enable people *to be observers of themselves, while acting*. Its ultimate would not be *passiveness*, but *maximum consciousness*. One would 'transcend' himself by noting his own foibles. (Burke, 1984, pp. 170–171)

As Rueckert (1994) reminds us, "Burke is not really interested in comedy as a dramatic form but as an attitude toward history, *a habit of mind*, a perspective, a critical/analytic way of looking at and examining the drama of human relations as it unfolds in history" (p. 117; emphasis added). Moreover, the maximum self-consciousness (as a habit of mind) that Burke sees as the telos of what we might call "an ontologically appropriate" approach to education is a product of systematic critical reflexivity on "situation and personal resources," on ourselves as actors in our own dramas.

In this essay I begin by establishing dramatism as the launch pad for Burke's approach to education. From here I explore two orbits of critical reflexivity. First is self-awareness through critical reflexivity of the dialectical (and ironic) structure of symbols themselves, thereby facilitating becoming symbol-wise rather than symbol-foolish. This involves cultivating a "fearful appreciation" of *symbolic action*. The second orbit is self-awareness of the social and political *enactment* of symbolic motives that converts the dialectic of symbolic action into the drama of human relations. Politically, the ideal form for enactment of this drama is democracy, and thus Burke's idealization of education is concomitantly an idealization of democracy. The purposes of this essay are to offer a reading of Burke's "linguistic approach" to education, situating it within Burke's "dramatistic" perspective, to contextualize that approach in contemporary problems of and prospects for democratic culture, particularly as the concept of "democracy" itself is understood from within a Burkeian perspective, and finally to discuss the implications of the Burkeian approach to education as they relate to the revitalization of democratic culture in the United States.

Dramatistic Approach to Education

Burke's approach, in the words of Enoch (2004), constitutes "a pedagogy of critical reflection" (p. 273). Before proceeding further, it is important to contextualize Burke's approach in relation to the contemporary curricular landscape, with its heavy emphasis on "math and science" and the accumulation of factual knowledge capable of being objectively tested. What Burke proposes is fundamentally a *way* of looking at human symbol-use, not a limitation on *what* symbol-use should be looked at; that is, the "linguistic approach to problems of education" is a *perspective* on the *problems* of education, not a new educational program ready to cast out the old. Two keys to Burke's proposal are his dramatistic views of meaning and meaning creation, and analysis of linguistic tendencies.

Meanings and Meaning Creation

The dramatistic approach to education is an *encompassment* of the dominant modes of education; it does not erase but rather supplements.[2] Burke's orientation is evident in his depiction of a corresponding relationship between "semantic" and "poetic" meaning. Burke describes "semantic" meaning as relatively objective and factual, meeting "operational" tests, and fulfilling "the ideal of the logical positivists"; "the semantic ideal" is "the aim *to evolve a vocabulary that gives the name and address of every event in the universe*" (1973a, p. 141; emphasis in original). Meanings are thus either right or wrong, correct or incorrect: "The either-or test would represent the semantic ideal" (Burke, 1973a, p. 144). "Poetic" meaning is not the opposite of semantic meaning; it "*impinges* upon semantic meaning" without ruling it out (Burke, 1973a, pp. 142–143; emphasis in original). Poetic meaning is in the both-and: for instance, whereas semantic meaning "would try to *cut away*, to *abstract*, all emotional factors that complicate the objective clarity of meaning," poetic meaning "would derive its vision from the maximum *heaping up* of all these emotional factors, playing them off against one another, inviting them to reinforce and contradict one another, and seeking to make this active participation itself a major ingredient of the vision" (Burke, 1973a, p. 148; emphasis in original). The process is not without order; in a sense, poetic meaning must be adequate to "situation and personal resources": "'Poetic' meanings, then, cannot be disposed of on the true-or-false basis. Rather, they are related to one another like a set of concentric circles, of wider and wider scope. Those of wider diameter do not categorically eliminate those of narrower diameter. There is, rather, a progressive *encompassment*" (Burke, 1973a, p. 144; emphasis in original). The "poetic ideal would attempt to *attain a full moral act* by attaining a perspective *atop all the conflicts of attitude*" (Burke, 1973a, p. 148; emphasis in original).

This "maximum heaping up" of concentric layers of poetic meaning for the attainment of a "full moral act" is analogous to the sort of critically reflexive maximum self consciousness that Burke sets as the ideal for a dramatistic approach to education, and just as poetic meaning situates itself "atop" semantic meaning via "progressive encompassment," so too does Burke's linguistic approach to education, derived from the premise that humans are symbol-using (and mis-using) animals, situate itself atop educational practices that flow from the more restricted ontological premises, such as humans are "rational animals." As symbol-using (and mis-using) animals, we should seek through critical reflexivity to become maximally self-aware in our use of symbols and, reciprocally, their use of us. In the next sections of the paper, I will discuss Burke's understanding of what he sees as inherent tendencies of symbol systems, especially language. These are tendencies that often culminate in symbols using us (and making us symbol-foolish). He couches his perspective on language within a theory he calls "dramatism." After that, I will delineate a few of the dramatistic critical procedures, procedures that, taken together, constitute "correctives" to the potentially dangerous tendencies of language. A better understanding of the nature of our symbol systems combined with rigorous and routine application of dramatistic "correctives" constitute Burke's approach to education, his "pedagogy of critical reflection," an approach designed to guide us toward maximum self-consciousness.

Analysis of Linguistic Tendencies

Consistent with Burke's ontologically framed starting premise—that we are by nature symbol-using animals—a major part of Burke's "linguistic approach" to education is to help us as symbol using animals become more self-consciously aware of the processes of symbol use, including especially an awareness of how symbols may come not simply to frame our choices for us but indeed to make those choices. Although the full dramatistic system is quite extensive, I will limit my discussion to two inter-related tendencies that Burke sees within human symbol use.

Dialectical Pressure for Linguistic Purity

Burke is fond of paraphrasing Samuel T. Coleridge's observation that although we created symbols in order to generate categories by which to help us think, we too often allow those very categories to do our thinking for us. That is, in clarifying our concepts—or categories—we work diligently, even methodically, to make the categories purely distinct, to make them "pure" categories. Coleridge equates this with "common sense": when a "distinction has been so naturalized and of such general currency that the language itself does as it were *think* for us (like the sliding rule which is the mechanic's safe substitute for arithmetical knowledge) we then say, that it is evident to *common sense*" (1951, p. 158; emphasis in original). Burke relates this process to "substance-thinking," which he sees as an inherent tendency, an "entelechial" pressure or perfectionist goad, within human language use: "we take it that the principle of substance (and consubstantiality) cannot be eliminated from language. . . . [W]e would at least treat 'substance-thinking' as a universal motive of *language*" (1954, p. 260n; emphasis in original). This "substance-thinking" motive, or essentializing tendency, that Burke ascribes to language itself can in turn become enacted by humans when we take our categories, and our thinking, "to the end of the line." When a category is purified, or taken to the end of the line, murky areas of overlap between or among concepts are cleansed: differences become rigidified; indeed, they move toward antithesis, and "this is not that" becomes "this is opposed to that," and it gets enacted hierarchically as "this rather than that." The *difference* of dialectic becomes enacted as the *agon* of drama (see Williams, 1989).

Burke describes this "dialectic process" in the essay "Semantic and Poetic Meaning," which is included in his volume *The Philosophy of Literary Form*:

> ... there is a "dialectical process" whereby a difference becomes converted into an antithesis. You have, for example, noted that when two opponents have been arguing, though the initial difference in their positions may have been slight, they tend under the "dialectical pressure" of their drama to become eventually at odds in everything. No matter what one of them happens to assert, the other (responding to the genius of the contest) takes violent exception to it—and vice versa. Thus, similarly we find the *differences* between "Bourgeois" and "proletarian" treated, under dialectical pressure, as an *absolute antithesis*, until critics, accustomed to thinking by this pat schematization, become almost demoralized at the suggestions that there might be a "margin of overlap" held in common between different classes. (1973a, p. 139; emphasis in original)

The conversion of difference into antithesis/opposition gives rise to seemingly intractable polarization, which in turn contains motives for conflict and, potentially, war (Williams, 1989; Enoch, 2004). When this process is perfected, the categories do in fact do our thinking for us, as we rather automatically sort and act in the world in accordance with our hierarchical construction of categories.

Stereotypes offer a rather straightforward illustration of this: an observation of cultural difference, let us say, becomes purified and, in the process, rigidified or even reified, which in turn invites a hierarchical ordering of preference ("this rather than that" is but a restatement of "this is better than that"). "They" are that way; "we" are this way. Our way is better; their way is worse. Thus, we are better and they are worse. In this manner, a stereotype becomes a rigid construct that orders the world around us—or at least the people in the world—and we no longer recognize, perceive, or think about individual differences. Instead, the category stands in place of the individual, and the category does our thinking for us and makes our value choices for us. Just as this process operates in stereotyping, so too does it operate in language generally.

In this non-reflexive enactment of symbolic categories, we become somnambulant. Burke offers a description of propaganda and "ideology" to illustrate this process:

> We hear of "brainwashing," of schemes whereby an "ideology" is imposed upon people. But should we stop at that? Should we not also see the situation the other way around? For was not the "brainwasher" also similarly motivated? An "ideology" is like a god coming down to earth, where it will inhabit a place pervaded by its presence. An "ideology" is like a spirit taking up its abode in a body: it makes that body hop around in certain ways; and that same body would have hopped around in different ways had a different ideology happened to inhabit it. (1966, p. 6)

In Burkeian terms, action has turned to motion: the categories of the ideology have come to do our thinking for us, and the mediation of human consciousness (and the *action* of human choice that is thereby implied) has been supplanted by the rigidity of the categories (see Burke, 1978). We as humans somnambulantly dance the tune called by our symbols.

Identification and Perfection

If we come to think through our creation of symbols and the categories and meanings that they in turn create for us, we come to engage the world and each other through our enactments of those meanings. The process of using symbols or of naming is neither objective nor neutral; indeed, "something of the rhetorical motive comes to lurk in every 'meaning,' however purely 'scientific' its pretensions" (Burke, 1950, p. 172). That is, where there is language, there is meaning, and where there is meaning, there is persuasion; or, as Burke puts it, "Wherever there is persuasion, there is rhetoric. And wherever there is 'meaning,' there is 'persuasion'" (1950, p. 172). That which binds this process together is identification. We identify the world and each other through our language, our symbolic screens; psychologically, we may come to identify *with* the world and each other through some of those screens, and we come to be identified by, or to gain identity through, this process.

Burke views identification as psychological linkage between an inner "I" and both the perceptual categories, the thinking, facilitated through our symbol-use and the "attitudes" and roles that we absorb through social interaction. The term "identification" is common enough, but what Burke offers is a rhetorical and psychological appropriation of the term, an embedding of it within the theory of dramatism as a way of understanding human motives. Burke writes.

> The key term of the "new" rhetoric would be "identification," which can include a partially "unconscious" factor

to appeal. "Identification" at its simplest is also a deliberate device, as when the politician seeks to identify himself with his audience. In this respect, its equivalents are plentiful in Aristotle's *Rhetoric*. But such identification can also be an end, as when people earnestly yearn to identify themselves with some group or other. Here they are not necessarily being acted upon by a conscious external agent, but may be acting upon themselves to this end. In such identification there is a partially dreamlike, idealistic motive, somewhat compensatory to real differences or divisions, which the rhetoric of identification would transcend. (Burke, 1951, p. 203)

In *A Rhetoric of Motives* (1950), Burke describes the sweep of identification in similar terms: "And identification ranges from the politician who, addressing an audience of farmers, says, 'I was a farm boy myself,' through the mysteries of social status, to the mystic's devout identification with the source of all being" (p. xiv). The conscious identifying by the speaker with his/her audience constitutes a strategy of persuasion, a faculty or means of persuasion. The "unconscious" or "partially dreamlike" identification of an audience with a speaker (or of a speaker with the categories of his/her own discourse) constitutes a form of self-persuasion, culminating entelechially in a mystical merger of self and the ultimate ground for self. Indeed, the shadowy substance of self participates at all registers in the very process of identification (much in the sense that a thing's end may be understood as its essence, or substance; see Burke, 1950, pp. 13, 19), and at all levels the process of identification is itself both dialectical and rhetorical. Burke (1950) writes,

> A man can be his own audience, insofar as he, even in his secret thoughts, cultivates certain ideas or images for the effect he hopes they may have upon him; he is here what Mead would call an "I" addressing its "me"; and in this respect he is being rhetorical quite as though he were using pleasant imagery to influence an outside audience rather than one within. (p. 38)

However, since this rhetoric is reciprocal within the structure of the dialectic, is a "parliamentary wrangle" (p. 38), the "me" also "addresses" the "I," and just as we may yearn "unconsciously" to identify with others, we may also yearn "unconsciously" to identify more thoroughly with aspects of ourselves which we may have repressed or differentiated from our current configurations of identity (for a discussion of Burke and Freudianism, see Wright,

1994). It is this complicated dialectic which, through the agency of identification, is constitutive of identity formation. In *A Rhetoric of Motives* (1950), Burke elaborates on this process:

> The individual person, striving to form himself in accordance with the communicative norms that match the cooperative ways of his society, is by the same token concerned with the rhetoric of identification. To act upon himself persuasively, he must variously resort to images and ideas that are formative. Education ("indoctrination") exerts such pressure upon him from without; he completes the process from within. If he does not somehow act to tell himself (as his own audience) what the various brands of rhetoricians have told him, his persuasion is not complete. Only those voices from without are effective which can speak in the language of a voice within. (p. 39)

Through both the inward dialectic of, using Mead's terms, an "I" and a "me," a dialectic which may be conscious or not, and the outward dialectic between the self and the external world, including its multiform persuasive inducements of both a symbolic and nonsymbolic nature, a dialectic which again may be conscious or not, identity is born.[3]

In weaving together his dramatized incorporation and adaptations of Mead's symbolic interactionism and Freudianism, Burke constitutes a rhetorical understanding of "self" and human identity. Ambrester (1974) suggests that in Burke's framework, "the self is a dynamic process of becoming—a quest for identity" (p. 206). This quest for identity proceeds through a dialectic of outward identifications and inward critique of those identifications; in addition, whether conscious or unconscious, identification is constitutive of our construction of "self" and is motivational in the engagement of self in society: through our identifications we construct both our personal and our social identities.

As early as *Attitudes Toward History* (1937/1984; first edition in 1937) Burke saw these connections: "Identity is not *individual*." A person "'identifies himself' with all sorts of manifestations beyond himself" (p. 263; emphasis in original). In this sense, "'identification' is hardly other than a name for the *function of sociality*" (pp. 266–67; emphasis in original). Amid these tangled webs of identification, we strive toward identity. Some 35 years later, Burke (1973b) makes the same point: "Even when considered close up, the identity of the 'self' or 'person' becomes part of a collective texture involving language, property, family, reputation, social roles, and so on—elements not reducible to the individual" (p. 265). From within this dissolution, Burke

(1973b) suggests, a man "may *identify* himself" with "some special body more or less clearly defined (family, race, profession, church, social class, nation, etc., or various combinations of these)" (p. 268; emphasis in original).

Yet identification for Burke is not just social (as in imitation of role-playing behaviors) but also always linguistic: we identify both with and through our linguistic distinctions. For instance, I might come to make distinctions among humans based upon a scheme of racial categories (as Hitler did with the scheme of "Aryan" and "non-Aryan" races). I am able to order my perceptions through this scheme, categorizing people accordingly. Moreover, I could place myself within this ordering, thereby identifying with either "Aryan" or "non-Aryan." Unabated, the logic of my identification might compel me to affiliate with those similarly identified, and against those identified otherwise. The "purer" the category, the more compelling the identification may become, and the more closed our sense of identity becomes.[4] For Burke it is not so much "I think, therefore I am," but rather "I am, at least in part, what I think."

Just as a linguistic category undergoes "dialectic pressure" for perfection, so too do our corresponding identifications (and identities). The "entelechial" perfection of a mode of identification (e.g., I am a neo-conservative) makes one somnambulant with respect to enactments emanating from that identity. Here is where our categories "sleep walk" us through "automatic" responses to situations; that is, they do our thinking for us. In Burke's terms, "action" has turned to "motion." This is at the end-of-the-line, and it is in Burke's perspective precisely this which is to be most feared, for herein lie the motives not only for scapegoating but also for war, including the "perfected" war of nuclear obliteration (see Williams, 1989).

If the process by which linguistic difference can transform into hierarchy, orders of preference, and polarities (that are but incipient conflicts and the loci of motives for war and destruction) is one characterized by somnambulant symbolic use (enacting our "symbol-foolishness"), then perhaps the way out of such a calamitous condition is greater self-reflexive awareness of how we use symbols and how they use us. Self-awareness of these processes opens space for critical intervention, for arguing with self or others for changing course before coming to the end of the line. This is the orientation of comic criticism; as Rueckert (1994) puts it, comic criticism

> is a frame of acceptance dedicated to the amelioration of individual lives in society, largely by means of knowledge of human error [in symbol use] and a whole series of salvation and transcendence devices that stress a both/and rather than an absolutist either/or, US versus THEM attitude. It is

> a mind-set committed to negotiation, education, and peace; one that is always opposed to the closed confrontational mind-set that so often leads to violence, killing, and war. In fact, Burke even says that war and the comic perspective are incompatible. . . . (p. 118)

Therein lies the imperative for a linguistic approach to education: to promote critical reflexivity and self-consciousness as antidotes for reductionist rationality that pursues categorical thinking for its own sake, that takes its categories to the end of the line, and that is conflictual and driven toward conquest, both of others and of nature.

Self-Awareness through Critical Reflexivity

Traditional approaches to education that are based on such partial anecdotes as "humans are rational animals" reinforce a reductionistic motive structure. Burke instead suggests that a "linguistic approach" to education, based on the more encompassing anecdote of "humans as symbol-using animals," would work to develop a critical self-reflexivity about symbol use, both of others and ultimately of our own selves as well.[5] Self-awareness through critical reflexivity of the dialectical (and ironic) structure of symbols themselves thereby facilitates becoming symbol-wise rather than symbol-foolish. In promoting this sort of maximum self consciousness as the desired objective of our educational processes, Burke offers an array of pedagogical techniques designed to move students along the path toward such critical awareness. Two that I will discuss here are indexing and pentadic analysis.[6]

Indexing and Cluster Analysis of Structures of Symbolic Action

Indexing is a method of close textual analysis designed to disclose intratextual structures of meaning. When indexing a text, the critic "charts" word usages and relationships among them, "clustering" them into relational patterns. It is, Burke suggests, "a methodic study of symbolic action" (1954, p. 269). Although Burke is writing of literary criticism specifically, the method, I believe, can be generalized to all forms of symbolic action for which there is a text that can be analyzed:

> [T]he study of symbolic action in particular literary works should begin with the charting of "equations." That is: When you consult a text, from which you hope to derive insights as regards our human quandaries in general, you begin by asking yourself "what equals what in this text?"

And then, next, "what follows what in this text?" (1954, p. 270).

Burke later elaborated more fully on these indexical equations, adding the questions, "What opposes what?" and "What becomes what?" A rubric of four intratextual structures of symbolic action emerges: *association* (what goes with what?), *opposition* (what opposes what?), *progression* (what leads to what?), and *transformation* (what becomes what?). (See Burke, 1964; Rueckert, 1969, esp. pp. 24–27) These indexical equations provide a "kind of 'short-cut' which we consider primary" in "the analysis of particular linguistic structures" (1954, p. 270).

Indexing the structures of symbolic action in a text becomes a way of "seeing" those structures, of a critical "yielding" to the text without "surrendering" to it: "The study of such 'equations' is a way of *yielding without demoralization*" (1954, p. 270; emphasis in original). It facilitates what Burke calls symbolic "hypochondriasis," which is his term for the sort of self-reflexivity practiced by a hypochondriac. In Rueckert's interpretation, "hypochondriasis" "means that one should study the symptoms and causes of one's own illness in order to better understand it so that one can learn how to treat it and live with it" (1994, p. 121). At the point of hypochrondriasis, critical reflexivity becomes a possibility, and with that possibility comes as well the possibility of greater freedom from symbol-foolishness:

> . . . consider the difference between the equation "reason equals respect for authority" and the equation "reason equals distrust of authority." Such equations are studied, first of all, in a non-normative, nonpreferential way, the assumption being that the best function of education is in giving us a free approach to such linkages, which otherwise tend to call forth automatic responses, making us in effect somnambulists. (1954, p. 270n)

Indexing is a preparatory step toward a "full moral act": it has the potential to rouse us from a somnambulant condition, to become more self-aware of linguistic compulsions (our own as well as those of others): "For, if certain elements equal 'good' and certain elements equal 'bad' (or, what is often more important, if certain elements equal 'socially superior' and certain elements equal 'socially inferior'), then in contemplating the 'dynamics' of such 'equations' (their implied hortatory value), do we not contemplate the very essence of human foibles?" (1954, pp. 270–271)

"Ratios" and Pentadic Analysis

Although dramatism's pedagogy of critical reflexivity starts with indexing, it does not end there. Through indexing, a critic can discern structural equations of symbolic action operating within a text; through pentadic analysis, a critic can discern the *motives* of a given text. For Burke, all texts contain motive structures; moreover, motives, in Burke's understanding, are *in* language: they *are* the pentadic structures Burke calls "ratios." These motive structures can be discerned through diligent application of a set of terms derived methodically from the contemplation of drama: Act, Scene, Agent, Agency, and Purpose (see Burke, 1945, pp. x–xvi, 3–20, 127–320). These are then structured by the text into the featured or dominant relationships, which Burke calls *ratios* and by which he may be harkening toward the radical root of the term, for example, "reason." The motive structure is in the enacted relationships among these terms as they appear in featured ratios.

What do these look like? A good example comes from Brummett's (1979) analysis of the discourse of pro and anti gay rights arguments in Florida several years ago. The analysis represents the pro gay rights argument as claiming homosexuality is an expression of who a person *is;* therefore, suppression or non-recognition of homosexuality is a denial of identity and personhood and a denial of their right to enact their identity. This is an agent/act ratio: the nature of the agent (person) shapes ("determines") the act. The argument against recognition of gay rights claimed that homosexual *acts* make people into homosexuals, so by suppression of the acts, society can control/impede/eliminate the "spread" of homosexuality. This is an act/agent ratio: the act makes the person into who he/she is. Each ratio represents a motive structure, and the controversy in Florida at that time could be understood in terms of those differences in motive structure.

Or let us consider a hypothetical example: Suppose that a student arrives late to class. When asked why, the student says, "My alarm did not go off and then the traffic was terrible, on top of which there were no parking spaces, so that I could not arrive on time despite my best efforts." Dramatistically, it would be noted that in the text scenic factors (clock, traffic, lack of parking) dominate (shape, determine) the act (arriving late). Motivationally, then, this is a scene/act ratio. Alternately, a different student may arrive late and, when queried in a similar manner, may say, "I don't know. I try to get here on time; I really do. But I just can't seem to get anywhere on time. I am always late." Here, the act of being late may be interpreted as simply an expression of the nature of the student: being late is part of his/her nature. This is again the agent/act ratio.

By reflecting critically on symbol-use and the texts that we construct through our symbols, we can bring to awareness these motives structures. Again, this self-awareness of symbol-use through critical analysis keeps us alert to, conscious of, the dangers of lapsing into somnambulant states of enactment. A dramatistic approach to education featuring such procedures for developing critical reflexivity as indexing and pentadic analysis aims at attaining a maximum consciousness of the ways we use symbols and the ways they symbols use us.[7] Burke (1954) reminds us, "Education, as so conceived, would be primarily admonitory" (p. 271). Critical reflexivity warns us against compulsive rushes toward the end of a linguistic line, either conceptually through the dialectic of symbolic action or in social enactment, in the drama of human relations; the ensuing "comic perspective" preaches criticism as a habit of mind and patience as an attitude of choice. Burke writes, "'Dramatism,' the approach to the human situation 'linguistically,' in terms of symbolic action, fulfils its purposes only in so far as it makes methodical the attitude of patience. The 'dramatic' may thunder. It should. The 'dramatistic,' in a commingling of techniques and hypochondriasis, will 'appreciate' man's ways of thundering" (1954, p. 271). The dramatistic approach to education is preparatory for life, not a self-contained institutional objective: "We can never sufficiently emphasize, however, that we are thinking of education as a tentative, preparatory stage in life, not as a final one" (Burke, 1954, p. 287). The critically reflexive, comic habits of mind are preparatory for habits of living.

Self-Awareness and Problems of Democracy

Through critical reflection, through the attainment of maximum self-consciousness, we are able to transform linguistic somnambulism, or the motion-like enactment of our linguistic categories, into purposive action constituted through conscious choice, and with such purposive action comes the prospect of freedom. In other words, self-awareness of the social and political *enactment* of symbolic motives converts the dialectic of symbolic action into the drama of human relations. At a collective level this brings with it a dialectical tension between *the competitive* and *the cooperative*, a tension that Burke sees as both the core and challenge of "democracy."[8] For Burke, a dialectical process is one of transformation,[9] and Burke understands "democracy" to be an institutionalization of the dialectical process. Moreover, he understands the dialectical process of linguistic transformation synechdochally through the process of an idealized democracy: *A Grammar of Motives* (1945) is centrally concerned with the dialectical processes of transformations of linguistic distinctions or categories as they occur through a "central moltenness" or "alchemic center" (pp. xii-xiii) that is not itself random or amorphously formless but rather "Constitutional" (pp. 323–401). The transformational processes of Constitutional democracy are synechdochally representative of the processes of linguistic transformation, and vice versa. Burke's orientation toward what Enoch has termed "critical reflexivity" as an educational ideal is part-and-parcel of Burke's understanding of a concentricity between maximum consciousness of how we use symbols and how they use us as a condition of *action* and individual freedom, which in turn requires a self-consciousness of the dialectical processes of transformation and rhetorical processes of identification, and Constitutional democracy, which negotiates the dialectical tension between the competitive and the cooperative at a collective level, in the great "drama of human relations."

Democracy as Institutionalized Dialectic

In response to a 1939 article by William Heard Kilpatrick calling for increased attention to education as a means of preserving and promoting democracy and as an antidote to indoctrination through propaganda, Burke writes,

> To approach those [issues], I should begin by adding one more term to his [Kirkpatrick's] "education-ethics-intelligence- personality-freedom-democracy" equation (as against the "propaganda-indoctrination-authoritarianism" equation). *This added term would be "dialectics."* In conformity with Mead, as I understand him, *I take democracy to be a device for institutionalizing the dialectical process, by setting up a political structure that gives full opportunity for the use of competition to a cooperative end.* All full scope to the dialectic process, and you establish a scene in which the protagonist of a thesis has maximum opportunity to modify his thesis, and so mature it, in the light of the antagonist's rejoinders. (Burke, 1973a, p. 444)

It is important to note that for Burke dialectic is not ultimately resolutional: a stable, ultimate transcendence is never attained, even in theory. Rather, dialectic is always transformational, always on-going (Williams & Young, 2002, p. 9); by extension, democracy also is never "finished." It remains "the always unfinished task of making social choices and working toward public goals that shape our lives and the lives of others" (Colby, et al., 2007, p. 25). Moreover, the "habits" of democracy must constantly be re-created anew. Branson explains, "The habits of the mind, as well as the 'habits of the heart,' the dispositions that inform the democratic ethos, are not inherited. As Alexis de Toqueville pointed out, each new generation is a new people that must acquire the knowledge, learn the skills, and develop the dispositions or traits of private and public character that undergird a constitutional democracy." Democracy "must be consciously reproduced, one generation after another" (Branson, 1998).

Democracy, as an institutionalized dialectic that requires re-creating in each generation, is fundamentally a "communication system" (Williams & Young, 2002, p. 8). "Democracy," Branson notes, "is a dialogue, a discussion, a deliberative process in which citizens engage" (1998). Or, as John Dewey put it, "Democracy begins in conversation" (as cited in Geyer, 2008, p. 10). This interpenetration of democracy and conversation, or discussion, or talk is not accidental; rather, it is the substance of democracy. As Keith puts it, "Democracy is governance through talk" (p. 2). Of course not all talk is the same, and here it becomes the role of dialectical and rhetorical self-awareness, of critical reflexivity and maximum consciousness, to lead us toward better choices for action, toward symbolic and political wisdom rather than foolishness or somnambulant enactments of catastrophic implications of our symbolic constructions.[10]

Perhaps here we approach Dewey's vision of democracy as "a *personal* way of individual life" (1940, p. 148; emphasis in original), a habit of living, a notion entirely consistent with the Burke's critically reflexive maximally conscious enacting of the institutionalized competitive-cooperative dialectic.[11] Dewey's elaboration suggests as much:

> Democracy is the belief that even when needs and ends or consequences are different for each individual, the habit of amicable co-operation—which may include, as in sport, rivalry and competition—is itself a priceless addition to life. To take as far as possible every conflict which arises—and they are bound to arise—out of the atmosphere and medium of force, or violence as a means of settlement, into that of discussion and of intelligence, is to treat those who disagree—even profoundly—with us as those from whom we may learn, and in so far, as friends. A genuinely democratic faith in peace is faith in the possibility of conducting disputes, controversies, and conflicts as co-operative undertakings in which both parties learn by giving the other a chance to express itself, instead of one party conquer by forceful suppression of the other—suppression which is none the less one of violence when it takes place by psy-

> chological means of ridicule, abuse, intimidation, instead of by overt imprisonment or in concentration camps. To cooperate by giving differences a chance to show themselves because of the belief that the expression of difference is not only a right of the other persons but is a means of enriching one's own life-experience, in inherent in the democratic personal way of life. (p. 151)

As a way of living, democracy enters the realm of the habitual: it is a way of interacting with others that stresses, among other things, the give-and-take of conversational exchange, the enactment of dialectic, of difference. It is as a habit of living, a way of interacting, a particularized competence in communication that democracy is ultimately realized. Dewey comments that "democracy is a reality only as it is indeed a commonplace of living" (p. 150).

Burke clearly saw linkages between his "linguistic approach" to education and Dewey's perspective: "we can say that *ideal* democracy does allow all voices to participate in the dialogue of the state, and such *ideal* democracy is the nearest possible institutional equivalent to the linguistic ideal" (Burke, 1954, p. 285).[12] From a Burkeian perspective, a thing's ideal is its "end," or *telos*, and as such it is also its "essence," and in this manner the linguistic process and the democratic process may be seen as "consubstantial."[13] Here then is where the orbits of concentric reflexivity merge: through critical reflection on linguistic processes, on the dialectic of symbolic action, we attain a maximum consciousness of our own symbol use (and mis-use) thereby preserving our own freedom for action, and by extending this critical process into the social orbit we attain the democratic ideal of an institutionalized dialectic in which all voices can participate. The habits of mind of comic criticism become the habits of living of "the democratic personal way of life." A linguistic approach to education in the trajectory of the linguistic ideal is thus also directed toward the democratic ideal. Consistent with Keith's (2007) claim that "citizens need an education which enables them to participate effectively in their particular [political] system" (p. 5), there are compelling reasons to take seriously Burke's pedagogical program.

Problems of Democratic Education

It has become almost commonplace to acknowledge the deplorable condition of American education relative citizen preparation. Even as numerous efforts are underway to revitalize civics education in elementary, secondary, and higher education, report after report documents lamentable deficiencies in civic knowledge, civic skills, and civic dispositions, including civic engagement (see Branson, 1998; Colby, Ehrlich, Beaumont & Stephens,

2003; Colby, Ehrlich, Beaumont, & Corngold, 2007; Comber, 2003; & Intercollegiate Studies Institute, 2007). As discouraging as these reports are, the need for a pedagogical approach that encompasses knowledge acquisition within a more comprehensive linguistic approach such as Burke's is apparent when one's considers the corresponding deficiencies in students' communication skills, including not only advocacy and listening (see Zompetti, 2006a; Zompetti, 2006b) but also critical reflexivity. As Keith (2007) notes, "Contemporary civic education has been more focused on knowledge than communication skills" (p. 11). It is thus not surprising that civic skills, including the fundamental communication skills required to engage effectively in democracy as talk, conversation, dialogue, or dialectic, are sorely deficient (see Hogan, Andrews, & Williams, 2008, esp. pp. 1–21; Williams & Young, 2007; Williams, 2008; Zompetti & Williams, 2008). Yet, as Comber (2003) points out, in order "for citizens to be capable of fully engaging in civic and political life, they must possess a minimum of civic skills. Civic skills include personal communication skills, knowledge of political systems, and the ability to critically think about civic and political life" (p. 1).

Ideally for democratic enactment, such critical thinking would extend to the linguistic ideal of critical reflexivity and maximum consciousness about symbol use and mis-use, for it is that ideal which makes us symbol-wise rather than symbol foolish and that thereby facilitates both purposive and potentially wise *action*. As Colby, Ehrlich, Beaumont, and Stephens (2003) insist, "If a college education is to support the kind of learning graduates need to be involved and responsible citizens, its goals must . . . include the competence to act in the world and the judgment to do so wisely" (p. 7). Burke's approach to education "offers a theory and practice of language study" (Enoch, 2004, p. 273) designed to habituate the critical reflexivity needed for both symbol-wisdom and, by extension, social-wisdom.

Conclusion

In the concluding sentences of *The Open Society and Its Enemies: The Spell of Plato*, Karl Popper (1971) notes, "But if we wish to remain human, then there is only one way, the way into the open society. We must go into that unknown, the uncertain and insecure, using what reason we may have to plan as well as we can for both security *and* freedom" (p. 201). If we wish to become fully human, fulfilling our ontological trajectory as the symbol-using animal, we must learn to reflect critically upon our own uses of symbols, including their uses of us, and to strive not only in our educational systems but also in our lives to attain a "maximum consciousness" about our condition in the world and the choices that we make. Then, and only then, will we develop the "habits of mind" fully resonate with "living democracy" and sustaining the possibilities for truly open societies: "Linguistic reflection, Burke points out, is the institutionalizing of an attitude; it habituates students into responding to literature and life with careful and critical thought" (Enoch, 2004, p. 291). That is, we need "conscious" habits; democracy is a habit of living, but it is not a habit of addiction or conditioning. It is a habit of self-conscious, self-aware choice operating within a bureaucratization giving sway to freedom and equality. Democratic life is not somnambulant; it is conscious enactment of symbolic action, of maximally aware choice, not sleepwalking to the tune of a category or ideology. By attaining maximum consciousness we also attain, as in Burke's discussion of the poetic ideal, "*a full moral act* by attaining a perspective *atop all the conflicts of attitude*" (1973a, p. 18; emphasis in original), a perspective which perpetually opens us to *choice* and keeps us in the self-conscious realm of action. As British philosopher Herbert Spencer is reported to have once remarked, "The great aim of education is not knowledge but action" (as cited in Herrera, 2008, p.7).

Critical reflexivity and maximum consciousness generate purposive action while warning against symbol misuse. They create the prospect of freedom in both the orbit of the dialectic of symbolic action and the orbit of the enacted drama of human relations. The ensuing tensions between the competitive and the cooperative are negotiated collectively within the institutionalized dialectic of Constitutional democracy.[14] The *ideals* of Burke's linguistic approach to problems of education and of conceptions of democracy as conversation, talk, dialogue, or institutionalized dialectic are co-terminous, and thus the trajectories toward the ideals are consubstantial: a linguistic approach to education that can vitalize and animate our very humanity can concomitantly vitalize and animate our enactments of democracy. If education were to embrace seriously Burke's encompassing definition of human and derive its pedagogical program in accordance with it, we might produce the habits of mind requisite to purposive action, human freedom, and Constitutional democracy. Or, as Burke puts it, "The best I can do is state my belief that things might be improved somewhat if enough people began thinking along the lines of this definition; my belief that, if such an approach could be perfected by many kinds of critics and educators and self-admonishers in general, things might be a little less ominous than otherwise" (1966, p. 21).

Notes

1. Although this essay was for a long time relatively neglected by critics and Burke scholars, Burke himself was quite pleased with the essay, as he crowed to his life-long friend Malcolm Cowley in a September 22, 1954 letter: "I just saw the

proofs of it ["Linguistic Approach to Problems of Education"]—and bejeez, I was delite. It's not just an essay, it's an ORATION. My sense of inferiority among all them pedigreed eddicaters made me vow to do my damnedest towards the stating of my position—and I feel I really got it said. A bit slow on the pick-up, but then it moves along as rip-snortin as the poor old baystard when he's pig-stewed—but sans hangoverish regrets, praise God" (personal communication, September 22, 1954). Perhaps it would be more accurate to say that Burke "Old Crowed" his delight to Cowley.

2. In "Linguistic Approach to Problems of Education," Burke writes, "In sum: So far as the curriculum is concerned, its specialties would be left pretty much as they are, the biggest division being a variant of the 'Cartesian split,' in this case involving the distinction between 'natural motion' and 'symbolic action.' But, as with semantics generally, dramatism would place special stress upon the purely terministic elements that might otherwise be mistaken for sheer 'objective fact' in the nonlinguistic sense. For instance, laboratory equipment being linguistically guided in its construction, one should expect even the most objective of instruments to reveal a measure of sheerly 'symbolic' genius. When considering acts in life, one may have to cut across the special realms of curriculum specialization, in so far as such acts themselves cut across these realms" (1954, p. 282 n.4).

3. Lake (1997), drawing upon traditions including Burke and Mead, approaches a similar discussion in these terms: " . . . identity is better understood as a dialectical site where these tensions [between essentialist and conjectural orientations] mediate each other. Further, the self is an arguer, always engaged in both internal debate and in dialogue with others about the proper balance between these tensions. Or, if suspicious of this personification, we might say the one's self *is the argument* in which one engages about identity. One's life is thus the enactment of one's self, which is to say the performance of this argument" (p. 68; emphasis in original).

4. In "The Rhetoric of Hitler's 'Battle,'" Burke describes in detail Hitler's use of "congregation through segregation," victimage, and other techniques to transform "regular Germans" into blood-lusting Aryans inhabited by Nazi ideology (1973, pp. 191–220).

5. Burke tends to equate traditional understandings of human "rationality" with but this aspect of human's symbol-using capabilities, and then he views rationality as the human genius for tracking-down the implications of our creations, linguistic and otherwise, for "perfecting" and "purifying" our categories, our dialectical desire for not just difference but opposition. Burke writes, "The Logological concept of our species as the 'symbol-using animal' is not identical with the concept, *homo sapiens*, the 'rational' animal—for whereas we are the 'symbol-using animal' *all* the time, we are *non*rational and even *ir*rational *some* of the time. " (1981, p. 182; emphasis in original).

6. Indexing and pentadic analysis are perhaps the most prominent of Burke's procedures for criticism. Enoch (2004) discusses Burke's unique pedagogical approach to the use of debate that he advances in "Linguistic Approach" (1954, p. 287). But there are many other associated "angles" that Burke proposes for better understanding of symbolic action, including the purification-guilt-redemption

cycle, logological analysis of words and The Word, "terministic screens," "representative anecdotes," and many others. Ultimately, Burke's advice for critics is to "use all there is to use" in better appreciating our modes of symbol use (and mis-use).

7. These critical orientations can, and should, be combined with other forms of pedagogy. Burke cites the example of debate, or at least a modified form of debate designed to enhance reflexivity concerning the appeals of modes of appeal employed in the debate. Burke proposes the following as a pedagogical exercise for the promotion of critical reflexivity about the function of symbolic goads and motive structures: "... were the earlier pedagogical practice of debating brought back into favor, each participant would be required, not to uphold just one position but to write two debates, upholding first one position and then the other. Then, beyond this, would be a third piece, designed to be a formal transcending of the whole issue, by analyzing the sheerly verbal maneuvers involved in the placing and discussing of the issue. Such a third step would not in any sense 'solve' the issue.... Nor would we advise such procedures merely as training for the art of verbal combat. For though such experience could be applied thus pragmatically, the ultimate value in such verbal exercising would be its contribution toward the 'suffering' of an attitude that pointed toward a distrustful admiration of all symbolism, and toward the attempt systematically to question the many symbolically-stimulated goads that are now accepted too often without question" (1954, p. 287).

8. Many theorists of democracy recognize the tension between the competitive and the cooperate as implicit in any understanding of democracy. See Fontana, Nederman, and Remer, esp. pp. 4–19.

9. Burke equates the "dialectical" with "a series of terms in perpetual transformation" (1950, p. 38).

10. Frans van Eemeren offers a somewhat similar perspective on the relationship between democracy and dialectical processes involved in "critical discussion": "Democractization is an act of institutionalizing uncertainty: of subjecting all interests to competition. It is inside the institutional framework for processing conflicts offered by democracy that multiple forces compete. Although the outcome depends on what the participants do, no single force controls what occurs. Here lies the decisive step towards democracy: in the devolution of power from a group of people to a set of rules" (pp. 71–72). The rules themselves are negotiable and mutable through the same process of argumentation.

11. Eberly's depiction of a "citizen-critic" moves in this same direction.

12. Dewey's influence on Burke probably exceeds the direct textual evidence. As Enoch (2004) points out, "It would have been difficult for Burke to escape Deweyan ideas during his years [as an teacher] at Bennington College (1943–1961), since the school itself was explicitly founded upon Dewey's educational theories" (p. 278).

13. Through the process of identification, two things that are apart my become "substantially" one: they are "both joined and separate" (Burke, 1950, p. 21).

14. In a discussion of the conceptual variations of "democracy," William Keith (2007) builds on Jane Mansbridge's distinction "between unitary and adversary democracy" by correlating those dialectical polarities with their respective communication practices: "agonism and cooperation are the communication elements that

correspond to adversary and unitary democracy" (p. 332). Adversary democracy values "debate and the clash of ideas"—it is adversarial. Unitary democracy "will focus more on discussion and the attempt to find consensus" (Keith, 2007, p. 332). Keith's point is not that one form is better than the other but rather "that they should maintain a productive tension between the two." The goal in any given context is to find the "equilibrium point between struggle and cooperation" in order to produce a "quality deliberation" that might in turn produce a wiser outcome (Keith, 2007, p. 333). The "betweenness" of struggle and competition locates the same conceptual space as Burke's oxymoron "competitively cooperative," and Keith's goal of locating the "equilibrium point" is in effect a call for greater critical reflexivity or enhanced self-consciousness that is presumed to lead us toward wise choices without being symbol-foolish, at least not too often or for too long.

References

Ambrester, R. (1974). Identification within: Kenneth Burke's view of the unconscious. *Philosophy and Rhetoric, 7*, 205–216.
Branson, M. S. (September 1998). The role of civic education: A forthcoming Education Policy Task Force position paper from the Communitarian Network. Center for Civic Education. Retrieved October 29, 2008, from http://www.civiced.org/papers/articles_role.html.
Brummett, B. (1979). A pentadic analysis of ideologies of two gay rights controversies. *Central States Speech Journal, 30*, 250–61.
Burke, K. (1945). *A grammar of motives*. New York: Prentice-Hall.
Burke, K. (1950). *A rhetoric of motives*. New York: Prentice-Hall.
Burke, K. (1951). Rhetoric—old and new. *The Journal of General Education, 5*, 202–209.
Burke, K. (1955). Linguistic approach to problems of education. In N. B. Henry (Ed.), *Modern philosophies and education, The fifty-fourth yearbook of the National Society for the Study of Education, Part 1 of 2* (pp. 259–303). Chicago: National Society for the Study of Education.
Burke, K. (1964). Fact, inference, and proof in the analysis of literary symbolism. In S. E. Hyman (Ed.), *Terms for order* (pp. 145–172). Bloomington, IN: Indiana University Press.
Burke, K. (1966). *Language as symbolic action*. Berkeley, CA: University of California Press.
Burke, K. (1973a). *The philosophy of literary form* (3rd ed.). Berkeley, CA: University of California Press.
Burke, K. (1973b). The rhetorical situation. In Lee Thayer (Ed.), *Communication: Ethical and moral issues* (pp. 263–275). New York: Gordon and Breach Science Publishers.
Burke, K. (1978). (Nonsymbolic) motion/(symbolic) action. *Critical Inquiry, 5*, 401–416.
Burke, K. (1981). Variations on "providence." *Notre Dame English Journal, 13*, 155–83.

Burke, K. (1984). *Attitudes toward history* (3rd ed.). Berkeley, CA: University of California Press.

Colby, A., Ehrlich, T., Beaumont, E., & Stephens, J. (2003). *Educating citizens: Preparing America's undergraduates for lives of moral and civic responsibility.* San Francisco: Jossey-Bass.

Colby, A., Ehrlich, T., Beaumont, E., & Corngold, J. (2007). *Educating for democracy: Preparing undergraduates for responsible political engagement.* San Francisco: Jossey-Bass.

Coleridge, S. T. (1951). Biographia literaria. In D. A. Stauffer (Ed.), *Selected poetry and prose of Coleridge* (pp. 109–428). New York: Modern Library College Editions.

Comber, M. K. (2003, November). Civics curriculum and civic skills: Recent evidence. CIRCLE Factsheet. Retrieved October 29, 2008, from http://www.civicyouth.org/PopUps/FactSheets/FS_Civics_Curriculum_Skills.pdf

Dewey, J. (1940). Creative democracy—the task before us. Reprinted in J. Gouinlock (Ed.) (1986), *John Stuart Mill, John Dewey and social intelligence* (pp. 146–151). New York: Teachers College Press, Columbia University.

Eberly, R. A. (2000). *Citizen critics. Literary public spheres.* Urbana: University of Illinois Press.

Enoch, J. (2004). Becoming symbol-wise: Kenneth Burke's pedagogy of critical reflection. *College Composition and Communication, 56,* 272–296.

Fontana, B., Nederman, C. J., & Remier, G (2004). Introduction: Deliberative democracy and the rhetorical turn. In Fontana, B., Nederman, C. J., & Remier, G. (Eds.), *Talking Democracy: Historical Perspectives on Rhetoric and Democracy* (pp. 1–26). University Park, PA: Pennsylvania State University Press.

Geyer, C. (2008). "Deliberative skills for citizenship." *The Key Reporter, 73*(2), 10.

Herrera, J. D. (2008, February/March). Democracy in action. *Public Purpose,* 7–9.

Hogan, J. M., Andrews, P. H., Andrews, J. R., & Williams, G. (2008). *Public speaking and civic engagement.* Boston: Pearson.

Intercollegiate Studies Institute. (2007, September). *Failing our students, failing America: Holding colleges accountable for teaching America's history and institutions.* Retrieved October 29, 2008, from http://www.americancivicliteracy.org/

Keith, W. M. (2007). *Democracy as discussion. Civic education and the American forum movement.* Lanham, MD: Lexington Books.

Lake, R. A. (1997). Argumentation and self: the enactment of identity in *Dances with Wolves. Argumentation and Advocacy, 34,* 66–89.

Popper, K. (1971). *The open society and its enemies. The spell of Plato.* Princeton, NJ: Princeton University Press.

Rueckert, W. H. (1969). Kenneth Burke and structuralism. *Shenandoah, 21,* 19–28.

Rueckert, W. H. (1994). *Encounters with Kenneth Burke.* Urbana: University of Illinois Press.

Van Eemeren, F. H. (2002). Democracy and argumentation. *Controversia: An International Journal of Debate and Democratic Renewal, 1*(1), 69–84.

Williams, D. C. (1989). Under the sign of (an)nihilation: Burke in the age of nuclear destruction and critical deconstruction. In H. W. Simons & T. Melia (Eds.), *The legacy of Kenneth Burke* (pp. 196–223). Madison: University of Wisconsin Press.

Williams, D. C., & Young, M. J. (2002). Introducing controversia. *Controversia: An International Journal of Debate and Democratic Renewal, 1*(1), 8–11.

Williams, D. C., & Young, M. (2007). Argumentation and education: Preparing citizens in cultures of democratic communication. In F. H. van Eemeren, J. A. Blair, C. A. Willard, & B. Garssen (Eds.), *Proceedings of the sixth conference of the International Society for the Study of Argumentation* (pp. 1495–1501). Amsterdam: Sic Sat.

Williams, D. C. (2008). Argumentatively competent citizens: building blocks of democracy. In F. H. van Eemeren, I. Z. Zagar, D.C. Williams (Eds.). *Understanding argumentation: Work in progress* (pp. 219–225). Amsterdam: Sic Sat.

Wright, M. (1994). Burkeian and Freudian theories of identification. *Communication Quarterly 42*, 301–310.

Zompetti, J. P. (2006a). The role of advocacy in civil society. *Argumentation, 20*, 167–183.

Zompetti, J. P. (2006b). Listening and intercultural communication: viewing international debate as a means of improving listening effectiveness. *Controversia: An International Journal of Debate and Democratic Renewal, 5*(1), 85–101.

Zompetti, J. P., & Williams, D. C. (2008). The pedagogy of civic engagement: Argumentation and public debate as tools for democratic living. In T. Suzuki, T. Kato, & A. Kubota (Eds.). *Proceedings of the third Tokyo conference on argumentation* (pp. 312–318). Tokyo: Japan Debate Association.

Contributors

Elvera Berry (Ph.D., University of Buffalo) is professor of communication and director of the communication program and the honors program at Roberts Wesleyan College (Rochester, NY), where she has taught undergraduates in multiple disciplines for over three decades. An active member/officer in the Kenneth Burke Society and its affiliates in the National Communication Association (NCA) and Eastern Communication Association (ECA), Dr. Berry was instrumental in establishing the ECA Kenneth Burke Interest Group and serves on the ECA Executive Council. Having known Kenneth Burke and benefited from William Rueckert's insights on her dissertation committee, Dr. Berry is a frequent Burke presenter/panelist and avid promoter of Burkean studies and criticism. Special research interests include Burkeian perspectives on higher education curriculum and pedagogy; on liturgy, sermons, and worship; and on such topics as inclusive language, German literature and translation, and the rhetoric of national/world events.

Bernard L. Brock (Ph.D., Northwestern University) was an award-winning, emeritus professor and co-director of the Center for Arts and Public Policy (CAPP) at Wayne State University in Detroit, Michigan. He passed away on March 31, 2006 at the age of 73. He specialized in research and teaching in contemporary rhetorical theory and criticism with applications in political campaigns and social movements. He identified with and specialized in Kenneth Burke's dramatistic rhetorical theory. Dr. Brock authored and co-edited five books, including *Making Sense of Political Ideology*, *Methods of Rhetorical Criticism*, *Kenneth Burke and the 21st Century*, *Kenneth Burke and Contemporary European Thought* and *Public Policy Decision Making*. He also authored over 60 journal articles and book chapters and wrote over 30 op-ed pieces in a variety of newspapers.

Kenneth Burke (1897-1993) is the author of many literary, critical, and other works over his lifetime. His books include the landmark volumes, *A Grammar of Motives* (1945) and *A Rhetoric of Motives* (1950), which were to be part of his Motivorum trilogy. The third and final volume in the trilogy was published posthumously in 2006 as *Essays Toward a Symbolic of Motives: 1950-1955* (Parlor Press). He has been hailed as one of the most original thinkers of the twentieth century and possibly the greatest rhetorician since Cicero.

Bryan Crable (Ph.D., Purdue University) is an associate professor and chairperson in the Communication Department at Villanova University. His research primarily examines the rhetorical theory of Kenneth Burke, placing it in dialogue with existential phenomenology and contemporary communication theory. Dr. Crable also has focused on Burke's personal and intellectual relationship with African-American novelist and critic, Ralph Ellison. Portions of this project have already appeared in the volume *Kenneth Burke and His Circles*, edited by Jack Selzer and Robert Wess, and in *Rhetoric Society Quarterly*, earning the 2003 Charles Kneupper Award. In addition, he has published a dozen other chapters, essays, and reviews in such venues as *The Quarterly Journal of Speech*, *Rhetoric Review*, *Argumentation & Advocacy*, *Human Studies*, *Western Journal of Communication*, and *Communication Quarterly*.

Mark E. Huglen (Ph.D., Wayne State University) is an associate professor of communication at the University of Minnesota, Crookston; and University of Minnesota CIC ALP Fellow. He is co-author of the books *Poetic Healing: A Vietnam Veteran's Journey from a Communication Perspective, Revised and Expanded Edition*; *Making Sense of Political Ideology: The Power of Language in Democracy*; and *Argument Strategies from Aristotle's Rhetoric*. Journals publishing his articles include the *American Communication Journal*; *The Review of Communication*; *The Electronic Journal of Communication/La Revue Electronique de Communication*; *KB Journal*; *Kentucky Journal of Communication*; and *North Dakota Journal of Speech and Theatre*. Dr. Huglen is a former coeditor of *KB Journal*, He received the Distinguished Service Award from the Kenneth Burke Society, as well as the Most Supportive of Diversity Award from the UMC Black Student Association.

Andrew King (Ph.D., University of Minnesota) is Hopkins Professor of Communication at Louisiana State University. He is editor of *KB Journal* and a former editor of *Quarterly Journal of Speech* and the *Southern Communication Journal*. A past president of the Kenneth Burke Society, Dr. King's research interests are in the rhetoric of power and in Burkeian studies.

James F. Klumpp (Ph.D., University of Minnesota) is professor of communication at the University of Maryland. His research studies contemporary rhetorical theory and American rhetorical discourse. Primarily, he is a rhetorical critic interested in the use of discourse to affect social structure. Dr. Klumpp's work in contemporary rhetorical theory concentrates on Kenneth Burke and the European continental critics. He is a former member of the Board of Directors of the Kenneth Burke Society. He is coeditor of *American Rhetorical Discourse*, the most comprehensive anthology of American speaking now in print. His latest co-authored book, *Making Sense of Political Ideology: The Power of Language in Democracy*, critiques current practices in political communication from a Burkeian perspective and argues for the importance of effective rhetorical processes in a well-functioning political democracy.

Erica J. Lamm is a doctoral student in the department of communication at the University of Maryland at College Park.

Rachel McCoppin (Ph.D., Indiana University of Pennsylvania) is an assistant professor of literature at the University of Minnesota, Crookston where she teaches literature, humanities, and ethics courses. Her publications include "Questioning Ethics: Incorporating the Novel into Ethics Courses" published in a book entitled *Teaching the Novel across the Curriculum* edited by Colin Irvine and published by Greenwood Press and "'God damn it, you've got to be kind:' War and Altruism in the Works of Kurt Vonnegut" published in a book on the Life and Works of Kurt Vonnegut edited by Dr. David Simmons of Northampton University and published by Palgrave Macmillan. Dr. McCoppin also published an article entitled "Creating American Literature" in the journal *Teaching American Literature: A Journal of Theory and Practice* and coauthored an article entitled "Being Actively Revised by the Other: Opposition and Incorporation" in the book *Teaching Ideas for the Basic Communication Course*.

Peter M. Smudde (Ph.D., Wayne State University) is assistant professor in the School of Communication at Illinois State University. He received a Wisconsin Teaching Fellowship for 2005–2006 from the University of Wisconsin System while he was on the faculty at the University of Wisconsin-Whitewater (2002–2008). He came to academe in 2002 after 16 years in industry in the fields of public relations, marketing communications, and technical writing. Dr. Smudde's primary research and teaching interest is the application of Burke's ideas (and contemporary theories of rhetoric) to pedagogy and industry, especially public relations. Dr. Smudde has presented numerous papers in communication, rhetoric, and other topics at regional, national, and international conferences. He has published articles in *Communication Quarterly, Communication Teacher, Corporate Reputation Review, International Journal for Strategic Communication, Public Relations Journal, Public Relations Quarterly, Review of Communication, Technology Century, Technical Communication* and *Visible Language*. Dr. Smudde published *Power and Public Relations* (coedited with Jeffrey L. Courtright) and *Public Relations as Dramatistic Organizing*, which is his own Burkeian study of public relations. A portion of the latter work was published in *Kenneth Burke and His Circles* (Parlor Press), edited by Jack Selzer and Robert Wess.

Richard H. Thames (Ph.D., University of Pittsburgh) an associate professor in the Department of Communication and Rhetorical Studies at Duquesne University, considers himself fortunate to have studied with Kenneth Burke during his visiting professorship at the University of Pittsburgh. A founder of the Kenneth Burke Society, Dr. Thames edited the *Kenneth Burke Society Newsletter* for over a decade and now serves on the editorial board of the *KB Journal*. His publications include "The Writings of Kenneth Burke, 1968–1985" and "A Selected Bibliography of Critical Responses to Kenneth Burke, 1968–1985" in *The Legacy of Kenneth Burke* as well as "A Flawed Stone Fitting Its 19th Century Setting: A Burkeian Analysis of Russell Conwell's 'Acres of Diamonds' Speech" in *Speaker and Gavel*, "Nature's Physician: The Metabiology of Kenneth Burke" in *Kenneth Burke and the 21st Century* edited by Bernard Brock, and "The Gordian Not: Untangling the *Motivorum*" in the spring 2006 *KB Journal*. Dr. Thames is currently editing a critical edition of Burke's unpublished "Symbolic of Motives." Thames served as an Associate Editor of *Quarterly Journal of Speech* from 1998–2001. His interest in Burke encompasses his interests in the rhetoric of science and the rhetoric of religion.

Robert Wess (Ph.D., University of Chicago) is emeritus professor of English at Oregon State University, and he was president of the Kenneth Burke Society (2005–2008). He also taught English at the University of Texas at Austin. He was recipient of the Society's Distinguished Service Award in 1999. His book, *Kenneth Burke: Rhetoric, Subjectivity, Postmodernism*, was published by the Cambridge University Press in 1996. He and coeditor, Jack Selzer, published *Kenneth Burke and His Circles* in 2008 from Parlor Press. Journals publishing his articles include, among others, *Modern Philology, Bucknell Review, the Minnesota review, The Eighteenth-Century: Theory and Interpretation, Pre/Text,* and *ISLE: Interdisciplinary Studies in Literature and Environment*. Conferences where he's given papers include among others the

National Communication Association, the Modern Language Association, the Association for the Study of Literature and Environment, the Rhetoric Society of America, the Kenneth Burke Society, and the International Association for Philosophy and Literature.

David Cratis Williams (Ph.D., University of Kansas) is associate professor of communication at Florida Atlantic University. He is coeditor with Greig Henderson *of Unending Conversations: New Writings by and about Kenneth Burke* (2001), published by Southern Illinois University Press. Dr. Williams has published numerous articles in books and journals, including work published in *Unending Conversations: New Writings by and about Kenneth Burke, The Legacy of Kenneth Burke* (edited by Herbert Simons and Trevor Melia and published by University of Wisconsin Press in 1989), *Encyclopedia of Rhetoric and Composition: Communication from Ancient Times to the Information Age* (1996), and *Philosophy and Rhetoric* (1990). Dr. Williams has also presented many conference papers and participated as a panelist, respondent or debater at major scholarly events, including the Triennial Conferences of the Kenneth Burke Society and annual conventions sponsored by National Communication Association, International Conference on Argumentation of the International Society for the Study of Argumentation, Eastern Communication Association, and Southern States Communication Association. Dr. Williams has also been involved in the discipline and Burke studies through invited lectures and presentations.

Index

Abelard, P., 137
acculturation, 87
action, xi-xii, xiv-xv, xvii-xviii, 3–10, 17- 21, 31- 34, 40–41, 60–61, 67–69, 70–71, 73–74, 76–77, 79–82, 94–96, 98–106, 109–113, 122–124, 143–149, 151–152, 158–159, 188–198, 202–206, 217- 230
active learning, xii
ADDIE model, 112–114
administration, xviii, 11, 125, 155, 163
admonitory, 13–14, 18, 28–29, 33, 61, 67, 74, 78, 83, 86, 93, 175–176, 208, 221; negative, xiv, 12, 14, 16, 19, 26, 28–29, 34, 56, 60, 65–66, 73, 74, 84, 98, 109, 119, 162, 169, 176; thou-shalt-not, 19, 22
advocacy, 225, 231
aesthetic, 46, 48
Alibali, M. W., 152, 165
Allen, M. J., 109, 112
Ambrester, R., 216, 229
American Council on Education, 187
Anderson, F. D., 59
Andrews, J. R., 225, 230
Andrews, P. H., 225, 230
animality, 4–5, 6, 19, 22, 65, 195, 205
ante-bellum reforms, 62
Antolin, M. F., 203, 206
Appel, E. C., 60
Aristotle, 4, 7, 17–18, 21, 31, 37, 46, 127, 142, 144, 150, 164, 215
Arnold, Matthew, 46, 48–49, 116–118, 168

art, 8, 14, 26, 31, 44, 45, 48–49, 56–57, 65, 67, 73, 90, 112, 119, 126, 128, 141, 176, 185, 191, 194, 228–229
artificial, 21, 194, 198
Arts and Crafts movement, 48
Ashton, L., 182, 185
attitude, 11, 13–15, 17, 18, 25, 26, 30, 36, 38, 56, 67, 74, 84, 88–89, 96, 98–99, 104–106, 121, 135, 147, 159, 160, 162, 185, 187, 204, 209, 211, 218, 221, 226, 228
authority, 20, 31–32, 41, 66, 117, 159, 173–174, 194, 219
Axtelle, George E., 11, 40, 111

Barry, P., 116–117, 126
Beaumont, E., 225, 230
Benne, Kenneth, 3, 7- 11, 36, 40, 111, 187
Benne, Kenneth D., 3, 7–11, 36, 40, 111, 187
Bennington College, 43, 50–51, 228
Berkeley, George, 38, 60, 90, 112, 164, 167, 185–186, 206, 229–230
Bernasconi, R., 204, 206
Bicard, D. F., xix
Bicard, S. C., xix
Bichelmeyer, B. A., 112
Bishop, John, 48
Blakesley, D., xv, xix, 50, 57, 60
blindness, symbolic, 192, 194, 199, 202
Bloom, Benjamin, xv, 116
Booth, Wayne, 51

239

both-and, 31, 66, 71, 110, 175- 178, 180–183, 211
Bowen, W., 171, 185
Bowers, C. A., 171–175, 185
Bracey, G. W., xiii, xix
Bransford, J. D., 100–101, 112–113
Branson, M. S., 223, 225, 229
Brock, B. L., xi, xviii, 60, 65, 69, 90, 96, 104, 112, 165
Brown, A. L., xix, 47, 107, 112
Brubacher, Prof., 4
Brummett, B., 220, 229
Bruna, K. R., 203, 206
Buber, M., 77, 90
Burchell, D., 117, 126
bureaucracy, 11, 40
Bush, G. W., 155–158, 163–164, 207

Carson, Rachel, 52
Carter, C. A., 60
Casey, L. B., xix
catharsis, 17
Cheney, G., xviii, xix, 56–57, 60, 111
Chesebro, Jim, xii, xix, 51, 59, 111
choice, xii, 52, 66, 68, 71, 73, 82–83, 86, 102, 130, 137–138, 143, 145, 147–148, 153, 160, 162, 164–165, 214, 221, 226
Christianity, 48
Cicero, 75, 141
citizen critic, xvii, 94, 96, 103–104, 111
civic engagement, xviii, 225, 230–231
civic skills, 225, 230
Clark, B. B., 122–123, 126
cluster agon, 98
Cobb, T., 102, 112
Cocking, R. R., 112
Coetzee, J. M., 122–123, 126
cognitive motivational outcomes, xii
Colby, A., 223, 225, 230
Cold War, 46, 54, 170, 175, 177, 185
Coleridge, Samuel T., 212, 230
Comber, M. K., 225, 230
communication, xv-xvi, xix, 12, 21, 39, 43, 46, 49–60, 64, 66, 71, 73, 76, 83, 103, 106, 111, 126–127, 137, 139, 143, 147, 186, 188, 206, 223–225, 227, 229, 231
communism, 56, 139
community: mythopoeic, xii, xiv-xv, 20, 42, 48, 57, 73, 78, 80–84, 89, 115, 118120, 124, 146, 154, 196, 204
community responsibility, xii
conflict, 11, 55, 80–81, 83, 142, 184, 213, 223
constructionism, 174, 179–181
constructivism, xii, 99, 103–107, 110, 113
constructivist pedagogy, xvi, xvii, 92, 100, 103
consubstantial, 11, 41, 69, 92, 99, 103, 212
consubstantiality, 11, 41, 69, 92, 99, 103, 212
contradictions, 46, 50, 53–54, 56, 118
conventions, 59, 93, 98, 109–110, 117
conversation, 65, 115, 118–120, 128, 136, 141, 147, 223, 225–226
Cooney, W., 150, 165
cooperative educational movement, xii
Corngold, J., 225, 230
cosmocentric, 182
course design, 108, 138
Cowley, M., 48, 66, 90, 92, 113, 227
Cowley, Malcom, 48, 66, 90, 92, 113, 227
Cox, Margaret, 43, 49, 56
Crable, B., xvii-xviii, 187, 205–206
Crane, R. S., 167–168, 184, 186
Crawford-Mason, C., 154, 165
critical reflexivity, 208, 210–211, 218–223, 225, 228–229
Crocean, 31
Cross, C., 150, 165
curriculum development, xii

Dante, 41, 135–136
Darwin, Charles, 63, 91
Davis, T. F., 126
De Bono, E., 59, 60

De Gourmont, Rémy, 54
De Santillana, George, 40
de Toqueville, Alexis, 223
deduction, 129, 131–132, 134, 142, 208
definition of man, Burke's, 4, 65, 93–94
democracy, xvi, xviii, 24, 61, 63, 65, 73, 77, 82, 91, 116, 210, 221–226, 228, 229, 230, 231; democratic culture, xviii, 210
devil terms, 98
Dewey, John, xv, 110, 112, 116, 118, 169, 172–173, 186, 223–224, 228, 230
dialectic, 3, 21, 27–28, 33, 40, 57, 66, 82, 84, 107, 133, 142, 147, 206, 210, 212–213, 215–217, 221–226
dialectical, 3, 21, 27–28, 33, 40, 57, 66, 82, 84, 107, 133, 142, 147, 206, 210, 212- 217, 221–226
dialogical coherence, 120
Diderot, 15
Dillow, S. A., xiii, xix
Dilthey, Wilhelm, 54
Dinkes, R., xix
discourse, 10, 42, 45, 55, 57, 59, 66, 77, 83, 88, 98–99, 101, 109–110, 118, 128, 137, 155–156, 170, 179–180, 187, 192, 195, 199–200, 207, 215, 220
Diversions of Purley, 39
Dobyns, L., 154, 165
doctrine, 12, 25, 34–35, 48, 51, 53, 113, 170, 175, 177
dogma, 34–35, 177
Douglas, A., 112
drama of human relations, 6, 9, 69, 72, 91, 95, 208, 210, 221, 226
dramatism, xix, 9, 11, 25, 28, 34, 36, 38, 41, 50, 53, 60–61, 65, 68–69, 82, 86, 94–95, 111, 187–194, 197–199, 203–206, 210–211, 215, 220, 227; ratios, xix, 9, 11, 25, 28, 34, 36, 38, 41, 50, 53, 60–61, 65, 68–69, 82, 86, 94–95, 111, 187–194, 197–199, 203–206, 210–211, 215, 220, 227
Driscoll, M. P., 100, 101, 112
Drucker, Peter, xi
Duncan, Hugh Dalziel, 40, 66, 69, 77, 90, 112, 143, 165, 205
Duquesne University, 139, 142
Duryea, E., 63, 90

Eberly, R. A., 228, 230
ecological, 51, 53, 171, 173, 181, 183–185
ecology, 51, 53, 171, 173, 181, 183–185
economics, 117, 136, 194, 202
educational ladder, 22, 78, 85, 103, 120, 177
educational objects, 98, 100–101
Ehrlich, T., 225, 230
Einstein, Albert, 55, 168
Eisenhower, Dwight D., 54
either-or, 31, 110, 175–176, 180, 211
Eliot, T. S., 49, 59, 138
Emerson, Ralph Waldo, 28, 45, 47
Enoch, J., 94, 111, 113, 185–186, 208, 210, 213, 222, 225–226, 228, 230
entelechy, 56–57
equality, 158, 162, 226
equations, 12–13, 17–18, 29, 41, 84, 98, 173, 175–176, 192–193, 219–220
equipment for learning, 96
Escudero, M. P., 203, 206
essentializing, 181, 212

Farber, J., 159–161, 163, 165
farm, 60
fate, 17, 25, 184
Fergusson, Francis, 41
Fink, D. L., 108, 113
Fitzgerald, F. Scott, 49
Fontana, B., 228, 230
form, xviii, 5–7, 24, 27, 30, 35, 37–39, 41, 45, 49, 53–57, 60, 67, 77, 89, 95, 102, 109–110, 112, 118, 123, 128, 133, 135, 138, 140, 146, 164, 186,

196, 200, 206, 209–210, 215–216, 228–229
Foss, K. A., 111, 113
Foss, S. K., 111, 113
frame, xviii, 47, 49, 53, 56, 94, 103, 157, 161, 169, 189; acceptance, xviii, 47, 49, 53, 56, 94, 103, 157, 161, 169, 189; comic, xviii, 47, 49, 53, 56, 94, 103, 157, 161, 169, 189; passivity, xviii, 47, 49, 53, 56, 94, 103, 157, 161, 169, 189; rejection, xviii, 47, 49, 53, 56, 94, 103, 157, 161, 169, 189; tragic, xviii, 47, 49, 53, 56, 94, 103, 157, 161, 169, 189
Freed, J. E., 109, 113
freedom, 26, 31–32, 34, 71, 77, 115–116, 129, 161–162, 165, 201, 219, 221–222, 224–226
Freire, P., 125–126, 150–151, 165
Freud, Sigmund, 16, 46, 55, 111
Friesen, N., 100, 113
Frost, Robert, 52

Gaonkar, Dillip, 56
Garvin-Doxas, K., 56–57, 60
genius of the contradictory, 53–54
geocentric, 182
George, Stefan, 40, 55–56, 119, 145, 155, 163, 207
Gerth, Hans, 57
Gettysburg, 44
Geyer, C., 223, 230
Gillen, J., 113
Ginsberg, R.,, xiii, xix
goads, 17, 26, 28, 96, 228
God, 14, 25, 27, 37–38, 51, 133–134, 139, 167, 182, 227
god terms, 98
Goethe, 15, 29
golden mean, 32
Gozzi, Jr., R., 203, 206
grammar, 3, 5, 20, 60, 90, 111–112, 164, 186, 199, 206, 229
Great Depression, 46
Gredler, M. E., 113
Green, S. K., 107, 112–113

Green, T. D., 107, 112–113
Greenwich Village, 48–49
Griffin, C., 73, 90, 113
Griffin, L. M., 73, 90, 113
guilt, 12, 35, 228

Hadot, P., 45, 60
Hadot, Pierre, 45, 60
Hamil, B., 203, 207
Harlan, T., 113
Harris, James, 39
Hartley, Wesley, 187, 205
Harvest, William, 43, 57
Hayden, Donald E., 40
Haywood, H. C., 113
Hegel, George, 55
Henderson, G., 51, 53, 60, 206
Henry, Nelson B., 75, 90, 112, 126, 185, 206, 229
Henson, K. T., 113
Herbers, J. M., 203, 206
Hermes, 39, 60, 90
Hernandez-Serrano, J., 102, 113
Herodotus, 136
Herrera, J. D., 226, 230
Hewitt, T. W., xiii, xix
hexad, 98, 108–109
hierarchal psychosis, 30, 41
hierarchy, xiv, 33, 56, 60, 65–66, 72, 78, 82, 98, 103, 130, 147–149, 161, 165, 200, 217
historicizing, 181
history, 21, 34, 60, 62, 75, 90, 114, 117, 125, 127, 135–136, 164, 167, 174, 179, 184, 186, 192–194, 202, 209, 230
Hitler, Adolph, 55, 217, 227
Hitt, J., 204, 206
Hochmuth, Marie, 40
Hoffer, Eric, 139
Hoffman, C. M., xiii, xix, 152, 165
Hoffman, K. D., xiii, xix, 152, 165
Hofstadter, R., 63, 91
Hogan, J. M., 225, 230
Holford, J., 113
Hollywood, 30

Homer, 136
homiletics, 128, 135
hooks, b., 161–163, 165
Huba, M. E., 109, 113
Huglen, M. E., xvii, 115, 122, 126
human nature, 53, 117, 167, 186, 206
humanism, 94, 116, 124, 126
Hume, David, 38, 167
Hussar, W., xiii, xix
Hyman, Stanley, 30, 187, 189, 229
Hyman, Stanley Edgar, 30, 187, 189, 229
hypochondriasis, 13, 15, 74, 83, 95, 192, 219, 221

idealism, 10, 48, 55–56, 70, 78, 83
identification, 11, 56, 70–71, 78, 81–82, 84, 89, 107, 111, 119, 147, 191, 201, 214- 217, 222, 229, 231
indexing, 16, 17, 39, 40, 96, 109–110, 192, 218, 220–221
individualism, 63, 172, 176
induction, 62, 131–132, 142
insight, symbolic, 16, 19, 20, 44, 53, 61, 64, 70, 104, 119, 131–132, 146, 189, 192–193, 197–199, 201, 203
instructional design, 92, 104, 107, 112–114
Intercollegiate Studies Institute, 225, 230
intertextual structures: association, 133, 142, 219; opposition, 54, 116, 180–181, 183, 213, 219, 227; transformation, 42, 49, 52, 59, 111, 174, 176, 219, 221, 228
Islam, 37
Isocrates, 127–128, 140–141

Jarvis, P., 101, 113
Jay, P., 92, 113, 185
Jeffersonian values, 63
Jehlen, M., 181, 186
Jesus, The Christ, 55, 131, 133–134, 182
Johnson, M., 57, 145, 165
John-Steiner, V., 113

Jonassen, D. H., 113
Jones, Jean, 142
Julius Caesar, 30, 176
Jung, Carl, 55
justice, 6, 11, 17, 47, 122–123

Kant, Immanuel, 41, 53, 167
Karpov, Y. V., 100, 113
Keith, W. M., 223–225, 229–230
Kemp, J., xix
Kena, G., xix
Kilpatrick, William Heard, 222
kinesis, 18
King Jr., Martin Luther, xvi, 42, 56, 60, 133–134, 140, 165
King, A., xvi, 42, 56, 60, 133–134, 140, 165
Klumpp, J. F., xvii, 56, 60, 143, 147, 161, 165
Koestler, Arthur, 139
Korzybski, Alfred, 41
Kretovics, M. A., 152, 165
Kuh, G. D., 119, 126

Lake, R. A., 227, 230
Lakoff, G., 57, 145, 165
Land Grant College Act, 63
language: limitations, xix, 37, 66, 74, 107, 117, 161, 179, 209
language act, 145
law, 17, 26, 63, 119, 167
Leamnson, R., 105, 106, 113
learning, xii, xiv-xix, 3, 9, 17, 19, 61–62, 74, 79, 81, 85–86, 88–89, 90, 93, 94–95, 97–101, 103–113, 115, 121–122, 125–126, 128, 135, 137, 140, 153–154, 158, 161–164, 167, 169, 199, 202, 207, 225
learning communities, xii
learning environment, 93, 97, 99–101, 104, 106–107
Liberal, 11, 115, 117, 126, 141, 165
liberal arts, 64, 88, 118–119, 125–126
liberal education, 85, 116–119, 125–126
liberal humanist education system, 117

liberty, 24
linguistic metastructure, 61, 76, 83, 84, 86
Lips, D., xiii-xix
listening, 225, 231
literacy, xii, xvii, 54, 186, 199–200, 203, 206–207
literary criticism, 39, 42, 45, 111, 188, 218
literature, xvi, 7, 23, 40, 43–45, 4750, 52, 55, 63, 89, 112, 116, 122, 138, 142, 156, 163–164, 186, 191–192, 194, 204, 206, 226
Locke, John, 38, 150–152, 163, 165, 167
logic, logical, 3, 5–7, 38–39, 47, 53, 119, 142, 144, 194, 217
logology, 60, 61, 90, 112, 206
Longinus, 21, 55
Lott, T. L., 204, 206
love, 29, 30, 38, 43–44, 54, 66–67, 81, 105, 130, 134, 140, 150, 167, 196
Loveless, T., xiii-xix
Lyche, L. F., xiii-xix

Macbeth, 30, 176
Mahn, H., 100, 113
Maki, P. L., 109, 113
man: definition of man, 3- 6, 9, 12–16, 19, 21–22, 24–29, 32, 35, 37, 43, 48, 52, 58–59, 66, 90, 93, 95–96, 112–123, 166–167, 169, 173–174, 180, 187, 192, 194–195, 205, 208–209, 215, 217, 221
Mann, Thomas, 55
Martinez Aleman, A. M., 118–119, 126
Marx, Karl, 46, 118
Marxism, 25, 55
master tropes, 109
materialistic reductionism, 56
materiality, 32, 55, 171
math, xviii, 101, 155, 157, 203, 207, 210
May, S., xix, 39, 50, 58, 142, 203, 206

McCoog, I. J., xiii, xv, xix
McCroskey, J. C., xv, xix
McGhee, M. W., xiii, xix
McKeachie, W. J., 107, 109, 113
McMillan, J. J., xviii, xix
McNally, M. D., 121, 126
McPhail, M. L., 118, 119, 120, 124, 126
Mead, George H., xiii, xix, 215–216, 222, 227
Mead, S., xix
Melia, Trevor, 59, 112, 138–139, 142, 231
Meno, L. R., xiii, xix
mental structures, 101
metaphor, xiv-xv, xviii-xix, 53, 57, 59, 97, 112, 143–144, 147–157, 159, 161–163, 165, 205, 206
Mills, C. W., 46, 57, 60
Milton, John, 49, 50
modernity, 172, 174–176, 180, 183, 185
Molenda, M., 107, 113–114
Molière, 34
moments of contingency, 143
mortification, 14, 35, 51, 111
motion, 4–6, 8, 12, 18–22, 27, 41, 55, 62, 69, 71, 76–77, 79–82, 95, 103–104, 171, 183, 188, 190, 193–197, 202, 204–206, 214, 217, 221, 227, 230
motives, 7, 10, 12, 17, 30, 37–38, 40, 57, 60, 69, 75, 81–82, 90, 98, 104, 111–112, 145, 147, 153, 164, 176, 178, 183, 186, 190, 193, 206, 210, 213, 215, 217, 220, 221, 229; human, xi, xvi-xvii, 3–4, 6–7, 9–16, 18, 20, 22, 24, 27, 31–32, 34, 45, 47, 52, 55, 56–58, 61–63, 65–66, 68–71, 73, 74, 76, 82–84, 86–89, 94- 96, 99–102, 104–105, 108, 110, 116–117, 119–121, 124, 128, 136–139, 141, 143–150, 159, 161, 163–171, 173, 176, 179–180, 182–186, 189–202, 204–206, 209–210, 212, 214–216, 218–222,

225–227; motivation, 10, 145–147, 149, 190, 201, 205, 209; The Seven Offices, 75
Motivorum trilogy, 142
Mottet, T. P., xv, xix
Moyers, B., 182, 186
multicultural education, 115, 118–119, 125
multiculturalism, 115, 118–120, 125
music, 8, 194
Mussolini, Benito, 44
mystery, 11, 16, 28, 103, 191
mysticism, 10, 70, 78, 99, 202

naming, 109, 214
narrative, 50, 59, 131–132, 133, 157, 160
Nation at Risk, A, xix
National Communication Association, xi
National Society for the Study of Education, 90, 112, 126, 185, 206, 229
Nederman, C. J., 228, 230
negative: hortatory negative, 191
negative, the, xiv, 12, 14, 16, 19, 26, 28–29, 34, 56, 60, 65–66, 73–74, 84, 98, 109, 119, 162, 169, 176
negativity, 14, 19, 22, 27, 34–35
Nelson, S. W., xiii, xix, 75, 111
Nemesis, 17
neurotic, 21, 194, 198
Nevins, A., 63, 91
Nichols, S. M. C., xiii, xix
Nietzsche, Frierich, 55, 57, 118
Nixon, Richard M., 44
No Child Left Behind, xiii, 155–158
Norris, E., 122, 126
nuclear, 94, 170–171, 178, 217, 231; Big Technology, 93–94

occupational psychotic, 7, 64
Ogden, W. R., xix
Omer, L. S., 203, 207
ontological, 130
orality, 199

order, 6, 16, 17, 19, 22, 27–30, 33, 35, 45, 50, 53–56, 64–66, 71, 73, 74, 76–78, 80–82, 84, 86, 88, 90, 96, 98, 103, 112, 130–131, 133, 168–169, 188–189, 192, 196, 199–201, 211–212, 217, 219, 225, 229; terms for, 109–110
orientation, 9, 92, 95, 103, 109, 145, 150, 177, 227, 228
Orr, D. W., 181, 186
Othello, 30, 33, 39, 176

Panza, Sancho, 44
Pater, Walter, 48
pedagogical, xi-xii, xv-xvi, 99, 110–111, 113, 126, 162, 167, 170, 173, 176–184, 186, 209–210, 212, 220, 228, 230–231
pedagogy, xi-xii, xv-xvi, 99, 110–111, 113, 126, 162, 167, 170, 173, 176–184, 186, 209–210, 212, 220, 228, 230–231
Peeples, J. A., 187, 207
pentad, xi, 10, 11, 62, 68–71, 78, 84, 93, 98–99, 108–109, 111, 146, 191; act, 4, 10–11, 21, 23, 34, 38, 55, 57, 66, 69–71, 73–74, 76–81, 84, 89, 96–98, 120–122, 124, 134, 139, 141, 146, 156, 160, 181, 183–184, 191, 193, 199, 211, 213, 216, 219, 220, 225–226, 228; agency, xiv, 10, 47, 67–68, 70–71, 73, 76, 78–81, 84, 89, 146, 191, 216; agent, 10, 47, 54, 55, 59, 68, 70, 71, 73, 74, 77–78, 80–81, 84, 86, 89, 146, 191, 215, 220–221; pentadic analysis, 218, 220–221, 228–229; purpose, 10, 13, 28, 62, 68, 70–71, 73, 78–81, 84, 89–90, 94, 99, 121, 129, 135, 140, 146, 164, 166, 186, 191, 198; scene, 10, 27, 34, 48, 68, 70–71, 73, 75, 77–80, 89, 132, 139, 146, 191, 196, 220, 222
perfection, 6, 12, 21–22, 27, 57, 65–66, 72, 94, 98, 146–147, 169–170, 188, 212, 217

personhood, 81–83, 85–86, 88, 90, 220
perspectival imperatives, 67
perspective, xii, xv, xvii, xix, 11, 47, 50, 53–54, 62–63, 65–67, 70, 76, 78, 80–81, 84–85, 100–101, 108, 112–113, 122, 139, 152, 192
perspective by incongruity, 147, 161
persuasion, 36–37, 52, 66, 95, 139–141, 176, 214–216
Peterson, C., 60, 107, 114
Peterson, T. R., 60, 107, 114
Petraglia, J., xvi, xix
Petrarch, 135–136
philosophy of education, xi, xiii, xvii, 8, 10, 92–94, 103, 110, 150–151, 155, 158, 162, 187–188, 192, 195, 204
philosophy of teaching and learning, 42
physiological, 8
piety, 37, 50, 178–180, 182
Planty, M., xiii, xix
Plato, 13, 24, 27, 116, 127, 148–150, 155, 163–165, 196, 203, 225, 230
Platz, D. L., 203, 207
poetic, xiv, 10, 22, 39, 45, 48, 69, 71, 76, 78, 84, 96, 104, 111, 211, 226
poetic humanist, xiv
politics, xix, 121, 128, 170, 192
positivism, 94
Pound, Ezra, 44
power, xi, xvi, 18–19, 29, 33, 42, 44, 46–48, 50, 53, 55–58, 60, 67, 70, 77- 80, 82, 84, 99, 116, 118, 120, 140, 144–145, 147–148, 152, 157, 159, 161, 163–164, 176, 190–191, 193–194, 196, 198, 201, 209, 228
pragmatism, 10, 18, 60, 70, 78, 99
Prelli, L. J., 59
preparatory withdrawal, 15, 61, 74, 83, 96
preparatory withdrawal, technique of, 15, 61, 74, 83, 96
problem-based learning, xii, xvii, 92, 101, 110, 113

professional training, 64
professional writing, 108; technical writing, 107–108, 109
Provasnik, S., xix
psychology of form, xvii, 128, 132–133, 137, 140
public speaking, 128, 130, 132, 134–135, 138, 142, 154
purification, 12, 178, 191, 228

Quintilian, 167–168

rationality, 4, 11, 18, 148, 218, 227
ratios: dramatism, 69, 78–81, 146, 191, 220
Raup, R. Bruce, 11, 40, 111
realism, 10, 70, 78
reconciliation, 66
redemption, 35, 48, 228
Reiser, R. A., 100, 114
religion, 33–35, 46, 54, 60, 90, 112, 121, 141, 177, 179, 182, 186, 192, 206
Remier, G., 230
representative anecdote, 108, 228
revolution, 161
rhetoric, xii, xv–xvii, xix, 3, 37, 57, 60, 62, 68, 73, 77, 90, 93, 110–113, 119, 124, 126–128, 134–135, 138–140, 142, 165, 167, 180, 186, 194, 206, 214- 216, 229
Richards, I. A., 48, 60, 144, 165
Richmond, V. P., xv, xix
rights, xiv, 5, 14, 32–33, 35, 118–220, 229
ritual, 8, 22, 73, 147–148
Rorty, R., 115–120, 124, 126, 145
Rotherham, A. J., xiii, xix
rounded education, 128, 140–141
Rountree III, J. C., 60
Rudolph, F., 62, 91
Rueckert, W. H., 66, 69, 90–91, 185–186, 205–206, 209, 217, 219, 231
Russett, C. E., 63, 91
Russo, J. P., 48, 60
Ryder, Nova, 142

sacrifice, 30, 35, 47, 55
Safire, William, 44
Saint Augustine, 59
Sajé, N., 153, 165
Salkever, K., 118–119, 126
Santayana, George, 22
scaffolding, 100, 103
Scholes, R., 114
science, xiii, xvii-xviii, 12, 55, 57, 63, 89, 101, 104, 127, 136–138, 141, 167–168, 172, 174, 183–184, 188, 193–194, 198, 202–203, 207, 210
secular, 14, 25, 28–29, 34–37, 48, 54, 67, 73, 75, 104, 142, 177–178
Seigel, M. A., 185–186
self revision, 115, 121–124
self-destruction, 203
semantic, 41, 227
Seneca, 42
Sensenbaugh, R., 203, 207
service learning, 121–122, 125–126
Shakespeare, 168
Shaughnessy, M. P., 109, 114
Shaw, George Bernard, 55
Siegler, R. S., 152, 165
simplicity, 21, 138
sin, 29, 35
Skinner, B. F., 85, 91
Slater, C. L., xiii, xix
Slavin, R. E., 100, 114
Smith, B. Othanel, 111
Smith, W., 91
Smyth, J., 203, 207
Snyder, T., xiii, xix
Snyder, T. D., xiii, xix
socialization, 67, 89, 116, 135–137, 140, 201, 205
socioanagogic, 6, 27–28, 33, 40, 194, 197, 200
sociology, 40, 136, 140, 188, 194
Socrates, xv, 45, 149
somnambulism, 18, 221
Southwell, S. B., 185–186
speeches, 129–130, 132–133, 142, 155
Spinoza, Baruch, 38
Staton, A. Q., 187, 207

Steinmann, Jean, 45
Stephens, J., 225, 230
stereotype, 213
stereotyping, 213
student development, xii
student retention, xii
substance, 5, 10, 25, 27, 38–39, 41, 52, 62, 69–70, 84–85, 99, 109, 199, 200, 212, 215, 223
symbol-foolish, 4, 208, 210–211, 217–219, 229
symbolic interactionism, 216
symbolicity, 5, 65, 95, 190, 194–196, 198–202, 204–205, 208; extra-linguistic, 6, 38; extrasymbolic, 6; extraverbal, 4, 171, 190; linguistic, xvi, xviii, 3, 6, 8, 11–12, 15–16, 18, 21–22, 24–32, 36–38, 41, 48, 61–62, 65–69, 72–73, 75–76, 78, 80–86, 88–89, 96, 103, 138, 141, 144, 146–148, 157, 163–164, 166, 169, 174, 176, 178–179, 188, 194, 196–198, 208, 210–212, 217–219, 221, 224- 227; nonsymbolic, 4, 6, 19, 171, 188, 190, 193–197, 200–202, 204, 216; subverbal, 4; symbol-using, xvii, 3, 4, 6, 8, 14, 17, 19–20, 22, 24–25, 30, 33, 36–37, 65, 73, 75, 90, 166, 169, 178, 184, 188–190, 192–193, 197, 199, 201, 205, 208, 211–212, 218, 225, 227; word-using, 8, 65
symbol-wise, 4, 111, 113, 186, 208, 210, 218, 225, 230

Tartuffe, 34
Tate, Alan, 48, 49
teaching, xii, xv-xix, 24–25, 33, 42–43, 45, 47, 49, 54, 59, 61, 73, 75–77, 79–81, 84–85, 88, 91, 93, 96, 98, 101, 104–111, 113–114, 128, 135–136, 139–141, 152–153, 155–156, 162, 164, 179, 199, 203, 230
technological psychosis, 65
Ten Commandments, 14

terminological screen, 61, 82
Thames, Richard, xvii, 59, 127
Themis, 17
theology, 34, 135, 139, 185, 194, 202
Thoreau, Henry David, 45
Thurston, Beverly, 54
Tindall, T., 203, 207
Tooke, Home, 39
Torrens, K., 56–57, 60
trained incapacity, 53, 147
transcendence, 12, 17, 22, 31, 46, 51, 55–56, 182, 191, 218, 222
Trapp, R., 113
Troilus and Cressida, 33
true education, 135, 137, 140–141, 150, 155
Trunk, B., 150, 165
tyranny, 24

Ulysses, 33
Umbach, P. D., 119, 126
universal education, 150, 155
University of Maryland, 153–154, 165
University of Pittsburg, 138
Urciuoli, B., 125–126

Van Eemeren, F. H., 231
Vann, R., 203, 206
verbal pyramid, 27
Veysey, L. R., 63, 91
victimage, 12, 17, 30, 73, 96, 204, 227
Vygotsky, Lev, 100, 113–114

Walker, M. U., 122, 126
Walvoord, B. E., 109, 114
war, 11, 14, 30, 50, 94, 115, 118, 176, 178, 213, 217–218
Warren, Robert Penn, 48–49, 51

weapons, 14, 38, 93, 170–171
Weber, Max, 54–55
Weigle, S. C., 109, 114
Weisinger, Herbert, 41
Welty, G., 107–109, 114
Wertsch, J. V., 114
Wess, R., xvii, 166, 182–183, 186
White House, The, 165
Whitehead, D., 203, 207
Whitman, Walt, 43, 44
Williams, D. C., xviii, 51, 53, 60, 206, 208, 212–213, 217, 222–223, 225, 230–231
Williams, G., xviii, 51, 53, 60, 206, 208, 212–213, 217, 222–223, 225, 230–231
Williams, Tennessee, xviii, 51, 53, 60, 206, 208, 212–213, 217, 222–223, 225, 230–231
wisdom, 12, 29, 45–47, 58, 67, 80–81, 110, 124, 141, 165, 173, 223, 225
Womack, K., 126
World War I, 54; Great War, 54
World War II, 54
Worrell-Carlisle, P. J., 121, 126
Wright, M., 46, 57, 203, 206, 216, 231
Wright, N., 46, 57, 203, 206, 216, 231

Young, M., 222–223, 225, 231

Zeno, 137
Zilsel, Edgar, 40
Zlotkowski, E., 125, 126
Zompetti, J. P., 225, 231
zone of proximal development, 100, 103, 113